The Evaluation of
Composition Instruction

The Evaluation of Composition Instruction

Second Edition

Barbara Gross Davis
Michael Scriven
Susan Thomas

Teachers College, Columbia University
New York and London

Published by Teachers College Press, 1234 Amsterdam Avenue, New York, NY 10027

Library of Congress Cataloging-in-Publication Data

Davis, Barbara Gross.
  The evaluation of composition instruction.

  Bibliography: p.
  Includes index.
  1. English language—Composition and exercises—
Study and teaching—Evaluation.   2. English language—
Rhetoric—Study and teaching—Evaluation.   I. Scriven,
Michael.   II. Thomas, Susan, 1947–   .   III. Title.
PE1404.D38   1987   808'.042'07   87-9348
ISBN 0-8077-2850-0

Manufactured in the United States of America

92 91 90 89 88 87   1 2 3 4 5 6

To Paul Diederich
who led the way

Contents

Preface   xi

How to Use This Book   xiii

Introduction   xv

1 ■Basic Evaluation Concepts   **1**
   1–1   Preliminary Considerations   1
   1–2   Formative and Summative Evaluation   3
   1–3   Holistic and Analytic Evaluation   4
   1–4   Credibility and Bias Control   6
   1–5   Evaluation Effort and Cost   7
   1–6   Intended and Unintended Effects   9
   1–7   Phases of an Evaluation   10
   1–8   The Key Evaluation Checklist   10
   1–9   Final Reports   24
   1–10   Implementation and Utilization of Evaluations   25
   1–11   Evaluation Design—Scientific and Administrative   26
          Scientific Design   26
          Evaluation Questions   27
          Nontraditional Parts of Scientific Design   33
   1–12   Evaluating Writing as a Skill   34

2 ■Aspects of Composition Instruction   **40**
   2–1   Issues in Composition Instruction   40
          Overview   40
          Recent Developments   46
          Computers and Writing   47
          Summary   51

2–2   Ways of Describing Composition Instruction   52
       Preliminary Considerations   52
       Description of Program Approaches   53
       Examples of Approaches and Programs   55
       Descriptions of Program Context   59
2–3   Professional Development Activities   61
       Research on Staff Development   62
       Issues for Evaluators   63
       Examples of Professional Development Programs   64

3 ■ Aspects of an Evaluation   68
3–1   Student Writing Performance   68
       Preliminary Considerations   69
       "Found" Test Data   78
       Student Grades in Composition Courses   80
       Published Tests and Research Instruments   81
       Locally Developed Tests   85
       "Found" Writing Samples   94
       Judgments by Students: Self- and Peer-Assessments 95
3–2   Student Attitudes and Beliefs About Writing   97
       Preliminary Considerations   97
       Self-Report Measures   99
       Observations   106
       Review of Program Records   107
3–3   Other Student Indicators   108
       Surveys of Students' Writing Activities   108
       Student Enrollments   110
3–4   The Process of Teaching Writing   111
       Preliminary Considerations   111
       Methodology Inventory   112
       Composition Questionnaires   115
       Structured Interviews   116
       Classroom Observations   117
       Students' Perceptions of Teaching   119
       Evaluation of Writing Assignment Topics   121
       Standardized Measures of Teaching Expertise   122
3–5   Teachers' Attitudes and Beliefs About Writing   123
3–6   Teachers' Professional Activities and Leadership Roles 126
3–7   Training Activities   127
       Formative Evaluation by Participants   127
       Summative Evaluation by Participants   130
       Evaluation of Training by Nonparticipant Evaluators 134

		Evaluation of the Impact of Professional Development Activities	135
3–8	Program Administration	136
	Preliminary Considerations	136
	Key Dimensions	137
	Guidelines for Use	137
3–9	Costs	139
3–10	Side Effects	146
3–11	Replications	150

4 ■ Assembling Evaluation Components   **153**
| 4–1 | Vignettes | 153 |
| 4–2 | Case Study: An Evaluation Plan for the Program "Training College Faculty Across Disciplines to Teach Writing" | 160 |

References   **197**

Additional Reading   **207**

Select Bibliography Related to Evaluation of Composition Instruction   207

Case Studies of Writing Project Evaluations and Local Writing Assessments   209

Technical Reports of the Bay Area Writing Project Evaluation   210

Instruments for Evaluating Composition Instruction   210

Glossary   **213**

Index   **223**

About the Authors   **231**

Preface

During the six years that have elapsed since we completed the first edition of this book, research and evaluation of composition instruction have increased dramatically. In this second edition, we have updated references and resources and added new material to reflect recent developments in the field.

The first edition was an outgrowth of our work in evaluating composition instruction and, in particular, evaluating a large-scale professional development program for composition teachers, the Bay Area Writing Project. The evaluation was funded by the Carnegie Corporation of New York, whose concern that the lessons learned should not be buried with the final report led to a supplementary grant to develop this handbook. Alden Dunham, our project officer at Carnegie, was always exemplary in his warm encouragement and flexibility.

Our evaluation efforts have been significantly improved by the critical questions, challenges, and steadfast good will and humor of those whom we evaluated. Our special thanks thus go to the Bay Area Writing Project/National Writing Project Network and, in particular, to Director James Gray and his associates, Miles Myers, Mary Kay Healy, Keith Caldwell, and Jerry Camp.

Many others contributed to the work on the first edition. For discussions and written comments that helped shape our work in progress, we particularly wish to thank Catharine Keech. Our good fortune has also included a panel of reviewers who helped us clarify our ideas and add to our references of promising practices in the field. They include Paul Diederich, Joe Dominic, Mike Gish, Bruce Joyce, Walter Loban, Miles Myers, Ken Williams, and Lynn Wood.

How to Use This Book

- If you know very little about evaluation or composition instruction, we suggest you use this handbook as a reference. You may have to turn to some of the listed references for more details on specific topics, especially quantitative evaluation concerns, but you should not have to go elsewhere for explanation of the principles and practices.

- If you know a good deal about composition instruction but little or nothing about evaluation, you could omit Chapter 2 (Aspects of Composition Instruction) but should read the Introduction and Chapters 1 (Basic Evaluation Concepts), 3 (Aspects of an Evaluation), and 4 (Assembling Evaluation Components).

- If you have a general background in evaluation but no specific experience in evaluating writing projects—you could skip Chapter 1 (Basic Evaluation Concepts) and read Chapters 2 (Aspects of Composition Instruction), 3 (Aspects of an Evaluation), and 4 (Assembling Evaluation Components).

- If you have a background in evaluation and are familiar with current methods in composition instruction, go straight to Chapters 3 and 4; you can look over the subheadings or the beginning of these chapters and decide which parts are of particular interest.

Introduction

Serious evaluation of composition instruction has emerged as a common practice only in the past few years. The following vignettes illustrate some of the questions evaluators frequently face.

Vignette A. Several teachers have designed and tried out a new writing program. They are enthusiastic about its effects, reporting great success in improving student writing performance. The school principal is pleased with the program but finds the pressures for accountability too great to ignore. The program is to be evaluated.

- Can the principal or teachers use state (or district) test data to evaluate success?
- How can teachers and the principal be sure that observed outcomes are due to the program and not to other factors?

Vignette B. College administrators compared a new way of teaching the first composition course with a traditional course, using a standardized test of editing skills and easily collected information including comparative performance records of each group of students in subsequent composition classes. On the basis of these data, they found no apparent differences between students enrolled in the innovative course and those enrolled in the traditional offering. They decided to discontinue the innovative course because of its cost (it involves tutorial assistance for students). The faculty who developed the innovative course protest, requesting one more chance to teach and evaluate the course. The administration agrees, but provides no financial support for the evaluation.

- Who should be involved in conducting the evaluation?
- What kinds of measures might best reflect differences between the two programs?
- How can evaluation costs be kept low?

Vignette C. An urban school district is offering inservice training in composition. Participation is voluntary, and about 30 percent of the teachers enroll. During their inservice training, teachers request a district-wide assessment of student writing performance to determine the strengths and weaknesses of their new teaching strategies. Teachers who did not enroll in the program object. Some are afraid they might be compared unfavorably to teachers who have had inservice training. Others object to giving the administration yet another accountability measure.

- Which types of evaluation methods are likely to give teachers the most useful information regarding student writing performance?
- How can the anxieties of the nonparticipant teachers be reduced?
- Can the results of this student writing evaluation be used for evaluating teachers?

Vignette D. A large state now has several National Writing Project sites. The Higher Education Commission is currently considering a proposal to fund an evaluation of these writing projects. The aim of the projects is to improve student writing performance by improving their teachers' attitudes and practices. The projects do not offer a single recipe for teaching writing, but rely on a process of making teachers aware of a wide variety of teaching practices.

- What types of evaluation instruments could measure changes in teachers' attitudes, beliefs, and practices?
- How might an evaluator relate findings about changes in *teachers* to improvement in *student* writing?
- Can the program's impact on participating teachers and their students be usefully assessed without reference to changes in nonparticipating teachers?

Vignette E. A classroom teacher returns from a professional conference eager to try a new approach for teaching expository writing. It will involve dropping some required readings from the department course syllabus and substituting new materials that she will prepare. She decides—and gets permission—to try out the new approach in two of her four classes. She picks the two for which she feels it is most suited—the classes in which student motivation and achievement are currently highest.

- If the new curriculum seems to the teacher to be an improvement, what claims can be made about its generalizable effectiveness?
- What data could be *inexpensively* collected to determine whether the new approach works better with one type of student rather than another?
- What are the best evidence and arguments with which to persuade the department chair and school principal that the new approach should be continued as an option beyond the trial period?

As these vignettes illustrate, evaluation of composition instruction—whether in a single course or a whole program—typically includes not only investigation of student writing performance, but also a study of the process of teaching writing, the context of composition instruction, aspects of program support (e.g., faculty development), and a host of other issues. This guide provides practical assistance and resources on all these matters for teachers, administrators, and professional evaluators working at the elementary, secondary, and postsecondary levels. (Brief answers to the questions attached to the vignettes, with cross-references to relevant sections of the handbook, can be found in Chapter 4.)

We have been forced to treat certain important topics somewhat superficially because of limitations of space. But we hope we have provided a clear commonsense introduction to scientific evaluation. Our approach is scientific because it includes sound evaluation design and measurement procedures, treated systematically and comprehensively. But the language and content are designed to be accessible to classroom teachers who are inexperienced in evaluation as well as to professional evaluators who are relatively unacquainted with the complexities of composition instruction.

Because evaluation has far-reaching concerns, we provide a comprehensive checklist of many relevant topics and issues rather than a few general guidelines or principles. We feel this approach is flexible enough to be adapted to specific situations while providing some useful common standards for comparisons across programs, curricula, products, or processes. No one regrets more than we do the complexity of serious evaluation. But we hope that this book will help readers understand why so many considerations are crucial to serious evaluation.

We have organized the book to provide easily accessible information on the various topics that arise in designing and conducting an evaluation.

We begin, in Chapter 1, with basic concepts of evaluation. In Chapter 2, we provide an overview of the components of a writing program as a background and context for comparing and contrasting composition program features. Chapter 3 describes eleven components of an evaluation of a composition program. Although some components need not be studied in some situations, the list shows the range of data that may be required about a composition program. Chapter 4 discusses briefly how to fit the components into an overall evaluation of composition instruction. Finally, a glossary of evaluation and writing terms, and annotated references for further reading, are included.

Primary responsibility for the main chapters was: Scriven, 1; Thomas, 2; Davis and Thomas, 3; Davis, Scriven, and Thomas, 4. All chapters were based on many rounds of mutual criticism among the authors. There are some overlaps, as is common in such handbooks, and they provide multiple but not inconsistent perspectives on some key themes.

Evaluation of composition instruction is a relatively new field, and we recognize that there will inevitably be shortcomings in this guide. We encourage readers to provide us with critical responses and suggestions so that we can improve this book and our own efforts. We also wish to acknowledge the existence of other, well-known evaluation models that offer alternatives to our own approach (references to these can be found in "Additional Reading"). We offer our approach as one we have found to be effective through extensive and varied evaluation experiences.

The Evaluation of
Composition Instruction

1

Basic Evaluation Concepts

1-1 ■ Preliminary Considerations

Perhaps the most important message of this book is that the evaluation of composition programs is not the same as the measurement (or judgment) or improvements in student writing performance. Important though the latter is as a component of a serious evaluation, it is no more than a component. A great deal of resentment about evaluation can be laid to the common practice of equating it with mere testing. Testing bears exactly the same relationship to the evaluation of composition instruction as costing does; one would be ill-advised to make a decision about implementing or abandoning a composition program without knowing its effects on student performance to about the same extent that one would be ill-advised to make that decision without any information on its cost. But testing and costing are still only two of a dozen crucial components in an evaluation of composition instruction. The *political context and constraints* affecting a composition program are often just as important as cost or changes in writing performance, since they affect what a program could reasonably be expected to do, and they may be key ingredients in its success. The *side effects* of a program may be very serious—such as student distaste for an important novelist such as Hemingway because of the frequent assignment to "write in the style of Hemingway." Conversely, there may be extremely important and beneficial side effects of composition instruction, such as better appreciation of the style of a contemporary writer used as a model. To these components we might also add a need for an evaluation to look at certain *ethical questions* in writing instruction—for example, learning what plagiarism is, respecting the right of human privacy in reporting evaluation assessment results, and

1

recognizing and avoiding use of sexist language. Even then we have not exhausted the crucial dimensions of evaluation. In this chapter we provide a checklist of the various considerations that ought to be investigated in the course of doing an evaluation, although the extent to which each of these is critical will naturally depend upon the resources available and the purpose as well as the importance of the evaluation.

The vignettes in Chapter 1 illustrate the range of questions that evaluation can address specifically and effectively. This is a good moment to stress that in reality one does not have a choice about doing an evaluation—the only choice consists in how well to do it, so that it will provide reliable guidelines for decision making. Every teacher, parent, administrator, or student in the course of his or her work must evaluate it from the standpoint of measuring improvements—this is the nature of any serious professional or educational process. In education we are so pressed for time and for financial and personnel resources that it is foolish to be undiscriminating about how we spend them. A writing teacher wants to be selective about the approaches that he or she uses; the same principle applies to a student writer, and to an administrator considering which approach to support. The effective use of one's time presupposes an evaluation of the alternative ways to use it, and planning for the effective use of one's time in the future requires evaluating the way in which one is currently using time. Evaluation is simply insurance against waste.

We are often on the receiving end of evaluations—a role that makes us all apprehensive. On the other hand, every time we go shopping or start planning how to use our personal time and resources, we perform the role of evaluator. It is part of the social contract to accept both roles. A good evaluation shows us whether we have saved time and effort and whether we have done something worthwhile. It is not a trivial task. In evaluating composition instruction the crucial question is whether the current programs, or innovations to replace them, are worth the effort they involve or would involve. Discovering that they do in fact produce some positive results is not adequate evidence to answer this question, although we will certainly want to be sure of that point. We also have to look at the question of whether programs or innovations will expend too many resources in order to achieve those results. Again, "opportunity cost" is one of the main issues that an evaluation addresses: What else could have been done with the same resources? What were those resources (the cost problem)? Were there any bad or good side effects? Was the absolute size of the gain worthwhile? Was there due regard for the ethical considerations?

So evaluation turns out to be a much broader topic than one might think at first sight. It is emerging as a new discipline in its own right these days, a far cry from the common stereotype of evaluation as an application of "tests and measurement" technology. Although evaluation involves a great deal more than that, it does not involve anything else particularly technical. As can be seen from the examples just given, each of the considerations is really a commonsense consideration. The trick with evaluations is to remember to check all of these commonsense points and to bring them all into a balanced and appropriate perspective before making a final decision about a particular teaching approach or writing program.

1-2 ■ Formative and Summative Evaluation

It is worth making a distinction between two general kinds of evaluation that crop up all the time, the purpose of each being rather different, but the need for each being so commonsensical that we should keep them both in mind all the time. The first is called *formative evaluation;* it is evaluation aimed at the improvement of an ongoing enterprise. So, for example, if students engage in a prewriting effort and get some reactions to it from other students or a teacher, prior to producing a revised version of the composition, those evaluations were formative evaluations. Similarly at the program level, if a teachers' round table is convened to react to a new program after it has been running for a few weeks of a one-year trial period, complaints or suggestions that emerge from that discussion are formative evaluation suggestions. Thus, formative evaluation is done for the purpose of improving a program that is still in the process of development or implementation and this kind of evaluation is given to the people who can still effect improvement. Formative evaluation is a crucial part of doing anything worthwhile, if the project takes any period of time at all. It may be entirely critical, but its intentions and process are clearly dedicated to improvement. Composition instruction programs need formative evaluation just as much as individual student writers need it.

By contrast, *summative evaluation* is done for an external client or audience, and its main purpose is not to improve an ongoing enterprise but to report on the quality of a project for purposes other than improvement. Such purposes might include selection of people to go into an advanced or remedial composition class, purchase or adoption of materials or a program for implementation in a particular school or college, or refunding/rehiring of a program or person. The results of this kind of evaluation may eventually include the improvement of whatever it was that was evaluated, but that is not the primary aim. The results may get back to the people in charge of the original program, but that is not the primary audience. When buying a car, one makes a summative evaluation of the cars available; the intention is not to improve the design—which is fixed as far as purchasers are concerned—and the results of the evaluation are not in fact going to be sent to the people who are in charge of improving automobile design. But of course, the eventual result of a large number of people making such evaluations is often the improvement of the model, so the results of their evaluations do in fact get back to the design teams. But that is not their purpose. In composition instruction, summative evaluation is the crucial kind of evaluation for purposes of selecting a program, a composition instructor, materials, and students for the award of prizes or referral for special help. It is just as important as formative evaluation and just as widespread. The checklists that we suggest here apply equally well to both kinds of evaluation. The difference is in the audiences, the reporting procedures, and the choice of design.

Formative evaluation can actually begin even before a program has started, with reference to the various plans for the program under discussion. Evaluation of these plans in the hope of improving them is of course a formative evaluation of them and a kind of preformative evaluation of the program that will eventually result. Thus, in an important sense, evaluation of a program begins even before the program itself is initiated. Again, to measure improvement due to a program, one must have baseline data collected before the program begins. So the common assumption that one can bring in the evaluators "once the program has settled down" leads to less useful, or—for some purposes—useless results.

1-3 ■ Holistic and Analytic Evaluation

It is important to distinguish two kinds of approaches to or designs of evaluation, which we call *holistic* ("of the whole") and *analytic* ("of the parts"). Both formative and summative evaluation can be done either way. The bare minimum or holistic kind of formative evaluation simply involves reporting on how well a student or a project is doing overall. Where possible, it is desirable to go beyond this and give some details of any discovered imperfections in the part or process, "microevaluations" that can be tied to remediation. That is an analytic approach. Suppose that you are learning to shoot at a target with a rifle. Minimal formative evaluation would simply consist in saying how far from the bull's-eye each shot landed. It is evaluation, of course, because the further the shot is from the bull's-eye the less good it is. It is holistic, because it does not break the activity into parts; it merely gives an overall rating. But, it would be more useful as formative evaluation if we could say something about the shooting style that would improve the accuracy of the shooting. For example, the shooting instructor might say, "You are snatching at the trigger pull—just squeeze it slowly." Even though this detailed kind of formative evaluation is more useful, do not assume that minimal formative evaluation is not worth having. If you know that you are not doing well at midstream, even if not why, you can at least vary things that seem weak—if the worst comes to the worst, systematically vary each variable—and see whether a better result is obtained at the next formative evaluation. There are many areas where it is not possible to give the microevaluations and recommendations because we do not know enough about what works to be able to substantiate such claims. For example, in the *teaching* of writing, although there are a great many popular general formulas for what is effective, the fact is that certain approaches work very well for certain instructors dealing with certain classes, and do not work well for other instructors—or even for the same ones dealing with a different group of students. So one has to be very careful not to act as if there were an ideal way to teach composition, or jump quickly into recommendations. In general, it is advisable to stay with holistic formative evaluation, unless there are rock-solid connections to recommendations. Evaluators are not normally experts on writing program remediation; they may in fact be more objective as evaluators if they have no preferences for one type of program over another.

In the evaluation of student writing, the "holistic assessment method" yields an overall judgment of quality without recommendations for improvement, or indeed without any identification of the exact strengths and weaknesses of the performance. Since a holistic assessment can be achieved fairly reliably and rather quickly (and hence inexpensively), it is quite widely used and is very valuable in determining whether there has been an improvement in the overall quality of composition in a particular class or school. Such data are exactly what one needs for evaluation of programs for improving student writing. However, holistic assessment is not very useful for telling particular students what they should do to improve; for that, one needs more than a minimal formative evaluation. One needs some kind of analytic formative evaluation. In an analytic formative evaluation, one is able to determine the merit of various parts or components or dimensions of the performance and not just the performance as a whole. In analytic scoring of compositions one might, for example, be able to say that the punctuation is poor (or good), the sentence construction is not so good, and the development of the ideas is unclear. Notice that even when we have a diagnosis like this it does not follow automatically that we have a constructive remedial suggestion, since we may not know how to teach in such a way as to improve a student's punctuation. What we have done is narrow the focus of our formative evaluation. We have pointed to a particular area where improvement is needed, even if we cannot tell exactly how to achieve the improvement. In the medical situation from which we draw the term *diagnosis*, the doctor will not always be able to cure a condition once it has been diagnosed, but it greatly increases the chances of cure if we can give diagnostic or microevaluation and not just holistic evaluation.

There is some evidence to suggest that holistic evaluation can be more reliable than analytic evaluation—i.e., the total evaluation resulting from combining the microevaluations. So one must not assume that diagnostic evaluation is in general better; it's better for some formative purposes, not in general.

The formative/summative distinction is important in conceptualizing the purpose of an evaluation, its audiences, and the form of its reports. The distinction between holistic and analytic is particularly helpful when trying to design (or interpret) an evaluation.

1-4 ■ Credibility and Bias Control

One distinctive feature of evaluation concerns the question of credibility. When merely trying to determine good methods for measuring student writing performance, we look for procedures that are reliable, valid and cost effective. When we start talking about evaluation instead of measurement, however, we have to discuss credibility in addition to reliability and validity. For evaluation, particularly summative evaluation, is likely to involve judgmental elements, which are open to dispute. In such situations it is of the greatest importance to try to minimize the possibility that the evaluation won't hold up under subsequent attack. The best way to ensure that it will hold up is to arrange that it be conducted by people who have good credibility with the major parties involved: the teachers and the administrators. It is best to have at least some representative of the teachers and some representative of the administrators on an advisory board for—and perhaps even on the operative team that conducts—a summative evaluation that can seriously affect the welfare of either party. Not only does it improve the credibility of the results, but it improves the quality of the evaluation as well, since the interested and experienced parties will often make suggestions that would not have occurred to somebody with a quite different perspective. Parents, tax-payers, and employers might also be involved in certain evaluations that were intended to be credible to them.

An extreme example of this problem arises in the case of evaluating a Black Studies program. If a white evaluator is used as an external evaluator, he or she may have real difficulty in establishing rapport with program staff members, who may be suspicious of the motivation for the evaluation; conversely, a black evaluator from the program's staff (an internal evaluator) might run into a credibility problem with the audience to whom he or she reports. Obviously, the appropriate solution is to use a team with both white and black, both internal and external, members. In the same way, with summative evaluations of writing projects, it is almost always essential to use a team, or an advisory group to the evaluators, that includes representatives of the major interested parties—which may include parents or future employers and perhaps students, as well as teachers and administrators.

Internal evaluations are in general cheaper, easier to set up, and less transitory and internal evaluators tend to be better informed about the program. However, internal evaluations are more likely to "miss the wood for the trees," to be affected by personal biases, to be self-congratulatory or self-protective, and consequently to lack credibility to external audiences. External evaluators have the mirror properties. A hybrid involving elements of the two kinds is an obvious improvement. There are several common varieties: an internal evaluation team *and* an external one (as in school accreditation), an external consultant to an internal team or evaluator, an internal consultant to an external team or evaluator, and so on.

The internal versus external issue is just one aspect of what is sometimes called bias control. Using an atheist to evaluate a department of religion raises problems of bias just as does using only religious folk. Again, the solution lies in teams, or consultants, for each group. When contracting an evaluation with a professional, one expects to hear intelligent suggestions as to such arrangements. When doing one's own evaluation—perhaps of one's own work—one must make a real effort to have outsiders look at the design, execution, and interpretation with a critical eye.

1-5 ■ Evaluation Effort and Cost

A word about the range of effort involved in doing an evaluation. In everyday life, individuals do low-effort, inexpensive evaluations, often at a nearly instinctive level, for example, when shopping. Even though the effort involved there is minimal, it often pays off very well. (Those are the cases where someone is commended for "good judgment.") Sometimes, in one's role as a consumer, one goes a step further than careful consideration and does a little research, such as by using *Consumer Reports*. That little extra expenditure of effort often pays off many times over. In making a major commitment to the purchase of a home or a portfolio of investments for retirement, a person often picks up an extra book or two—or even takes a special workshop or course—in order to be in a better position to make an evaluation of the alternatives. Often enough, that's a bargain, too. Much of a professional's activity—not just an occasional moment or day—involves making, improving, or applying evaluative considerations, whether the professional is an instructor, administrator, consultant, or evaluator, and whether the professional area is architecture or writing. That raises the cost, but, done well, it can still pay off handsomely. At this stage, however, we do have to begin to look hard at the question of whether the evaluation is worth its cost. And when we begin to consider bringing in a professional evaluator from outside, the very expertise we are hiring should tell us to look hard at the costs as well as the benefits.

Of course, it is not only professionals who are concerned about something as fundamental as composition instruction. Parents, would-be writers, students who know they will need reasonable writing skills for most vocational commitments, and workers in almost every area are frequently concerned with composition instruction because it can affect them or their children or their friends, employees, and supervisors. The time they spend on evaluation has to be considered a cost, and the key question is whether the benefits resulting from that investment of time— benefits such as the selection of a better program or the improvement of an existing program—are worth more than the time.

Fortunately, the answer to the cost question will usually look good for evaluation of basic skills like composition, because the benefits are so large and lifelong. The big investment in the move back to the "basics" in education may or may not do us any good on balance. That is not always obvious without some fairly careful investigation—in other words, an evaluation. Evaluations range in effort from almost nothing up to six- or eight-figure budgets; but it is important to remember that *one can nearly always do very useful evaluation at a very modest cost.*

Although there is rarely a better reason for doing anything than there is for doing evaluation, that no longer holds true if the cost gets out of hand. It is just as foolish to spend a great deal of money on an evaluation that could at best save only a little money or produce a small gain as it is to spend too little when it could be done well for somewhat more and would then save a great deal or produce large gains in quality.

1-6 ■ Intended and Unintended Effects

Clients for an evaluation—usually those who commissioned the program—are typically very anxious to have the program or project evaluated against their goals for it. Of course, those goals should not be ignored, it is important for planners to find out whether they have succeeded in what they have been trying to do. But it is not professionally adequate to evaluate a project solely against the goals of its designer or manager. Our previous remarks (in 1-1) about the crucial importance of looking for side effects must be reemphasized. Programs (and personnel, and so forth) have to be evaluated in terms of what they do, whether or not they intended to do it. So one has to evaluate programs by looking for all the effects they had and not just at their success in attaining their stated goals. This calls for considerable ingenuity. For example, it is not too hard to select tests that relate to the intent of the program, but it requires careful study of the actual writing done in the program and the attitudes of those who go through it to discover whether there have been other effects that were unintended. It may be necessary to undertake a fairly systematic investigation in order to locate these other effects. Although for the most part in what follows we talk about the search for success in attaining the goals of a writing program, it is just as important not to neglect the search for side effects. These side effects may include the adoption of certain writing styles as personal styles, change in manners of verbal address so as to avoid stereotypical use of pronouns, acquisition of certain subject matter knowledge that happens to be present in the writing sample materials, and so on. And remember: if the goals are rather narrow and esoteric, the basic question of whether the students' writing has improved in the straightforward ways becomes a side-effects issue and must be checked. So side effects can easily be the death knell of a program—or its salvation. Like the side effects of insecticides, they often turn out to be more significant in the long run than the intended effects or lack of effects.

People sometimes feel that the idea of evaluating a program against criteria other than those defined by its goals is essentially unfair. They ask, Why should a program be criticized for not doing what it did not try to do? The double answer is: a program must be judged for what it did, intended or not—that is how history is told; and a program must also be judged for what goals it selected, against the needs of those it was supposed to serve and the resources it had available. It is entirely wrong to suppose that the selection of goals is either beyond criticism or that—even when faultless—it defines the search area for an evaluation. (Of course, casual and inappropriate criticism of a program for not meeting some other set of goals preferred by the evaluator is patently illicit.)

With these cautions, we proceed to list the various phases of an evaluation, and then to the key evaluation checklist.

1-7 ■ Phases of an Evaluation

Six different phases in the process of evaluation can be identified, though in many cases of simple evaluation they will not always be distinct. In other cases, different people will handle different phases. The checklist we are about to discuss can be used in all these phases, although certain checkpoints are of primary concern for only some of the phases.

The phases to be distinguished are:

- Previewing the evaluation—sketching a design for purposes of estimating its cost, negotiating arrangements to conduct it, and assigning responsibilities
- Designing the evaluation in detail (a preliminary design is necessary in order to do the costing, but constructing or selecting the instruments, or identifying samples, takes more effort and should be completed before making final arrangements)
- Conducting the evaluation—gathering the data, doing the observations or interviews, and so forth
- Synthesizing and interpreting the results
- Reporting the findings in an appropriate way and making recommendations when appropriate
- Evaluating the evaluation itself to see whether it meets reasonable standards of cost effectiveness, professional ethics and so forth (for credibility, this is of course best done by an independent critic, but evaluators should make sure it is done)

1-8 ■ The Key Evaluation Checklist

This checklist has two rather distinctive characteristics. First, virtually all of the checkpoints have to be covered in any serious evaluation. They are not just desirable—they are necessary. Putting it another way, an evaluation design that does not investigate each of the checkpoints is vulnerable to repudiation as not having established the evaluative conclusion to which it is said to lead. In certain checklists, such as a checklist for evaluating houses, one is prepared to trade off some considerations against others; for example, one might be willing to trade off a guest bedroom against easy access to public transportation. In a checklist for experimental and evaluation designs, however, few if any such trades can be made. If one does not investigate cost, for example, then there is usually a great big hole in any conclusions that one can draw from the evaluation. One can hardly recommend buying or using a program or procedure without knowing its cost. So the first point to remember about this checklist is that one cannot do an evaluation by taking account of most of it and crossing one's fingers about the rest. The least that is acceptable is a mental analysis of each point, to see whether it constitutes a serious threat in a particular case.

The second feature of this checklist is its iterative or cyclic nature. One cannot finish with each point and move on to the next, never to return. One handles a particular checkpoint as well as possible at a certain point in the evaluation, goes on to later checkpoints, and then finds that it is necessary to come back and revise one's conclusions about the earlier ones. This process of "cycling" through the checklist several times is not a sign of inefficiency in one's first approach to a given checkpoint, it is a sign of this particular kind of investigation. For example, the answers to the first few questions on the checklist (which concern the nature of whatever is to be evaluated, the background and context, the resources available for evaluation, and so forth) are usually provided in the first instance by those who commission the evaluation, the clients. In some cases the client and the evaluator are one and the same. One usually finds, as the evaluation proceeds, that the real nature of whatever is being evaluated was not at all well portrayed in the initial description by the client. People who are very close to something are often unable—and sometimes unwilling—to get a good perspective on it. Still, one cannot disregard their view of the matter; it is often the most important view, and anyway one will probably have to make a decision about what kind of an evaluation to do, and indeed whether to do one at all, on the basis of their description. So one listens very carefully as the teacher describes the approach to be evaluated, or the program director discusses the composition program, or the students talk about their project. One does not treat their description uncritically, however, any more than one assumes that an evaluation should only investigate the project's stated goals.

With those cautions, let us proceed to the checklist.

Checkpoint 1A: What Is to Be Evaluated? Here we need a description of exactly what we are to evaluate. Is it the program or method used in a course, the combination of a method and a particular teacher, the content of an essay, or its style as well as its content? This is the classic example of the checkpoint that we think we can handle very easily but end up refining as we work through the evaluation. Whatever it is that we are supposed to evaluate, let us call it the *evaluand*. It is unfortunate to have to introduce a special term for this, but the other candidates (such as *subject* or *object)* turn out to be ambiguous. So we begin by getting the clients' description of the evaluand, and later on we will get other descriptions of it from participants in the program or others knowledgeable about it. Putting all these together at the end will give us our best shot at describing the reality we were seeking to appraise.

Checkpoint 1B: What Kind of Evaluation? *The same kind of question needs to be answered about the evaluation itself. This "phantom question" turns up at every checkpoint and for a very simple reason. An evaluation is itself a product and hence something that can be evaluated. Since the checklist proposed here is intended to be a universal checklist for doing all kinds of evaluations, it should apply just as well to evaluating evaluations (called* meta-evaluation) *as to evaluating compositions or composition instruction or the instruction of composition instructors. So it is quite a good exercise in explaining the meaning of the checkpoints, to explain not only how they apply to the primary evaluand (the composition instruction program) but also to the evaluation itself. We call the latter the "B" checkpoints, by contrast with the "A" ones, which are (or imply) questions about the evaluand we were called upon to evaluate. We will italicize the text referring to the B checkpoints to keep it clearly distinct.*

Checkpoint 2A: Background and Context of the Evaluand. Here we consider a series of questions about the evaluand—its origin, development, authors, and so forth. Why should we bother with such questions? Sometimes they are not worth the trouble, as for example when we are simply evaluating a single student writing assignment. Yet sometimes, even in such a case, these questions may be very helpful in understanding the reason for the present level of performance, and that is in turn very useful for formative evaluation purposes. In the case of a large-scale writing program, the list of questions is quite formidable:

- When and for what reason was the program introduced?
- What are the intended effects (what is it hoping to accomplish)?

- Who are the intended users (clients or consumers—these might be students or teachers or principals of other schools)? Who were the originators or developers?
- Who are the present "stakeholders" (advertisers, managers, sponsors, godfathers, supporters, endorsers, and so forth)?
- Who are the present power holders (superiors, decision makers, responsibles, influentials)?
- What is thought to be the current performance of the evaluand by the various parties referred to above, and on what basis do they make these judgments?

These questions are useful in getting a sense of, for example, where the pressures will be, and where detailed proof will be required of results because they are contrary to expectations.

Checkpoint 2B: Background and Context of the Evaluation. *We now must ask the same kind of questions about the evaluation effort that we were just asking about the program. What are the purpose and hoped-for results of this evaluation? Have there been any prior evaluations? Are there any concurrent evaluations? Are future evaluations proposed or expected? Here it is helpful to get as many details and reasons as one can, or an explanation of why they are not available. Are there any perceived constraints on the evaluation—both with respect to doing it and with respect to implementing any results from it? We mean political, psychological, or social constraints rather than constraints on time and resources.*

Checkpoint 3A: Resources Available for the Evaluand. This checkpoint is sometimes called the "strengths assessment." One might think of the resources checkpoint as relating to the question of the feasibility of the program or project for the individual or staff or group of school sites that is involved. It requires identifying what resources are available and whether they are adequate for optimum program functioning or improvement.

Checkpoint 3B: Resources Available for the Evaluation. *Often the most important resource constraint refers to time; so we begin by clarifying the deadline for the evaluation and whether it is absolute or preferable. Starting time is also something to be clarified; when must it begin, when is the earliest that it could possibly begin? Are there any other critical dates by which time a preliminary report must be submitted? What personnel, financial, and expert resources are available? Who* *is the contact person on the client's staff? What support staff, what equipment, what records are available?*

Checkpoint 4A: Legal, Ethical, Political, and Other Valid Process Considerations. There are always some moral considerations that come into any serious teaching effort. As school and university administrators are only too aware, a number of legal constraints are becoming increasingly important; and there are also political constraints in many cases, even on individual writing programs. These may concern the use of certain materials that are attractive to the teacher but not to the governing board, the way in which reports are given to the parents, and so forth. The term "political" is here used not derogatorily, but in a general sense which involves most practical social considerations.

This checkpoint also covers aesthetic and euphoric or hedonic considerations, the status of which is: "other things being equal, take these into account." For example, other things being equal, one should use writing models that have some literary merit; or, other things being equal, use models that the students enjoy reading. (These two considerations are sometimes in conflict!)

Checkpoint 4A does *not* cover "teaching style"—a process consideration—since there is no evidence that any one style is superior to any other. Of course a particular style might itself be the evaluand, in which case it pertains to the issues of Checkpoint 6A.

Checkpoint 4B: Legal, Ethical, and Political Constraints on the Evaluation. *Exactly what would we be obligated to produce in the way of "deliverables"—that is, what kind of reports, by when, and in what formats, media, and detail? What would the contract (if there is one) between the client and the evaluator look like? Where does the liability reside in the event of a legal issue? Who will provide liability coverage? Who will control release of the reports (preliminary and final)? Under what conditions can they be edited? Who will provide authorization for the use of staff, equipment, and records, by when and with notification to whom? What particular legal regulations apply to records and the protection of privacy and the rights of human subjects that impinge on this evaluation? What ethical constraints, apart from the ones embodied in the law, should be considered? What political constraints must be observed?*

In the light of the preceding considerations, the evaluators should now be in a position to make a preliminary estimate of cost and of whether the results would be worth the effort, and express interest in the work at that cost level. The client negotiates, accepts, or rejects the proposal. (Of course, such negotiations are unnecessary in the simple case where people are interested in evaluating their own teaching; but it is worthwhile to go through the checklist quickly, even in such cases, and make sure that these rather formal-appearing requirements are actually being covered.) In order to prepare a bid that is realistic and complete, one will have to look ahead down the checklist and make a rough estimate of the cost of handling the whole design.

Checkpoint 5A: Needs Assessment.   Who does or could benefit from the evaluand if they received it or some of its effects? For example, what kinds of students would benefit from this kind of program? What kind of benefit could result from trying to write in the style of Hemingway? The population that has these needs constitutes an appropriate target group for a program or an effort, but it is wise to check on how needs were determined. An evaluator will frequently find that needs have changed because of the impact of other programs, or that the original needs were misconstrued because of an error of inference. A common type of inferential error involves drawing the conclusion that students need remedial writing courses when they are not doing very well in writing. In fact the reason for students' poor performance may be inadequate performance by their present teacher, boring materials, disorder in the classroom, visual impairments, lack of parental support, and so forth. Before one jumps from a perceived deficit in performance to the conclusion that a particular program or strategy is the appropriate remedy, one must take care to have evidence that the particular strategy is the best treatment to use for the diagnosed condition. Needs are not the same as wants, and they are not the same as "whatever it would take to make everything ideal." Roughly speaking, needs are what it takes to maintain or attain a minimum satisfactory performance level: to be able to perform the usual school and real-world writing tasks in an effective way, not perfectly, but competently. Going beyond that is desirable, but not essential; it has second priority, it is an ideal, not a need.

Checkpoint 5B: Need for the Evaluation.   *Of course by now it will probably be clear why the client (or you) thinks the evaluation is needed. But is it really needed? This checkpoint serves to remind us to consider the different possible needs for the evaluation. There is the accountability need, the gathering of proof to document the effectiveness of the composition instruction, to justify continuance. There is the case for formative evaluation even if a satisfactory level of performance is achieved, because there is a need for improvement beyond the merely adequate. It's* *not quite a basic need, but the "need to improve" (beyond the minimum) is an important part of all professional commitment, and improvement is detected by evaluation. We conventionally use the needs checkpoint to bring in these higher aspirations.*

For the remainder of the checklist, we will give only a brief comment for the B checkpoint.

Checkpoint 6A: Delivery System.   Suppose you are evaluating a highly praised new composition program in which students are given internships as journalist-assistants on local newspapers. Describing how many hours a week they spend there and who is in charge of them is part of Checkpoint 1A, Description. As you look at needs, you realize that the need for disciplined copy-editing that is focused on accuracy plus "impact" on the reader is a generally acknowledged high priority. It is clear from the description of the program that this is part of what the copy-editors are trained to do with the interns. But is this instruction actually delivered? Are the needs *met?* That's what Checkpoint 6A is about.

The evidence we gather about delivery could conceivably be included under Checkpoint 1A as part of a full description of the program as implemented at this site, but it is conceptually better to distinguish between the program and a particular implementation of it. As an example, consider the evaluation of a composition program based on a textbook, which is a kind of packaged program in itself. The book may be excellent, but the delivery system—how it is used in the classroom—may be defective. One would not want to condemn the former for the sins of the latter. Separating out the program or product from the delivery system is not always possible, and it is not crucial for certain types of summative evaluation, but it is very useful for formative purposes. It is a simple example of analytical evaluation (as opposed to holistic), and it is so often useful to make this particular distinction that we built it into the checklist. It has the special merit of reminding the evaluator to focus on the "degree of implementation"—on whether what is supposed to be delivered is actually delivered.

The delivery system may include the training of teachers; it may include the promotional campaign for a book. What is included depends entirely on what is being evaluated. If one is evaluating the book as such, one does not look at the promotion. If one is evaluating the book's impact, one would. If evaluating a federally funded composition program of which the book is the core, both promotion and teacher training would need to be examined. As another example, consider an approach to encouraging students to write by asking them to keep a diary. In the evaluation one must look very carefully at what often turns out to be the slip between the cup and the lip—namely, failure to actually bring the students in contact with the new method as it was supposed to have been presented. Even in evaluating a product or a particular performance by an individual student, for example a writing assignment, the delivery system is quite important. The content of the composition is independent of the particular way in which it is written or typed or presented—the "delivery system." But a bad delivery system can lead to a serious underestimation of the quality of the composition itself. For these reasons it is worthwhile to examine the delivery system of composition and composition instruction.

Checkpoint 6B, which refers to delivering the evaluation, reminds one of the importance of report formats and presentational efforts; it is not enough to write a technically good report, the contents and significance must also be communicated.

Checkpoint 7A: Market: Who Does or Could Receive the Evaluand?

Now we are moving away from the question of who would benefit from the evaluand to the question of who would or could actually receive it. This is what we call the "immediately impacted population" as opposed to the "target population"—the intended recipients. (By population we mean who or *what*—so as to cover environmental impacts as well.) The market is the group of people or things who are directly affected by the evaluand as it is in fact delivered or, if we are still in the planning stage, those who would be affected. Once we've looked at the delivery system and thought about ways to improve it, we will also get ideas about potential markets. The potential market for a computer-assisted composition instruction program is limited to those schools that could afford it. But that market would be greatly enlarged if federal funds were provided. Notice that this question is quite different from that of who could benefit from or who needs it.

Checkpoint 7B reminds one to look carefully at ways to increase impact by enlarging the "market" for an evaluation. Who could you send it to who would be influenced by it?

Checkpoint 8A: Effects of the Evaluand—People/Types/Amounts/Duration/Proof.

We typically evaluate a product, project, or program in terms of its effects, although to some extent it can be evaluated in terms of intrinsic characteristics such as aesthetics or ethical characteristics (Checkpoint 4A). But for the most part, when we talk about evaluating a composition instruction program, we mean trying to determine what sorts of changes it produces in its participants. We must also look at others who are indirectly impacted: parents, siblings, employers. That's the "people" aspect of the effects checkpoint; it must cover the market and everyone else affected.

We need to look for different types of effects, including intended effects and unintended or side effects. Such effects will probably vary with different impacted populations. A program may have one effect on lower-achieving learners in the class and another effect on advanced students and quite another on parents. Inservice training programs for teachers of composition may have significant effects on participants and quite different and adverse side effects on their nonparticipating colleagues. A program might succeed with experienced teachers but not with beginners. The effects may be in the direction of cognitive gains, social skills, attitude changes, and so on. An evaluation cannot simply focus on the narrow question of what effects of those planned actually occurred to the target population, ignoring all side effects by type or person affected.

Amounts. We must ask to what degree the various types of effects are produced. Here is where psychological measurement comes in, and we are also likely to need statistical techniques and sometimes computer assistance when dealing with large amounts of data. Once the types of effects have been determined, the matter of measuring their size is somewhat more straightforward. Of course, the fact that there *are* effects, and that they are of a certain size, does not tell us whether they are of value or if they are worth what they cost. For that we have to look at other checkpoints.

Duration. How long do the effects last? The bad news is that good effects are, roughly speaking, better the longer they last—but the longer they last, the longer it takes to find out why they lasted that long. When we want to know the answers from an evaluation quickly, so we can implement or replicate a program at many sites where the need is severe, it is trying to have to wait a long time. People rarely have that much patience, so programs are continually implemented prematurely, and long-term effects are rarely monitored. (After all, who wants to hear the bad news after having already committed resources? The answer should be, we the taxpayers, parents, and future employers.) One might ask whether short-term effects could be used as indicators that long-term ones will occur. It is true that programs without short-term effects are unlikely to have long-term ones; but the reverse is not necessarily the case. The Hawthorne effect (the positive effect of being a subject in any experiment) will often make a program look good in the short-run, while under study, but will not stay around for long.

At this checkpoint we refer to the durability of the effects. There is also the question of the durability of the program. Is it dependent on the leadership of one person whose health is somewhat precarious? On federal or state funding that may be cut back? Those questions are covered under the next checkpoint, although some aspects of them may be picked up at this checkpoint.

Proof. Are these apparent effects *really* effects or are they merely coincidental occurrences? Here we have to rely upon a careful evaluation design to eliminate alternative explanations. We must distinguish between general changes due to maturation, or due to changes in the social composition of the student body or in the general morale of the school, and effects due to a particular program or teacher. In a small-scale evaluation, an individual writing assignment, the problem of distinguishing effects arises in terms of whether the apparent merit of the composition that we are grading resides in it or in the fact that it is the last one in the pile that faces us tonight!

Checkpoint 8B, effects of the evaluation, reminds one to consider the actual *impact* of the evaluation and not just its validity.

Checkpoint 9A: Generalizability.

Would this evaluand have the same effects if it were in a different type of school situation, geographical location, or physical environment? This is, of course, a crucial matter where one is considering multiple replications of what may be an important innovation in the teaching of composition. For this reason the development and formative evaluation of innovative programs should involve several stages, progressing gradually from the intensive preliminary "hothouse" stage, through field tests at remote sites, to what are sometimes called "hands-off" trials where not even technical assistance is provided. The kind of generalization that is involved in generalizing from a sample of students' work to conclusions about their writing skill is part of Checkpoint 8A. Here we are concerned with the generalizability of the whole combination of the evaluand and its impacts: Can it be effectively replicated at other sites? We need to look at whether the delivery system is generalizable, whether the market is generalizable, whether the past pattern of effects is generalizable to the future, and so on. A good way to summarize the aspects of generalizability is under the headings of generalization to:

- Other people (salability)
- Other places (exportability)
- Other times (durability—of the evaluand and the need for it)
- Other versions (modifiability)

The terms in parentheses are not precise but simply useful mnemonics. The durability of the evaluand deserves repeated stress. One does not want to install a new program in composition instruction if its publisher will not be around next year. Many innovations in instructional technology have let us down because they were not around for long—that is something we should be sensitive to under "generalizability to future times."

A most important kind of example concerns the vocational needs of the future; one would be ill-advised to base a massive investment in arithmetic training upon the assumption that there will always be a general need for exact arithmetic calculation without the help of a calculator. Is it possible that small hand-held devices that will accept speech input and will fit into a slot in the side of an electric typewriter to produce written output will make much of the physical process of composition unnecessary? What effect would this have on composition instruction? Would it make obsolete considerations of punctuation and spelling? Questions like this must be addressed if we are talking about evaluating a program with any pretensions to a multiyear life span. They are not as important for evaluating a single writing performance, but their short-term analogy is still interesting and involves an attempt to judge whether a particular piece of composition has a long-term future. Reflecting on the shape of the future is a crucial part of much evaluation: it is not a precise science, but foresight—even if limited—is better than hindsight.

Checkpoint 9B raises the question of whether the evaluation has some larger significance, possibly an application to similar programs that have not been otherwise evaluated. It may, like the evaluand, have a hidden value.

Checkpoint 10A. Cost Analysis.   We must be deeply concerned not only with financial costs but also with costs such as time, labor, expertise, energy, and enthusiasm. We must look at direct and indirect costs and opportunity costs (the lost learning in some other subject that is displaced from the curriculum by increased time spent on writing). It is useful to try to do some breakout of costs against components—what would we save by doing without the tutors, the audiotape support system, and so forth. Cost analysis is sometimes very difficult and very often crucial. One of the great failures in the evaluation of innovative curricula is the failure to correctly estimate the massive cost of the human energy involved in making an innovative curriculum run successfully. We find to our surprise that when the same physical components of the evaluand are exported it does not go nearly so well. Although all the same "pieces" are there that surplus energy supply is missing. If we had done a decent cost analysis in the first place, we would have realized that the psychic drain was a part of the resources used up by the system.

Full-scale detailed cost analysis is a difficult task, but preliminary rough cost analysis is something we can all do. It is not often done seriously, with heartbreaking results in terms of programs that have to be abandoned because the true cost eventually emerges and is too much to manage. A really good and less expensive program could have been implemented and continued.

Checkpoint 10B raises the absolutely crucial question of the cost of the evaluation. It is crucial because evaluation expenditures often come out of program money and are in that sense "not productive." The justification of evaluation expenditures is that without them there is no way of knowing whether some or all of the program money is being wasted. Whatever the payoffs, the evaluation must meet standards of cost-effectiveness, just as it expects the evaluand to meet them.

Checkpoint 11A: Comparisons.   What else could have been done with the same resources that would have achieved similar or more important goals, or almost similar goals but using fewer resources? It is not enough to evaluate programs or efforts in a vacuum. If we are to make evaluation relevant to decision making, we need to evaluate the leading options. Moreover, comparative evaluation needs to look beyond the available options. One may also need to invent other possible combinations that might prove more cost effective or more effective. A nice example from consumer products evaluation was a decision made by *Consumer Reports*, when doing an evaluation of rug cleaners, to add as one of the products in the comparison stakes a diluted solution of a popular laundry detergent, not advertised or described as a rug cleaner. It turned out to do a much better job than the self-styled rug cleaners, at a fraction of the cost.

So many different approaches have been developed for teaching composition skills that classroom teachers as well as program planners need to make particular efforts to keep informed about the various options, and should be ready to consider alternatives or amendments to current programs as needed. Administrators of composition inservice programs often need to be reminded that they could dispense with some of the most expensive components in favor of simpler alternatives without any large loss of effects. (Of course the political constraints may make it necessary to obtain prestige by dressing up a good program in fancier clothes.) Comparisons do not even have to be between programs with the same goals; the notion of opportunity costs reminds us that we have to make even more far-reaching comparisons every time we make a curriculum decision. We may have to trade off a remedial writing program against advanced writing inservice courses, "apples against oranges," as everyone says in horror, forgetting that we do it every time we visit the market. So the comparisons checkpoint is very powerful and deserves much care and attention in the design, execution, and interpretation of an evaluation.

Checkpoint 11B requires one to ask whether there were better or cheaper ways to do the evaluation; or, in the planning phase, one must review several options and look carefully at their relative merits.

Checkpoint 12A: Overall Significance. What do all the preceding conclusions add up to? What is the bottom line? No additional investigation is required to cope with this checkpoint, but it may be the most difficult of all. Prior to reaching this point, one may have already done some "data crunching," using a computer, for example, in trying to determine the average effects of the program. That is one kind of synthesis. Again, one may have done considerable synthesis of data in order to get an overall cost picture. Now, however, the task is to pull together these many dimensions of the investigation into a set of conclusions, which may or may not include recommendations. This is a difficult task, and there are few rules for it. Of course, sometimes the overall picture is very simple: One option is best on most of the dimensions of the evaluation, and the remaining dimensions are not crucial to the needs of the impacted population. There are many other cases that require much more detailed analysis to a degree that is not covered by any general rules. When one comes to this point, detailed analytical discussions of the relative merits and strengths and weaknesses of the alternatives should be provided and weighed with considerable care. This may be quite a long process, and is virtually always best done by a team rather than one person working all alone. A team discussion often benefits from an advocate-adversary format, with one person or group role-playing one possible overall viewpoint and the others reacting—and then proposing, and defending another possible overall view. Some of the views defended should be more extreme than anyone expects to see in the report to be finally adopted.

Three Warnings About Synthesizing. One rather attractive method of synthesizing evaluation findings is in terms of cost-benefit analysis, which involves converting all gains and costs into dollar equivalents and then calculating the relative cost-benefit "potency" of each of the options. The first warning about this method is that one can very rarely give sensible cost equivalents for gains in such fundamental skills as composition skills. (This does not mean cost analysis should not be done, but that other common denominators besides dollars should be used, as for example in cost-effectiveness analysis.)

The second warning concerns the argument that one should only report the facts and "let them speak for themselves." This would be attractive if the facts were simple. But the facts are very complex, relate to a dozen dimensions that are qualitatively distinct, and interact strongly. Small changes in one dimension will often produce quite large changes in the overall conclusion if some other dimensions have a certain configuration, but produce no change in the conclusion if the other dimensions have a somewhat different configuration. So the combinatorial task is very difficult, and a good evaluator must acquire the skill. Typically, this will mean that the evaluator will have to get crucial information from the decision maker, such as important facts about the political constraints, as well as from consumers, but the synthesis is something that evaluators should be able to do better than anybody else just because of their experience and their detailed knowledge of the particular case.

However, the third warning is that there are times when the attempt at synthesis fails and one should let the facts speak for themselves, mainly because they are not speaking very clearly. Even here, the advocacy exercises mentioned earlier are frequently most illuminating.

Checkpoint 12B is the corresponding effort to pull the metaevaluation (the evaluation of the evaluation) together, to ask what its overall message is about the merit and worth of the evaluation. A metaevaluation is not necessarily a major undertaking, but one should get a reading on the impact of each checkpoint from the Key Evaluation Checklist when applied to an evaluation itself. Even on the smallest scale, metaevaluation can pay off. For example, when evaluating the writing of individual students, it is by no means a waste of time to look at the defects of the evaluation procedure, its cost, alternatives to it, and so on. The side effects of evaluation systems used in the past on student work have often been so negative for both students and teachers that the cry to abandon all grading has been widely raised. Here is where comparisons become useful, with alternative methods of evaluation besides the one in which the lonely teacher serves as judge, jury, and appeals court. One promising alternative developed in composition instruction has been to involve students in the response process. Peer feedback and response to drafts, and even to the final grades, are helpful as long-term formative feedback to students, not as punitive afterthoughts to a term's teaching commitment.

This final example illustrates two important points that are worth repeating. Evaluation, in some form, occurs regularly at all levels of instruction; students and teachers regularly, though often informally, evaluate one another and act upon their evaluations. The only means of keeping such evaluations fair and useful to the concerned parties is to regularly conduct metaevaluation. But keeping evaluations useful—for example, by providing steady formative output from them, may conflict with keeping them fair, because if the formative output is accepted the evaluator becomes a coauthor, with objectivity now compromised. The metaevaluator must look at this hazard and how to control it—by rotating evaluators through the project, using an occasional visitor to "keep everyone honest," and so forth. The synthesizing process in the metaevaluation must pay particular attention to the existence of bias control systems in the evaluation.

1-9 ■ Final Reports

The delivery system for a composition instruction program may be teachers, special instructors, teacher aides, or audiovisual media. The delivery system for a formative evaluation, on the other hand, is the set of reports and exchanges of a less formal kind that occur between an evaluator and a client once the evaluation is in progress (Checkpoint 6B). As we move through the various phases of an evaluation, we need to consider the importance of both designing the delivery system for the evaluation right from the beginning, and evaluating its success as part of the metaevaluation at the end. Unfortunately, the typical final report is too long, too technical, and too late. Evaluation, which should generally be designed to provide at least some formative element, should start early (usually before the program actually begins, during the planning stage), continue steadily, and report regularly, often in different ways to different audiences and clients. Verbal reports are sometimes much more effective and protective of the client than written reports; on other occasions, a written report is essential for accountability. Writing several versions of a report, each aimed at the problems of particular importance to a different audience or client, is frequently an appropriate procedure. Considerable attention should be given to graphic and dynamic presentations, since visual presentations of complex data are usually far more comprehensible than tabular presentations to anybody but the expert. Good reports are the first step toward good implementation as well as the last phase of the evaluation process.

The final report does not have to contain recommendations, although sometimes it should or must. But the evaluand may not need to be improved in any feasible way; and there are evaluations in which the purpose is purely summative—for example, oriented toward accountability. In such cases, there would be no need for recommendations unless the program was still continuing. As far as determining whether the money was spent appropriately and consistent with legislative guidelines, for example, such an evaluation may well involve no recommendation. Recommendations typically require more resources to substantiate than a simple grading or ranking, and when dealing with very large numbers of students or programs this is often simply not feasible. One can only say "pass/not pass" or "outstanding"; one cannot always go on to give the kind of detailed analysis on which one could then base some detailed formative suggestions. So, although holistic scoring of student essays is reliable and inexpensive and may be all that is needed to evaluate a writing program, it does not provide any basis for recommendations for improvement of individual student work. Without suggesting that it is in any way ideal, the reader is referred to the Bay Area Writing Project Evaluation Reports (Scriven et al., 1979) for an example of how an evaluation can offer detailed factual descriptions along with a brief summative synthesis with recommendations.

1-10 ■ Implementation and Utilization of Evaluations

Given that an evaluation may not be oriented toward recommendations or changes at all, it is obviously inappropriate to suppose that evaluations should in general be assessed in terms of whether they produce substantial effects in the evaluand or elsewhere. The principal criteria for judging an evaluation are whether it is correct and whether it was cost effective, and the "effectiveness" dimension may refer simply to determining accountability rather than to making recommendations. In general, effectiveness also includes comprehensibility, clarity, relevance, timeliness, unobtrusiveness, credibility, and robustness (i.e., immunity to errors of detail).

If one supposes the main index of the merit of an evaluation is whether its recommendations are implemented, as is common today, then one automatically saddles perfectly good evaluations with the sins of decision makers who failed to make use of the findings although they should have done so. It is much better to treat implementability as a measure of merit of the evaluation, and this only to the extent that the evaluation was intended to suggest improvements of practice at all. An evaluation should help in every way that it can reasonably be expected to in the direction of implementation, short of compromising its validity. It must, for example, speak to the real alternatives facing the decision makers or be deservedly regarded as poor evaluation. Where recommendations are provided, they should be clarified, if necessary, by repeated sessions with the client, and amplified into greater detail if that is requested (and budgeted). To put the evaluator into the role of somebody who has to secure implementation in order to win points, however, is to encourage the kind of salesmanship and pressuring on the part of evaluators that surely undercuts their primary commitment to objectivity and independence.

1-11 ■ Evaluation Design—Scientific and Administrative

It is worth distinguishing between two aspects of an evaluation design: the scientific design and the administrative design. The *scientific design* is the plan to find or create the data that will answer the questions that the evaluation is intended to address. It involves such matters as the selection of comparison groups, the construction of tests, and so on, within some constraints on procedures and resources. Beyond that, however, there is the problem of developing the logistics of the investigation: the "time line," the exact costs, the responsibility allocations, the sequencing of the tasks, the collection of permissions and contracts and payments, and so forth. Large-scale evaluations depend heavily for their success on effective *administrative designs*, which tackle these further questions, and even small scale evaluations benefit by taking a quick look at such matters. But we'll focus here on the scientific issues.

There are many interesting situations in which the only resource available is simply a certain amount of time on the part of one teacher who is also teaching the course that will be the object of study—but this happens to be a teacher who would really like to know something about the value of his or her contribution to students' learning. Much of what we say here bears directly on such individual cases, and our mention of administrative design considerations of a rather large-scale kind are not meant to imply that all those steps must be gone into in great detail for every kind of evaluation.

Scientific Design

In setting up the scientific design, one must first clarify the evaluation questions one hopes to answer and reduce them to a minimum. For example, there are major differences between the kind of design that is required to determine whether individual students have improved, and the kind of design that is required to determine whether the average performance of a class has improved. Similarly, there is considerable difference between the kind of design needed to determine whether the whole instructional package (the combination of inservice training, teacher, process used, curriculum covered, and materials) has produced improvement, and the kind of design needed to determine which of those components has produced how much of the improvement—a question that might be ten times as difficult to answer. The design task is not only to develop reliable answers to appropriate questions, but also to keep the total cost and time of the evaluation down. Creating an evaluation design that will operate within a certain cost framework, ethical framework, time constraints, and political constraints is all part of scientific evaluation design. These considerations are not to be relegated to the administrative design, although they have often been regarded in that way; they are part of the intellectual task of designing a practical investigation of practical questions. The administrative design checks and refines the details of costs and times, and then makes the detailed allocation and requisitions of the costs, equipment, staff responsibilities, and other resources according to the priorities and cost limits set by the scientific design. But the original scientific design has to ensure that the cost framework and work schedule are not too tight to get the required answers.

The particular object or objects of study—the evaluand—must first be clarified (Checkpoint 1A). Is it the individual student, the class, or the teaching package? In evaluating composition instruction this task can often be difficult because of the various ways teachers may use a specific method. Thus in evaluating different composition classes, it may be necessary to identify (and possibly even evaluate separately) large variations in use of the same technique or approach.

Evaluation Questions

The particular kind of conclusion that is of interest must also be clarified: for example, do we want a "grading" or a rank-ordering of students or programs? And here we rapidly discover that although there is plenty of interest in all of these matters, we are up against a set of resource constraints that may make it necessary for us to restrict ourselves to a careful investigation in one area rather than an uninterpretable investigation of a large number. Thus, context and background discussions about the evaluation frequently involve changing the set of evaluation questions in the light of what is feasible. Sometimes problems arise during the course of an evaluation which require amending the scientific design. Preferably, the evaluation team or advisory committee includes both administrators and conceptualizers (or can draw upon scientific designers as consultants), so that any necessary changes can be as true to the original evaluation purposes as possible. Scientific evaluation design is like the process of planning a sequence of roadblocks to pin down a fugitive. The ideal design of roadblocks leaves the fugitive no way out except to the police station: the ideal scientific design leaves only one possible explanation remaining at the end. But at the beginning one must have a clear question to guide the design—one must know how to recognize the fugitive.

One of the most serious errors in design involves the supposition that one can always directly infer conclusions about the merit of teachers of composition from evidence about their students' composition performance. Obviously, many other variables may be producing whatever absolute level of performance or even whatever change or lack of change occurs. There are, however, particular circumstances in which limited comparisons can be made and conclusions can be drawn about the relative merit of teachers—for example, when the students in the classes are randomly assigned from a school's population, the classes are of normal size, and the test and teaching effort focus on the same general aspects of composition skills. These demanding requirements on the design are imposed by the question you want to answer, and are incompatible with the requirements imposed by many other questions, such as what writing approach works best with gifted or bilingual students in this district?

So one must be clear at the beginning of the evaluation as to its main purpose, since it is not possible to obtain answers to all the interesting questions from some master design even if there were no constraints upon time and money. One can best illustrate how the type of evaluation question controls the type of design by looking at a series of questions related to student writing and at the designs that are required to investigate them.

The very simplest evaluative question one could raise would be, "How good is *this* essay on *this* topic on *this* day by *this* student?" Even this question is not an easy one to answer, and the appropriate procedure for answering it may involve issues of topic selection, the use of more than one judge, a fairly elaborate discussion of scoring criteria, blind grading procedures, and so forth. Nevertheless, this is what one might call the nucleus of more complex designs.

The next question in this sequence might be, "How good is this *student* on this topic on this day?" The inference from a single performance to a student's general capability involves at least some assumptions about motivation. If the student is not highly motivated on this day or for this teacher, the performance will not reflect his or her true capability. Appropriate designs for this question require attention to procedures for maximizing motivation, which typically means having the teachers very much on the side of the evaluation. Hence, even at this early stage, we see the need for handling one of the psychological constraints on evaluation—namely, the need to get assistance from people who may in fact be threatened by the whole evaluation project. It is a scientific design problem to reconcile these conflicting tensions.

The third question in this sequence would be, "How good is this student at *composition* on this day?" Here the design will clearly need to involve a wider sampling of the student's capability than is afforded by testing on a single topic. Other tensions begin to emerge: if we were to test the student on several topics, there might be a fatigue effect, a loss of motivation, or—pointing the other way—a reduction of tension. Any of these might weaken whatever conclusion was indicated by the score on the particular test. Empirical studies can assist us in answering such questions as, "How many essays can a student at a given age level write in succession without deterioration of performance through fatigue?" But in general it is not a matter of great importance to us to get an answer that applies to a particular day; we are more interested in the performance of a student at a particular period of his or her development—for example, during a given month. Here is a case where, by slightly relaxing one of the terms in the question, we can make it a little easier to answer.

Another way in which we can relax the specificity of the question parameters is by moving back from a question about the performance of a particular student to a question about the performance of the class. If we need to know only how good the class is at composition during this particular time interval, then we can give each student one topic to write about (though not the same topic), instead of having to give each of them several topics. This is an elementary form of what is called matrix sampling, and it has the great advantage of handling the problems of test overload and test resentment, both of which tend to weaken whatever conclusions we can draw from our findings. Notice that as we relax the precision of the question, we are often able to answer with greater certainty than before. When we move from requiring a measure of the student's capability on a particular day to the capability during a particular time interval, we are obliged to give tests on several days instead of one, but the trade-off is that we avoid the loss of certainty that arises because of the unknown size of the fatigue effect caused by writing extensively on one occasion.

All of the preceding questions concern the quality of particular student performances. We have not so far addressed the question of the quality of various types of composition instruction. If we want to turn our attention from inferences about the effects to inferences about the causes, then the inferences become considerably more speculative, though not impossible. In order to approach these causal questions, we need first to add another type of question about student performance. This type of question concerns changes in student performance. An example would be "How much has this class changed its performance between this time interval and a previous time interval (e.g., between the first three weeks of the fall semester and the last three weeks of the spring semester)?" Although at first it might seem that one can immediately determine this by simply using the previous kind of approach on two different occasions, and then subtracting one score from the other, a moment's reflection shows that this is not the case, because of the effects of the testing. We need to look at these in a little more detail.

Human beings have memories and acquire skills through practice, and those facts make educational evaluation a much more difficult task than evaluating the effects of altering a production line process on the quality of the product. In particular, we face the following design dilemma. We can either use the same topic or topics in the spring as we used in the fall, or we can change to another set. If we use the same topics, then we may not be discovering differences in performance capability but merely differences due to the so-called practice effect—to the fact that people have a tendency on many tasks to do rather better the second time they try the same task. This does not show that their composition skills have improved, only that their capacity to write compositions on this particular topic has improved. If, on the other hand, we use a different topic (or set of topics) in the spring testing program we will have to face the possibility that there is a difference in the level of difficulty of the topics and hence that we are not noticing a real difference in skill level but only a difference in task difficulty. This particular example illustrates a design problem faced by virtually every effort to evaluate composition instruction.

The design solutions for this dilemma are numerous, but two are particularly worth mentioning. First, we could use a set of topics for the essay, which we distribute among the class so that, let us say, six students write on each topic. In the spring we arrange that a different six students write on that topic. In this (matrix sampling) design we not only eliminate the practice effect but also average out any differences in topic difficulty. But no such design is possible if we must have answers about the changes in each individual student's performance across this period. Hence we cannot combine this design for program evaluation with the usual purposes of a teacher's use of tests—formative evaluation of each individual student.

A second design would involve trying to identify topics that are apparently similar in difficulty, and then going through a preliminary field test with students from similar schools, abilities, and age levels to see whether their average test scores, when they are asked to write about these topics, turn out to be closely similar. This approach would enable us to say that we had established the equivalence of the difficulty level of the two (or more) topics.

Thus to demonstrate that there has been a change in performance level involves quite a serious kind of design. If we now wish to identify the cause of this change, we face substantially greater difficulties. Suppose that we are trying to evaluate the contribution of the composition program, the particular instructor, the curriculum materials, or the particular teaching methodology. A number of possible factors could account for a difference in performance level between the beginning and end of an academic year.

One "competing cause" that might explain an observed improvement in performance level is "maturation," which may refer to merely genetic development but is more likely to refer to changes due to the general social and individual chain of experiences across this period of time. For example, students are (we hope) doing some writing in other courses they are taking and so their writing performance should be showing some slight gains even if there was no positive effect at all from the composition instruction we are trying to evaluate. It may be that the students' reading or conversation (or even television viewing!) may cause improvements in writing, most obviously because of increased vocabulary or range of interests. All of these factors are conventionally lumped together under the heading maturation, and it is essential that we eliminate these effects if we are to isolate the effects due to the particular instructional package (or one of its components). Here one usually starts considering *comparison group design.*

If we can identify a group of students closely comparable to the group that is to receive the instructional package in which we are interested, but which will not receive that package (but will instead continue with the regular instruction), and if we can test them at the same time at the beginning and end of the year along with the program group (the one that is receiving the instructional package to be evaluated), then we will be able to observe in the comparison group the effects due to maturation alone. If the program group shows a greater improvement, then we can attribute the extra improvement to the instructional package. The program group is often called the experimental group, but the term has adverse connotations—we are not so much "experimenting with" as "providing our best services for" this group and gathering evidence to show these services *are* the best.

If the comparison group—often called the control group—is located in the same school or institution, then it will also serve to "control for" any special efforts that are being made—for example, by a new administrator, department chair, or social studies teacher—to upgrade basic skills or specifically writing skills. Hence it will serve to control for what we might call irrelevant local efforts. If we cannot set up a comparison group (because the entire school or department is going to adopt the new approach), then we will have quite a hard time coming to any conclusions about the effects of the instructional package. This is a very good argument for trying to avoid a situation in which everybody jumps to a new approach.

Could we instead compare the gains in this school with those at another school that is not adopting the approach? The problem with doing that, of course, is that the other setting will be different simply in not having such an enthusiastic administrator or English department (or else *they* would be doing the evaluation!). It may be that enthusiasm, rather than the particular teachers or methods or content is producing the result. This is sometimes loosely called the "Hawthorne effect," and we need to be able to tell whether the results are due solely to enthusiasm, which tends to evaporate after a year or two. We would then find ourselves back where we started if there were in fact no long-term benefit accruing from the intrinsic merits of this particular program. And since one usually cannot wait several years before doing an evaluation, it is preferable to use comparison groups within the same school.

The preceding discussion concerns measuring improvement in a class's average performance. If we were trying to identify the cause of the improvement in a particular student's performance, the task would be much more difficult. In the first place, finding a matching student is much less easy than finding a matching class where the averaging process gives us some flexibility; though it's not enough to match just for average scores, we only need approximately equal distributions of scores, not one-for-one equivalence. Second, significant influences on a particular student are very far-ranging; they might include the influence of a parent, a sibling, a friend, or even a particular experience. It would be difficult indeed to eliminate all of these as alternative explanations for any improvement in performance that we are hoping is due to a particular instructional package.

Although it is not (in this respect) nearly as satisfactory to use other schools—or classes from other schools—as comparison groups, it may in certain cases be plausible enough. One needs to look carefully at the possibility that there has in fact been some overall schoolwide effort that could provide an alternative explanation: maybe this isn't a real threat in the particular case. Even in the absence of other schools, there is one remaining possibility, namely comparison with prior performances at this school by the preceding echelons of students. Again, it may only reflect a change in the times, or in external factors (e.g., Sesame Street's new program), or in overall Hawthorne effect, but it is better than no comparison at all. Getting these baseline data consists of calculating the rate of improvement during previous school years.

Nontraditional Parts of Scientific Design

In concluding, let us consider two nontraditional aspects of the scientific design. We have already mentioned that we need teacher cooperation. We may also need cooperation from school administrators in order to enter the classrooms. Now, why should the teachers and the administrators cooperate?

Good design tries very hard to arrange and announce and explain expected benefits, or payoffs, for all involved. That does not mean guaranteeing favorable results, it means guaranteeing informative and interesting results and, when possible, no punitive outcomes unjustly *or* unethically delivered. (It should be emphasized, however, that almost no sound evaluation can guarantee the total absence of critical outcomes.) Trying to arrange payoffs for all involved sometimes means doing more than the minimum required to answer the evaluation question of principal interest. For example, it is possible to find out whether a particular writing program is doing a good job without finding out whether individual teachers need to improve their contribution to that job. On the other hand, it will be more useful to the teacher to get an answer to the latter question. Similarly, matrix sampling designs save money and reduce test load on students—but they do not generate advice to individual students as to how to improve their writing unless provisions are made for additional analysis of student essays, which should be considered if the teachers feel students need the critique.

Of course, the best situation is one in which all participants are interested in doing the job well and find the evaluation worth supporting just because it will address the question of general effectiveness. After all, even if we cannot provide advice to individual students (because our budget forces us to matrix sampling), the students will still benefit if the best composition program is offered. One can often elicit support on this basis *if one makes the effort to properly inform program participants.*

There are also, of course, ethical reasons for explaining the function of an evaluation to those involved. Hence the scientific design must assign responsibility for informing participants and the cost/timeline must be calculated accordingly. By arranging anonymity and/or a database that will not permit individual evaluative conclusions that we do not need, we can often avoid unnecessary trouble and anxiety.

Another nontraditional aspect of design concerns the use of external evaluators. They may be district staff members, external to the particular school, or from a neighboring college. If they provide regular formative suggestions, they either become coauthors of the program (if the suggestions are adopted), or rejected suitors (if they are not adopted); in either case, they lose objectivity—and credibility. The evaluation design must address this problem. One solution is for the formative feedback to be only evaluative, not "therapeutic" (i.e., not including fix-it suggestions). Another is the rotation of evaluation staff through this project and on to others—the "authors" of suggestions are thus not also the evaluators of their own success. Another is the use of a metaevaluator.

The tenor of these remarks on nontraditional design is to make clear that considerations of fairness and usefulness to all are truly part of evaluation. Evaluation is not an alien imposition of scientific measurement. It is, and must be, a humane and commonsense process of improving and demonstrating improvement.

1-12 ■ Evaluating Writing as a Skill

It is essential to understand the peculiar status of mastery of an instrumental intellectual skill like writing or reading or reasoning or speaking Spanish, by contrast with mastery of a substantive intellectual subject like English literature or the history of philosophy or special relativity theory. The skills are in some sense content-free—loosely speaking, they represent knowing *how* to do something without knowing *that* something is the case. The first problem that affects validity arises from the terrible temptation to try to convert the skill into a subject, because subjects are easier to talk about, to teach, and to test. Thus we find teaching composition converted into teaching grammar, teaching reasoning converted into teaching the subject of logic, teaching Spanish converted into teaching Spanish literature or culture. If the conversion were licit, the evaluation would be much facilitated, and thus evaluators have happily followed teachers down the path of temptation. But the logic of the situation—the validity issue—sternly prohibits this move. There is not the slightest reason to think one can't learn to write well without any knowledge of grammar just as one learns to speak one's own language without the learning of grammar as a subject. Even if there is some reason to suppose that grammar helps (though it isn't essential), the valid summative test can test only composition skill and not grammatical knowledge, because that's the only performance we have direct reasons for valuing. In particular, individual students must be given full marks if their writing is excellent, even if they completely flunk grammar, because the grammar has no raison d'être of its own. In general, it is hard to justify time spent on grammar, not because it doesn't help at all, but because the same time spent on a direct approach to the improvement of writing helps more. But a few grammatical terms may be useful for communicating with students about their writing, and these can be learned very quickly. Learning any so-called principles of grammar is another story—they are hard even to state approximately, harder still to learn, and of unknown and probably negligible value in the improvement of composition. Hence tests of grammatical knowledge per se are simply—at this point—invalid components of an evaluation of composition skill.

Of course, grammar is a great deal easier to teach (and test) than good writing, just because it is a body of knowledge, a package of propositions. Good reasoning is like good writing (i.e., formal logic is a poor substitute for reasoning skill), while basic algebra is entirely different (the principles are precise, clearly stateable, and apply directly; and the skills can rarely be learned without knowing the principles).

So the evaluator should take great care not to confuse content knowledge with instrumental skills. What might seem to follow from this general principle is that we should use composition test topics that require no particular content knowledge: "What did you do last summer?" "Write a short story." "Tell us about something that concerns you deeply." But that is surely a mistake. Focusing on vacuous topics has two serious side effects; it rewards the skill of embellishing facile vapidities or phony phenomenology, and it diverts attention from the fact that instrumental skills are supposed to increase the skill with which something else is done—e.g., instructing, informing, directing. Of course, story writing skill is a kind of "something else" but a kind with virtually no repertoire value for children outside the writing class.

Becoming a writer is an unrealistic vocational skill for more than a few—but using writing well is part of almost everyone's vocational needs. Only those who become literary figures (if then) need the skill of writing about their own past or imagined scenes or streams of thought. For most people the value of writing lies only in its use for other, usually practical purposes and that is the only context in which it can be validly tested.

Of course, teachers who believe to the contrary will want to test their success in their self-appointed tasks (e.g., creative writing), but such tests are not valid tests of the composition skills that demonstrably need to be learned by all, the basic skills for which the taxpayer pays taxes. Tests of those basic skills must relate to their use on a task of independent validity—for example, the task of presenting the justification for a proposed course of action in a fully determinate context (as in a memorandum to one's boss or employees or fellow students, unionists or tax accountant). In the school context there are dozens of such tasks with concurrent validity, such as writing a report on a science project, and it is partly for this reason that "writing across the curriculum" has so much going for it—its tasks make sense to the student and are valid tests of writing skills.

It isn't easy to separate a student's knowledge of science from the writing skills—if the student knows no science, the writing is going to look "thin," but if the student knows a great deal the essay will look rich even if inelegant. But that effort at separation must be made by the composition teacher or by the science teacher. It must not be handled by converting the writing task into one that is meaningless to the student but easier for the composition teacher.

There are, of course, vast numbers of topics the composition teacher can set that do not require substantive knowledge of other subjects but still test a legitimate instrumental use of writing. The most obvious cluster of examples concerns current events on campus or in the world at large, hobbies, television, sports, and family affairs. Since students will differ in their involvement in these topics, allowing alternative choices of topic seems attractive and appropriate. However, teachers often encounter difficulties in compensating for differences in the difficulty of topics, they substantially overscore the efforts on the more difficult topics. (It is preferable to try very hard to match alternative topics for difficulty rather than assume the difficulty level can be compensated for in the grading process. That means, in particular, avoiding the common practice of offering one abstract or philosophical topic in a list of prosaic ones. Tests that do so thus represent another kind of invalidity.

Of course, any given class in a school curriculum serves many functions—and the same one may have different functions for different students. For example, discussion of the great philosophical issues of the meaning of life and the objectivity of ethics is sometimes to be found only in the English classroom, and one does not want to eliminate it from that last refuge. One must simply be clear that such discussions become part of the curriculum in their own right, and not use them as topics for the key tests of writing skills. Writing about such issues is no less an instrumental use of language just because relatively few people have a natural (or even arousable) interest in them. But requiring all or allowing some students to write on them as a test of writing, given the bias of teachers toward over-scoring such essays, is to build in too much reward for the proto-philosopher, in just the fallacious way that demands for orgies of introspection or retrospection or fantasy over-reward the proto-novelist.

One legitimate and important halfway house to philosophy is the requirement of skills in the analysis and presentation of arguments, since propaganda analysis and advertising analysis are vital skills for all, recognizable as such, and teachable to all. These skills can legitimately be taught in the process of teaching writing because they are part of almost all good functional prose. *The general skill of good writing cannot exist without good reasoning.*

Unfortunately, some English teachers think that to reward the logic is to reward something different from the writing (which is true) and hence it's inappropriate for the composition instructor to do this (which is incorrect). The extension of their approach is to give high marks for elegant nothings written on topics that require good arguments. To do so is like supposing you should teach reading without understanding because understanding is always subject-matter dependent and the reading teacher shouldn't be teaching subject matter. But there is a universal subject-matter—thinking—and some competence in that must be involved in all reading and writing, its teaching and its testing.

There is no useful skill of word-by-word reading without sentence-by-sentence and paragraph-by-paragraph understanding. It isn't necessary to insist on the reader having brilliant insights in order to avoid the empty shell of superficial reading. And similarly, it isn't necessary for one to give As for elegant nothings in composition in order to avoid the equal absurdity of refusing As to all but Einsteins. A logic curriculum is excessive; logic is essential.

Let's bring all this to bear on some examples that go beyond the substitution of grammar for writing. First example: the scoring key for a National Assessment of Educational Progress writing test, some years ago, which required the student to write about a color picture of a stag swimming across a river in a burning forest. The key made clear that describing what was there (i.e., doing what was requested) was completely unsatisfactory; one could get an A only by inventing some fanciful background story, something which was not requested. This is a totally invalid scoring key. Second example: in our comprehensive review of the literature for topics used in the evaluation of writing (Keech, 1979c) we found that the number of topics that involved any exercise of writing in the service of practical reasoning was negligible, despite the fact that the writing tasks that justify the view that writing is a basic skill either for further education or in later life are virtually all of that kind. This further illustrates the extent to which composition instruction has drifted toward so-called creative writing and away from functional prose. Third example: when I insisted on having one such task ("What is wrong with the following argument . . . ?") as one of the two topics we used for measuring writing performance in several thousand essays, the scoring key set up by the highly experienced professionals who did the grading did not incorporate a sound analysis of the elementary argument involved.

What's the moral of all of this? A valid scoring key in composition evaluation must absolutely require not only good writing but logical propriety: a relevant and/or reasoned answer where relevance and/or reason is requested. To award high marks for incompetent criticism or to withhold them from relevant and therefore limited description, is to reward incompetence and irrelevance, which is not only invalid in itself but a terrible message from the teacher.

To conclude, then. Teachers have been systematically trained to think and teach that good answers can include irrelevance, and that good commentary on serious topics can be identified without analysis of the merits of the case. These are serious and damaging assertions, but they are based on careful examination of the topics and rubrics used in the best professional grading efforts, set up and run by extremely experienced teachers and testers. These are people who are doing a great deal to improve composition, and they deserve great credit for that. Moreover, the trap into which they fall is a very easy one to fall into, and most academic philosophers fell into a similar trap as they developed the discipline of formal logic as an essentially useless introductory course. The philosophers substituted skill in doing formal logic for skill in reasoning on the plausible but false grounds that formal logic is the theory of reasoning and learning to apply it should therefore be very like learning to improve reasoning. The composition people, where they haven't substituted grammar for writing, have too often substituted skill in irrelevant writing for skill in writing on the plausible grounds that, since writing is an instrumental skill, writing about X should not be graded on knowledge of X but only on the intrinsic standards of good writing. Yet there's the rub: grading on the intrinsic standards of writing is abandoning the instrumental role of writing. Where X is reasoning, a case can be made that composition teachers should teach X, too; but the essential point is that they—and the evaluator—must require that the standards of X (e.g., logic, science, philosophy, or current news reports), as well as the standards of good grammar and other matters, be met, and that no other standards be introduced or substituted before they can claim a valid test.

There is no hope for high standards in composition instruction unless its developers and evaluators learn that even the emphasis on context, mode, and function we sometimes see stressed is not nearly enough. Teachers of reading and writing and speaking have to evaluate thinking or they teach nothing.

2

Aspects of Composition Instruction

2-1 ■ Issues in Composition Instruction

Overview

A comprehensive history of composition instruction in the United States has yet to be written. Some accounts of brief periods of a decade or so have appeared in the professional literature, as have histories on related subjects. (See *English Journal*, April and September, 1979, for histories of composition instruction; Applebee, 1974, and Hook, 1979, for related topics.) These reviews identify a number of provocative topics that deserve far more detailed attention than is possible in this brief section. Our purpose here is to identify what seem to be recurring issues and new developments of significance to composition instructors. (See also White, 1985, for a discussion of issues in teaching and assessing writing).

The Recurring Literacy Crisis. The widespread outcry about literacy problems is not the first crisis over language and its use in the United States. (See Piche, 1978; Judy, 1975; and Applebee, 1974, for more specific discussion of this point.) The following expression of concern voiced over a century ago sounds quite contemporary:

> Bad spelling, incorrectness as well as inelegance of expression in writing, ignorance of the simplest rules of punctuation, and almost entire want of familiarity with English literature, are far from rare among young men of eighteen otherwise well prepared to pursue their college studies. (Charles Eliot, President of Harvard, 1873)

Some time later, one of our most esteemed American authors, Henry James, along with other professionals, suggested that one source of the problem was "deterioration" of correct English into the polyglot forms of the immigrant masses. Their viewpoint is reflected in the words of another prominent educator of that period:

> Good English is a dead letter and each child uses his bastard speech unhindered and unafraid. (A. Searling, 1898)

Most professionals would vigorously disagree with this observation. However, the statement refers to a situation that may account for some of the current literacy problems, namely changing student populations. Other causes of the current crisis are undoubtedly peculiar to our time, though not restricted to the United States. The important point to remember is that the present situation is not a decline from some past age of competence; problems in literacy have consistently plagued American society. The causes are complex, interrelated, and in some cases beyond the control of the schools.

Diversity of Approaches to Teaching English and Composition. Response to any problems in English and composition instruction is compounded by English instructors' traditional independence and the resulting diversity of instruction at all levels.

> It would be presumptuous in any author to attempt to give rules or to lay down laws to which all the departments of English Composition should be subjected. (Richard Green Parker, author of one of the most widely used composition texts of the 1800s in 1841)

This situation has changed little from the turn of the century and may in fact have intensified, so that diversity is often considered a source of strength in a composition program.

> The diversities . . . are, perhaps, the basis for our program's greatest strengths, and the source of some of our most troublesome problems. If our teachers and students were all timid little persons of like mind, and if we could devise the proper hurdles for all students to jump over on their way to effective communication, then our days would be more serene. But then, of course, our program would not deserve to exist. There is no doubt that the presence of teachers with a variety of academic backgrounds and teaching philosophies lends an exciting vitality to our program. We learn from each other, and we are better for that. (Cleo Martin, Writing Supervisor, University of Iowa, 1978)

The rapid growth of high school elective programs during the late 1960s and early 1970s provides a more extensive example of the high value generally placed on diversity of teaching approach in English and composition. Few secondary schools reported using electives in the early 1960s. By 1977, in response to the National Council of Teachers of English (NCTE) survey of English department chairpersons, 78 percent reported some kind of elective program in operation (Applebee, 1978).

Although diversity of approach to composition can be lauded as an effort toward individualization, it can cause difficulties for evaluation, particularly in clearly describing a program content. This point will be discussed in a later section.

Definition of Writing Competencies and Language Standards. In large part the insistence on diversity of approach results from a recognition of the variety of skills necessary for writing competence. Some professionals have developed extensive lists of writing skills or competencies. (See Bereiter, 1979, and Mellon, 1978, for examples.) Though the general public often equates composition skill with grammatical correctness and legibility, these often constitute only a small proportion of skills identified by professionals. Other important skills often cited as necessary for successful writing include:

- *Motivation* to communicate in writing: willingness to write and confidence in writing; seeing writing as valuable for accomplishing personal goals
- Awareness of the unique *linguistic demands* or conventions of clear writing: sociolinguists are just beginning to document the differences between writing and speaking, and the additional linguistic demands of writing that go beyond rules for correctness. (See Mellon, 1978, for a description of "The Rules of the Writing Game" which describes these linguistic demands.)
- *Lexical and syntactic fluency:* an awareness not only of correct word meanings and sentence forms, but also of their most effective use for different audiences and different writing purposes
- *Understanding of discourse structure:* knowing how to structure longer pieces of writing so that they will be clear and meaningful; being responsive to the rhetorical demands of different situations—for example, how to adjust content and structure of writing to different audiences and purposes and make effective use of discourse modes or genre schemes
- *Psychological competencies: ideational fluency* or the ability to gener-

ate ideas about different topics; revision skill or the ability to clarify and refine ideas

- *Practice competencies:* knowledge of the different stages of writing (prewriting, composing, and rewriting) and how to make use of them in response to different task demands (e.g., impromptu, 20-minute writing tests require quite different efforts from week-long essay assignments)

The list is not meant to be either exhaustive or conclusive. It should serve to remind those who develop multiple-choice tests of grammar skills that they are not testing writing skills but only one small aspect of writing competence. This list should also suggest to program planners and evaluators that many different writing competencies can serve as the basis for the evaluation of student performance.

A related source of dispute is whether and how to adjust definitions of competence in application to special student groups. Much of the current debate about literacy concerns which versions of English to accept as standard or mainstream. Clearly a mainstream English exists; without it we could not understand national television programs, nor could we move freely from one region of the country to another. The quarrels result from attitudes toward and treatment of minority languages and dialects inside the schools and in society as a whole. Disputes arise over the problem of how heavily to weight correct mainstream usage on writing performance tests, and whether to penalize bilingual and bidialectal students for using their local spoken dialect in writing performance. There is no simple solution to these problems. Providing an egalitarian education in a multicultural context seems to carry with it an inherent contradiction: recognizing all language varieties as "equal," yet labeling one language variety as "the standard." Some multilingual societies seem to have faced this problem without the turmoil that has been generated here (Fishman, 1977). Yet other researchers have shown that in socially divided societies use of the mainstream language is often more highly valued and use of a minority dialect or language devalued (Lambert, 1973). This suggests that our problems originate in social relationships and may continue until the confusion of linguistic forms with social value ceases. In the meantime, however, program leaders and evaluators need to be aware of the problems involved in defining writing competence and language standards, and to recognize that the goals, outcomes, and evaluation of any program may be subject to dispute because of disagreement about the choice of standards. (See Gere and Smith, 1979, for a discussion of attitudes toward language and language change.)

Definition of Instructional Goals.   Educators have long debated the appropriateness of teaching a broad range of writing skills. Questions of what should be taught, how, and at what grade level continue to generate disagreement. Articulation and coordination of curriculum between grade levels have been rare; more often, instructors at the same level can reach agreement. Yet even then, consensus has not been unanimous. For example, college instructors have long deplored the need to teach college preparatory skills at their level:

> It is obviously absurd that the college—the institution of higher education— should be called upon to turn aside from its proper functions, and devote its means and the time of its instructors to the task of imparting elementary instruction which should be given even in ordinary grammar schools, much more in those academic institutions intended to prepare select youth for a university source. (Report of the Committee on Composition and Rhetoric, Harvard College Board of Overseers, 1892)

Yet more recently many programs for teaching such skills have been created at the college level in response to student needs.

Many teachers at the lower grade levels have insisted that training in practical communication skills was a far more appropriate role for them to assume than teaching the more academic composition skills, because until the late 1960s many students did not go on to college. In fact, NCTE was founded in 1910 by a group of such revolutionaries—secondary-level teachers who were tired of what they saw as inappropriate domination of high school curricula by college-level goals. They insisted that rather than dwelling upon rules of correct usage, instructors should teach grammar as an integral part of composition. By using oral and written work to deal with life's experiences, the student would be working for vocational and personal goals as well as for subsequent academic success (Hook, 1979, and *English Journal*, April 1979). Of course, this choice of goals for composition instruction has not been the only one. Other elementary and secondary teachers chose a solution to the debate that sounds remarkably contemporary:

> A reformation everywhere is demanded. It is being brought about, and so rapidly that most textbooks are stranded in the idealism of a decade ago, and many teachers are floundering badly in the new conditions. It is hard to keep pace with swift change, hard to know what it is all about, or why our duties are preached to us in such contradictory terms. Inspire is still the watch cry; drill in rudiments is soon to be the fact. (C. S. Ward, 1917)

The teaching of standards of correctness in rule-based learning exercises has long given many teachers some achievements that could easily be measured and readily provide a feeling of solid accomplishment. Though the goal of teaching correct standards of usage was superseded in popularity during the late 1950s and 1960s, it again gained support in the 1970s. Thus the latest demand for teaching "the basics" can trace its roots back to the beginning of this century, to another literacy crisis and a continuing debate about the purposes of composition instruction.

Working Conditions.   The conditions under which composition instructors work play an important role in determining their effectiveness. If one may generalize from research studies of secondary-level teachers, little improvement in working conditions has been made during this century.

   Daily class load.   In 1917 the average load of secondary teachers was 127 students a day. In the 1961 NCTE survey, teachers reported seeing about 130 students a day, and in a 1977 survey the figure was 121 students a day. Recent funding cutbacks have caused this number to increase in many places (Freedman, 1985).

   What has also remained constant is the time required for reading and responding to student writing. A study of the minimum time required for reading and marking a student essay so as to "teach thinking and writing" skills was 8.6 minutes (Dusel, 1955). Thus any one assignment given to 130 pupils would take eighteen hours to mark (even in a minimal fashion). Obviously this load would vary for elementary and college instructors, depending upon the number of students and the time spent on each essay. Nevertheless, it represents a considerable burden to assign very much writing.

   Extra duties.   Additional demands on composition instructors' time come from the extra nonteaching duties imposed upon them—sponsorship of school activities or other contributions of time and effort to the educational community. Growing bureacratization and shrinking budgets have increased these duties, leaving teachers with less time for such academic work as marking papers (Squire and Applebee, 1968; Applebee, 1978).

   Professional development.   Another problem, long detracting from teacher effectiveness, has been the lack, until recently, of opportunities for staff development training for composition instructors. Without opportunities for renewal and revitalization, teaching effectiveness inevitably suffers.

   These data illustrate some working conditions which limit the effectiveness of composition teachers at all levels. Any effort to improve or evaluate student and faculty performances needs to take such factors into account.

Recent Developments

In the midst of all these recurring issues and debates, it seems important to identify that which is new. One powerful influence on schools has been the call for new standards of accountability. Shrinking school budgets have led to adoption of the industrial model of performance-based accountability and a preoccupation with goal setting and measurable outcomes. In more than half of the states high school students must meet minimum proficiency requirements in writing skills before graduation (Fadiman and Howard, 1979). For many schools facing such requirements, the least troublesome response has been to develop tests for what is most easily measured, namely grammatical standards of correctness. Opposition to such practices caused NCTE to pass a resolution at its 1977 convention opposing legislatively mandated competency testing "until it is determined to be socially and educationally beneficial." Some professionals have turned such requirements to advantage and used proficiency test mandates as motivation to upgrade composition programs and to develop procedures for more sophisticated assessment of student skills. In three case studies at the precollege level, program participants stated that a variety of beneficial outcomes very likely would not have occurred had it not been for the mandated testing requirements. (See Thomas and Keech, 1979.)

In another widespread development, faculty in disciplines other than English, have been taking increasing responsibility for teaching composition (Griffin, 1982). At the secondary level this has taken the form of emphasizing writing across the curriculum where writing is used as a tool for recording and refining ideas in mathematics and science as well as in the social sciences. At the college level, adjunct courses have been developed for teaching writing skills specific to an individual discipline (e.g., science writing, business writing). Thus, it would seem that although excessive concern for performance outcomes can be abused, it can also provide the impetus for increased articulation among faculty and the improvement of writing programs.

Important changes have also emerged in the professionalism of composition teachers at K-12 levels, as indicated by the increasing numbers of staff development programs. An example is the rapid and widespread dissemination of the National Writing Project Network, which now includes more than 150 sites across the country. In addition, a variety of other training programs have been developed at the college level to assist the teachers of the newly offered composition programs. The heightened interest in topics related to composition instruction can also be seen in professional conferences and journals.

A fourth set of developments can be observed in the field of composition research, which now receives growing financial support from universities and federal agencies. This contrasts sharply with past practices; for many years it was estimated that for every $100 spent on reading research, only $1 was spent on writing research (Graves, 1978). More researchers are studying the writing processes of individual students and are beginning to provide empirical models of composing that teachers can use for diagnostic and planning purposes (Hillocks, 1986). The types of procedures used to assess writing skills are also receiving increased attention. In time, it is hoped that these efforts will result in more reliable and valid instruments for measuring writing competence. A third type of promising research involves developing and testing the effectiveness of specific instructional practices. Although past composition research has had little effect upon the actual teaching of composition and has sometimes been criticized for its quality, the alliances formed between university faculty and local school personnel (e.g., at the National Writing Project sites) suggests that this may not be the case in the future; there seems to be more opportunity now for joining experimental/ theoretical and practical expertise.

A national Center for the Study of Writing, funded by a federal grant in 1985, should help further these research developments. The Center, located at the University of California, Berkeley, School of Education, proposes four years of research on writing and the writer; the interactions of writing with reading, speaking, and computers; and writing and instruction. A major emphasis of the Center will be to involve teachers as collaborators in its projects in order to develop "research-sensitive practice and practice-sensitive research."

Computers and Writing

Since the late 1970s, composition instructors have found many uses for mainframe computers and microcomputers in a range of instructional contexts (Balajthy, 1985; Halpern and Liggett, 1983; Schwartz, 1985; Solomon, 1986; Wresh, 1984). The earliest software provided drills for basic grammar principles; more sophisticated programs now supplement instruction and practice in all aspects of the composing process: prewriting, composing, revising, rewriting, editing, and presenting a finished product.

Types of Instructional Software.   In general, instructional software can be classified into four categories. *Drill and practice* programs offer multiple-choice or fill-in-the-blanks questions. Correct answers are positively reinforced ("Good job!"), and the student proceeds to the next question. Incorrect answers elicit a prompt to try again. Composition programs of the drill and practice type usually test basic grammar. CRAM (Breininger, 1983) is an example of drill and practice software.

Tutorials provide some instruction, either before the student is tested or after the student selects an incorrect answer. Tutorial programs treat topics such as vocabulary, spelling, and grammatical concepts.

Simulation software requires students to make decisions about courses of action, analyze outcomes, and learn from the results of their decisions. The emphasis is on problem solving and logical thinking. Composition software of this type involves pattern-recognition and strategy development.

Integrative software, the most sophisticated, gives students the opportunity to manipulate concepts and ideas to learn thinking processes. Examples include LOGO, Rocky's Boots, and MaxThink.

Writing Programs.   *Word-processing* programs allow the student to revise a piece of writing without having to retype the entire piece. By eliminating the drudgery of retyping, word-processing programs may encourage students to spend more time making substantive changes in their work. Some instructors claim that these programs also make students more aware of the recursive nature of writing as a process in which revision begins almost as soon as composing leaves off. For reviews of popular word-processing programs, see Wiswell (1985) and Gallagher (1985).

Other writing programs respond in some way to the writer: *spelling checkers* indicate which words are incorrectly spelled; *text editors* flag certain expressions, word choices, and passive constructions. Grammatik (developed by Wang) and Writer's Workbench (developed by Bell Labs) are examples of this type of software. For descriptions and reviews, see Macdonald and associates (1982) and Seybold (1984).

Finally, *idea planners* and *idea processors* help the student structure the writing process by organizing blocks of text. Examples include ThinkTank, Executive Writer, and Thor. See Hershey (1985) and Seybold (1984) for reviews.

Description of Uses.   Teachers at all levels are now using computer programs to help students prewrite, organize their thinking, write, acquire readers' responses, rewrite, and prepare their work for final copy.

Prewriting programs include those that encourage invention by posing questions drawn from tagmemics or basic research investigation—"What is your thesis? What evidence supports your thesis?" Examples include WANDAH, INVENT, and Writer's Helper. These programs often save and store prewriting to be used at a later time when the student begins composing initial ideas into a longer, coherent piece. For a review of these programs, see Frase (1986).

Ordinary word-processing programs can also be used to encourage prewriting. Marcus (1985) describes a prewriting technique for developing fluency called "invisible writing with computers." Students turn down the monitor's brightness knob so that the monitor display is blank. They can then write for flow of thought rather than stopping to correct grammar, spelling, or punctuation. Marcus reports that invisible writing discourages local editing that is counterproductive at the beginning stages of the composing process.

Frase (1986) describes several computer programs such as Framework or Freestyle that help organize one's thoughts. This type of software can create outlines and hierarchical structures that aid students in organizing their ideas.

From prewriting and organization, a student can move easily to a first draft, using computer software such as WANDAH, Hypertext, or File Retrieval and Editing System (see Frase, 1986, for descriptions). Some of these programs allow students to comb through their text to gather related ideas and topics. Once a draft is completed, specific editing programs such as spelling checkers and text editors can help the revising process.

Computers can also make the text more easily accessible to others—peer writers or instructors—to read and to comment upon. Some systems provide dual screens, one for the student's text and one for instructor's comments. Others, such as RSVP (Kotler, 1983), allow a teacher to mark comments and typical errors (e.g., lack of supporting detail) on a student's text and then order a "personalized" letter to the student that discusses the errors and gives examples of correct or appropriate responses.

Other reported instructional uses of software include collaborative research and writing tasks intended to encourage dialogue among students. The program Seminar (Catano, 1985) allows students to comment on a collection of reading and lecture materials. The Communal Text Project (Catano, 1985) stores all writing done by students and instructors in a computer file as part of the basic course text that students can draw upon when they write their papers. In the elementary grades, computers assist students in composing collaborative texts; groups share story ideas and then type them into the computer. The electronic mail feature of many systems also encourages interaction and collaboration among students.

Reported Benefits.   Use of the computer for composition instruction is still too limited and recent to be documented fully in research and evaluation studies. However, anecdotal reports of positive impact come from teachers at all levels (Harris, 1985; Marcus, 1985; Rodrigues, 1985; Womble, 1984).

For younger students and beginning writers, for whom handwriting can pose a major obstacle, the computer's printed text seems to provide an incentive. Students like the "clean, professional" look. Instructors report that the printing of classroom "books" seems to give students more confidence and reduce writing apprehension. All the students' texts and teacher's comments (or computer-generated response letters) can be stored on diskette, making a printed record of student's progress readily available. Students also value the ease of making revisions, and some students seem more willing to rework a piece of writing. Seeing the text on the screen may allow students to regard it more objectively, which makes it easier for them to develop a sense of an outside audience.

Writers at all levels of skill—beginning, basic, advanced, college-level, and professional—report enhanced motivation to write and a more favorable attitude toward writing after working with a computer (Rodrigues, 1985; Womble, 1984). Students also value the experience of using computers, a tool many will encounter in their jobs after graduation.

Offsetting these glowing reports are other more critical assessments (Oliver, 1984; Harris, 1985). Limited resources that result in too few terminals for too many students keep some programs from being successful. Some instructors report that constraints in the software frustrate students, with keyboard operations or word-processing skills too difficult for some to learn. Other students are distracted by the constant opportunity for making changes in their text and worry about forgetting their deleted ideas. Some students are only able to make substantial revisions on hard copy, not on-line at the terminal.

Further, some faculty note that although an experienced writer can dismiss a computer's correction or notation if it doesn't fit the writer's meaning, novice writers are unable to make such distinctions. Conversely, some beginning writers who disagree vehemently with a computer's prescription conclude that all stylistic points are simply a matter of judgment.

A critical question raised by several researchers is whether the ease of editing and the number of changes students make actually improve the quality of their writing. Judgments are mixed, with a clear need for further research and evaluation. Some instructors observe that text editing programs may frustrate students or encourage them to "play it safe" by writing more simplistically than they might otherwise. Others note that the computer can positively affect the quality and quantity of time spent at each stage of the composing process (Marcus, 1985).

Finally, some teachers express concern that administrators might use computers to reduce actual instruction, increase class size, or limit peer-tutoring opportunities. The worst fears of instructors—that they might be replaced by computers—seem a long time from being realized. Software cannot teach students to think, nor does software eliminate the need for teachers. Students who use text editing programs often turn to the instructor for interpretation of the computer's responses.

To date, computers have proved to be increasingly sophisticated assistants, providing back-up support to teachers and motivational incentives to students. The continued refinement and development of software may lead to new ways of teaching composition and to improvements in students' writing skills.

Summary

Even this extremely brief and highly selective review of issues should help the evaluator and other professionals in the field understand that:

- The process of teaching composition skills is complex and can be successfully accomplished in many different ways.
- Definitions of literacy and writing competency are to some degree arbitrary, and the value of any instructional program is open to dispute if bilingual or bidialectual students are to be served.
- Appropriate goals of instruction for each grade level continue to be debated.
- Composition teachers continue to work under difficult conditions.
- Many of the most promising developments may come as a result of pressures for accountability measures and staff development.
- The increased knowledge resulting from growing research efforts may help provide new solutions for recurring issues.

With a clearer picture of these important issues, an evaluator can begin to place local debates into a broader perspective and offer program participants an enlarged view of their own aims and dilemmas.

2-2 ■ Ways of Describing Composition Instruction

Preliminary Considerations

The evaluation of writing instruction is especially problematic because the field lacks both a consistent descriptive vocabulary and a set of standard criteria for distinguishing one instructional approach from another. Some promising practices in composition instruction have been described (Keech and Thomas, 1979, Young and Larson, 1979), but none of these accounts will serve as a comprehensive guide to *all* the best techniques and strategies. Almost as rare are descriptions of combined individual practices and techniques which form complete courses or programs. (For brief descriptions of programs see Neel, 1978, and Squire and Applebee, 1968.) Phrases such as *growth-centered, process-oriented,* or *product-based,* are often used to express real and important differences in program emphasis or philosophy, but may obscure essential similarities in practice. Alternately, the range of practices applied under the rubric of a single approach to composition instruction is often so great as to baffle evaluators who wish to judge whether one method or technique of instruction is more effective than another.

These factors work to make the description and evaluation of instructional processes especially difficult. What is actually to be evaluated? Whole sequential programs? Individual instruction methods or materials? Philosophies of composition instruction? The behaviors of particular teachers? Composition instruction is sufficiently complex that we undoubtedly are evaluating all of these things and their interactions whenever we attempt to assess any of them. Any one of them may be important enough to affect student performance. Thus it seems essential to develop procedures which enable systematic description and comparison of them.

Yet evaluators may wonder, "If English educators cannot clearly characterize instruction in their own field, why should an evaluator try?" Without an understanding of the distinctions that can be made among approaches, however, the conceptual basis for a scientific evaluation is lacking. An evaluator's design and activities must necessarily be shaped and affected by the nature of the program being assessed: measures selected must be sensitive to evidence of progress toward program goals as well as to side effects or unexpected outcomes. Observations of program functioning may be uninterpretable without a clear grasp of intended aims of the instructional activities. Further, a comparative understanding of the various approaches to composition instruction can help an evaluator assess which particular educational factors significantly alter a specific program's effectiveness. In short, evaluators must hold as clear an understanding as possible of the range of program options, in order to evaluate a specific program and identify areas for possible improvement.

Description of Program Approaches

The following three questions can help evaluators—whether they are individual teachers or program-wide administrators—describe the focal points or key characteristics of composition program content.

- What causes of student writing problems have been identified?
- What are the stated purposes of composition instruction?
- What view of language learning and composition instruction is assumed or espoused?

Even though programs may include a wide range of approaches, these three questions can help establish points of similarity shared among teachers in the same program or in seemingly different programs. In discussing each of the questions, examples of approaches and programs will be described that make use of different views of language learning and composition instruction.

What causes of student writing problems have been identified? Although all three questions are closely related, this first one often becomes the basis for deciding the other two, because composition programs often originate in response to problems. For example, NCTE's survey of eighteen college composition programs (Neel, 1978) makes clear that most of them developed in response to changing enrollment patterns or newly emerging skills deficiencies in students.

The answer given to this question can reveal program developers' and teachers' views about language learning that affect the nature and functioning of the program. Is the cause of bad writing seen as inadequate skills practice? Or do the students lack certain conceptual understandings about how written language functions? Or are the problems more motivational in nature? Each of these reasons can result in a different approach to teaching composition. If key program staff members hold different opinions, the program may lack uniform focus and coherence. This characteristic is not uncommon in composition programs, nor one which is always considered a weakness.

What are the stated purposes of composition instruction? This question follows directly from the first one. Students may display a whole range of writing problems. The decision about which ones to address often depends upon the agreed-upon purposes of composition instruction and the view of language learning (or philosophy of composition instruction) that is held. In the 1950s, the professional consensus was that composition should be studied for "its practical value, its civilizing value, and the enjoyment it brought" (Hook, 1979). Most programs today, however, offer a more practical emphasis and teach skills necessary for success in school, success at work, or successful personal growth and fulfillment. Some programs choose only one of these purposes; others claim multiple goals. In fact, the skills necessary for accomplishing these goals are often interrelated. For example, clear organization of ideas would be a skill necessary for all three purposes. However, the instructional tasks might vary according to the purpose for which the skill was being practiced. Programs concerned with writing for academic success might require practice in the writing of research reports. But those conventions might be quite different from and inappropriate to the writing of memos or brief business letters. Identifying the intended purposes of a program, then, can help an evaluator begin to select appropriate measures to use in assessing student skills as well as possible side effects. This process also makes evaluators think about whether student needs are known and are likely to be met and whether adequate resources are available to support the program.

What view of language learning is assumed or espoused? One distinction often made about the processes of language learning is between those who believe that composition skills can be practiced in isolation from realistic communication experiences and those who believe that skills can be improved only as the need for them emerges from writing whole discourses for authentic communication purposes. This distinction might be characterized as *isolated* versus *integrated* skills learning. A pure isolated approach would have students use workbooks and exercises and never write complete discourses. A pure integrated method would have students writing only whole discourses—notes, letters, essays—to real audiences and learning correct usage only when necessary to communicate more clearly.

Another basic distinction can be made between *rule* or *form-governed* composition practice (which prescribes specific activities or a specific product, such as a precis or an essay of literary criticism) and *heuristically guided* activities, where more general considerations of the writer's purpose and intended audience help shape the topic. Instructors may also differ on the amount and kind of *linguistic knowledge* they believe is necessary for students to learn in order to write successfully. For example, one popular approach to teaching writing in the 1960s depended upon teaching students transformational grammar principles and procedures. Other program developers believe that if students learn about the principles of rhetoric or literary criticism, they will improve their writing skills.

Evaluators need to be concerned with these general distinctions so that they can accurately describe and characterize a particular program of instruction and compare it to another model or approach. In addition, these distinctions may be helpful in determining which evaluation questions to pursue and which instruments to administer. For example, a program that teaches students rhetorical principles of communication may best be evaluated by including an inventory of beliefs and attitudes about these principles in addition to measures of the quality of student writing. A skills-based program might be assessed more appropriately using analytic reading techniques or objective, short-answer exercises to test for specific skills mastery in addition to holistic assessment. An integrated approach merits holistic writing assessment; in addition, an inventory of students' beliefs and attitudes toward communication processes might also test for more particular course content.

Examples of Approaches and Programs

The following examples illustrate a range of options. Although not exhaustive, this list of approaches and programs based on different views of language learning and composition instruction can provide a starting point for an evaluator's more specific descriptive efforts.

We believe that the approaches distinguished below are most useful for identifying the general emphasis of instruction in particular cases. Because diversity of approach appears always to have been a hallmark of composition instructors, it may frequently be the case that an individual teacher incorporates several of the approaches described below into instruction for a single class. For example, a predominantly process-centered, language experience class may include some specific skills practice using one particular technique such as sentence combining. (Myers and Gray, 1983, describe a variety of approaches.)

Process-centered Approaches and Programs. These all focus on some type of process, either within the student or related to an instructional sequence. Some of these presume that writing skills should be used to facilitate and enhance natural cognitive and linguistic processes. Others suggest that instruction can be most fruitfully conceived of in terms of sequences of assignments. Many kinds of processes can serve as a focal point of instruction; hence, process-centered programs can be quite different in content and methodology.

Writing process approach. Composition researchers are paying increasing attention to composing processes, using observations of writers at all skill levels to understand all aspects of the writing process, from prewriting (development of ideas) through composing and revising whole discourses. Using insights from research and practice, instructors have designed a variety of techniques for teaching students about composing processes. (See California State Department of Education, 1986; Camp, 1983; and Griffin, 1982.)

Language experience approach. Moffett and Wagner (1976) offer one of the most comprehensive curriculum programs for developing communication skills, grades K-12. Students engage in a variety of speaking, listening, reading, and writing activities in order to learn how to establish relationships with different subjects and audiences. Skills are practiced in relation to realistic communication tasks.

Meaning-discovery approach. Berthoff (1978) argues that the process of composing is the process of making meaning out of chaos or of assigning order and form to complex phenomena. She believes that the best way to teach students to compose is to have them experience the different kinds of intellectual shaping processes that give some form to chaos or raw experience. She teaches students to identify cause-and-effect links and to develop ideas through comparison and contrast. Her approach seems to concentrate on the first stage of the writing process—prewriting or discovery of ideas. She suggests, however, that this discovery process and the refinement of meaning continues until the final draft is complete.

Conferencing program (University of New Hampshire). Murray (1980) teaches students using a technique he calls conferencing. He meets with students individually to help them discover what they want to say. The subject matter is the process of shaping and communicating meaning in writing to a real audience. The dynamic of face-to-face interaction encourages students to develop heuristics or "rules of thumb" to guide their own writing processes. In large classes teachers have successfully combined this technique with use of peer response groups.

Method- or Skills-centered Approaches. These approaches seek improvement of composition skills with a particular method of instruction or with students practicing specific skills. The distinction between method/

skill approaches and process approaches is often one of relative degree rather than absolute divergence. Compared to process approaches, method/skill approaches stipulate learning or teaching processes more specifically or comprehensively and implicitly embody a reductionist philosophy. They assume that all important constituent skills can be identified and practiced separately. Often they do not specify longer sequences of activities or processes that might apply to all phases and modes of written composition but are more concerned with developing specific competencies. They more often depend upon pragmatic rationale than upon psycholinguistic theory.

The models approach. One of the oldest methods of teaching writing skills involves asking students to imitate "models" of writing—single sentences, paragraphs, and whole discourses. The process of emulating good writing is believed to help students improve their own work (Richards, 1956).

Programs based on sentence combining. In this approach students are taught to write increasingly more sophisticated sentences through a series of exercises that combine different syntactic structures. This approach has been used at both the precollege and college level. Obenchain (1979) developed a set of curriculum materials using sentence combining exercises in conjunction with reading assignments to develop writing and thinking skills in high school students. Morenburg reported on a freshman composition program based almost exclusively on sentence-combining exercises (Daiker and associates, 1979).

Programs with writing skills labs. Some schools use individualized writing skills labs, where students report for a specific number of hours each week to complete exercises that allow them to practice specific aspects of writing skills. Units can be assigned to remediate individual writing problems, or they may constitute a writing skills curriculum that all students are required to complete. Work is often self-paced so that students may progress at their own rate and often may repeat the course once for credit. To the extent that such courses specify student outcomes, they are product-performance centered (see below). An interesting variation of this approach has been developed by Huntington Beach School District (California). Students work together in two different settings: in writing workshops they practice prewriting, revising, and other communication and composing processes, and in writing labs they study specific skills of correct usage.

Tagmemics approach. Pike (1964) drew upon extensive experience in linguistic analysis of discourse in formulating his own tagmemic model of discourse relations. Some composition courses teach his model specifically; others introduce students to its direct application in formulating written discourse, where students are taught to develop a topic by asking a specific set of questions about its relationships with other topics. For example, "How much change can the topic undergo without becoming something other than itself?" (What is its range of variation?) "What characteristically occurs with or around it?" (What is its distribution in specific contexts?) Repeated practice of this method is believed to develop students' capacity to identify more complex aspects of their topic and to approach writing from a more sophisticated perspective.

Product-performance-centered Approaches. These approaches and programs are most concerned with teaching specific skills, outcomes, or production of a particular kind of written product. To do so, they may employ any of the methods or approaches described in the previous sections; however their focus is on prescribed outcomes.

The five-paragraph essay. One of the most common traditional approaches to teaching composition uses the five-paragraph essay as a model. Regardless of topic or rhetorical mode (descriptive, narrative, expository, or argumentative) an essay is to be written in a set form, with introductory and concluding paragraphs and at least three paragraphs in between.

Programs coordinated by shared style sheets or marking systems. Some college-level programs concerned with improving expository writing focus their activities by using an agreed-upon set of response standards to student compositions. Instructors may choose different teaching texts and methods but use the same style sheets or rating criteria for placing students in the program, grading their papers during the course and evaluating their end-of-the-term tests. An example of this is the Subject A Program at University of California, Berkeley.

Adjunct courses in writing. At the college and university level opportunities to improve certain writing skills may be offered in courses taught in disciplines other than English or rhetoric. Such adjunct courses focus on the particular writing skills required by their associated discipline, such as the writing of scientific reports or philosophical essays. These courses may employ a variety of instructional approaches. (See Hancock and Moss, 1979, for course descriptions.)

Knowledge-centered Approaches. These draw upon the fields of linguistics, rhetoric, literature, or philosophy (language logic) for concepts and procedures that students must learn in order to become more competent writers.

Literature-based programs. The work of Frye (1973) and Bruner

(1960) was used to formulate new methods and materials developed in Project English curriculum centers in the early 1960s. Frye believed that analysis of four literary modes (comedy, romance, tragedy, and irony) provided the structural basis for all works of literature. Using Bruner's notion of the spiral curriculum, instructional programs for all grades were developed that involved written analysis of each of these modes.

Rhetoric-based programs. The University of Montana and the University of Texas at Austin both base their composition instruction on students' learning rhetorical guidelines for relating purpose, topic, and audience. They depend upon rhetorically based analysis of model compositions to serve as illustrative examples of good writing (Neel, 1978).

Logic-based programs. One of the oldest approaches to teaching students to write is to teach them first to think more clearly. Students at a California high school, for example, learn the axioms of syllogistic reasoning as tools for analyzing problems in organization and content. (This is regarded as *not* the way to teach clear thinking by people in the new "informal logic" movement. See Scriven, 1980.)

Descriptions of Program Context

Forces in the educational environment can shape the specific character of any approach or program. Evaluators need to be concerned with the following two questions as they describe how a composition program or approach operates in a specific setting.

What is the relationship of composition instruction to other language arts and other subject areas? One of the earliest controversies in English instruction centered on whether language arts should be taught in close relationship to or separately from composition instruction. The importance of an integrated curriculum has been affirmed by many professionals, including NCTE, but clearly this is an area of debate. The pressure in the 1970s for a return to the "basics" frequently forced English teachers to be concerned with developing specific student competencies, a task whose success is often more easily achieved by students' focused practice of specific skills. Though it may have discouraged use of an integrated language arts curriculum in some schools, the concern for teaching basic competencies has brought integration of another type: writing across the curriculum programs at the precollege level and special adjunct writing courses at the college level. Composition instruction is no longer considered the exclusive domain of English departments.

Attention to details of the total instructional program within and beyond the English language arts can help clarify the range of opportunities that students might have for *practicing* their writing skills, in effect, the real value an institution places on writing, which is often quite different from stated program goals. Unless students can see how writing accomplishes different purposes in quite separate contexts, they are likely to believe that writing for different audiences and writing for different purposes is an English teacher's fantasy. The following questions might help identify the value placed on actual use of composition skills:

- What is the role of composition instruction compared to instruction in the other language arts? Is writing practiced in isolation or is it closely related to other kinds of communication experiences?
- What role does writing play within the total curriculum? Are students regularly encouraged to clarify their thoughts in writing in both academic and nonacademic courses? Do they write for a variety of purposes and audiences?
- What course structures are used for delivering composition instruction? For example, are there only self-contained writing courses or skills centers? Or are there tutorials or adjunct courses that directly tie composition to other disciplines?
- What are placement and counseling procedures? Which courses are required? What is the range of elective options?
- Are there signs that writing is a valued activity among all members of the educational community? Are finished pieces of student writing prominently displayed? Is displayed writing read and valued by students and faculty? Is there a vigorous publishing program for student and, when appropriate, faculty writing?
- Can teachers and administrators be observed sharing and talking over pieces of writing among themselves as well as with students?

What are the contexts—social, educational, and institutional—in which writing instruction occurs and what constraints on writing instruction result from them? As powerful in shaping program content as any theories about composition instruction are the constraints present in an educational setting. Personal and professional interests of the faculty, goals imposed by parents or students, program and scheduling restrictions legislated for administrative convenience—all these factors influence the nature and format of a writing program, and their identification is important in identifying whose needs a program is serving and if unique circumstances determine a program's functioning. (See Myers and Thomas, 1982.) The evaluator, therefore, might ask: Are there prescribed texts and syllabi? How specific or flexible are departmental guidelines? What signs are there of direct administrative or parental supervision or mandates? Are teachers from other subject areas being reassigned to English instruction? (See Squire and Applebee, 1968, for a list of contextual circumstances that can affect composition programs.) Such an investigation can help uncover those factors in a school environment supporting or inhibiting optimum program functioning. Furthermore, prospective users of a program need this data to determine which factors are peculiar to a specific setting and which might be integral to the program itself and thus likely to appear when the program is replicated.

2-3 ■ Professional Development Activities

Another program component comprises regular opportunities for professional development, including preservice and inservice training programs for faculty, administrators, and other staff, as well as activities such as attending professional conferences or developing curricula. For ease of reference, all these activities will be referred to as training activities. Providing regular opportunities for such experiences seems crucial to the success of educational programs. For example, in their survey of high school English programs across the country, Squire and Applebee (1968) identified well-prepared, professionally active, ever-learning teachers as a prominent feature of outstanding programs. Yet support for giving even well-prepared faculty regular access to professional development opportunities is only slowly growing, and this is primarily as a result of faculty demands made in response to accountability pressures.

Composition teachers at all levels require training support because so few of them have received adequate preservice training. Data from three national studies suggest the extent of their needs. In 1961 the NCTE Committee on The National Interest and the Continuing Education of Teachers of English conducted a nationwide survey and found that only one-third of all English teachers at the precollege level felt adequately prepared to teach composition skills (Squire and Applebee, 1968). In a subsequent survey, 3100 English teachers in junior colleges in 1968 identified "training in techniques in teaching composition" as the overwhelming priority for preservice and inservice programs (Modern Language Association, American Association of Junior Colleges, 1969). A third descriptive study made in 1976 of eighteen freshman composition programs found that over 85 percent of the composition courses were taught by graduate assistants, many of whom lacked previous teaching experience (Neel, 1978).

Inservice training programs for precollege teachers of composition have been offered on a widespread basis only for the past few years. Prior to that time, composition teachers were expected to develop their skills as a result of training in some other discipline (such as literary criticism or rhetoric) or through inservice courses on teaching all the language arts. The National Defense Education Act Institutes, developed in the late 1960s, were among the first designed specifically for teachers of writing. These programs reached only a small number of teachers and did little to ease the general situation identified in the national surveys. Two developments have altered this bleak picture. The National Writing Project Network (with its central office at the Bay Area Writing Project, UC Berkeley) was created in 1977 to improve composition instruction at grades K-13, and it now includes more than 150 affiliated sites worldwide. The Network model aims to correct some of the problems of previous composition inservice efforts as well as to provide some valuable additions. The increased demand for composition courses at the college level has encouraged some schools to allow graduate students and in some cases undergraduates to assume teaching responsibilities and receive training to do so successfully.

Research on Staff Development

Before turning to examples of training programs, it seems valuable to note the findings of recent research on staff development. Considerable agreement exists among training experts regarding the factors that make for effective programs and lasting change in teachers (Roark, 1978):

- Successful inservice training is continuously responsive to participants' needs (training and participants are "mutually adaptive") with formative evaluation conducted regularly.
- The content and goals of the training need to be made clear to participants; attitudes, beliefs, and behaviors seem to be more difficult to change than specific instructional practices or knowledge of the subject matter.
- Participants learn best when they are active in the training and in tasks that allow for individualized response.
- Teachers need to try out techniques with opportunities for systematic feedback.
- Training is most successful if it is extended in duration and given by other practicing teachers.
- Programs that increase teachers' sense of efficacy (or their belief that they can make a difference) have the greatest impact.

- Programs are most successful when educators at all levels of responsibility are involved and supportive (i.e., teachers, program administrators, district administrators, and so forth).

These findings scarcely appear innovative; they incorporate generally
accepted principles of successful learning and institutional change. What
seems surprising is how seldom they have been implemented in staff
development programs. (For details on inservice research, consult Berman and McLaughlin, 1978; Nicholson and Joyce, 1977; Lawrence, 1974;
and papers from the National Institute of Education's Conference on
Professional Development, 1979.)

Issues for Evaluators

Because there is no single way to teach composition, there seems to
be no single inservice that which is helpful to large numbers of teachers.
(Cases where training assists faculty members in teaching a specific
course with a set syllabus might seem to offer an exception, but even
there different approaches might be adopted to teach the same content.)
The crucial question for the evaluator is the effectiveness of any training
in preparing teachers for their immediate academic responsibilities.
Research findings may be of little help because most research has been
done on the process of adopting or rejecting single innovations; very little
baseline data exist on the *amount* and *kind* of change that might be
reasonably expected from staff development training for composition
teachers (Thomas, 1978, and Thompson, 1978). Thus, the summative
judgment about the educational significance of any training rests almost
entirely on locally derived standards.

Training content and activities may exert only a limited effect on
teachers. Other contextual influences may be operating selectively, regardless of whether training occurs within individual schools and districts
or draws teachers from different educational environments. Important
contextual influences on inservice impact include:

- Who initiates and conducts the training
- Whether a needs assessment has been done and to what extent
  inservice content is responsive to teachers' perceived needs
- What the purpose of the training is (for general preparation or for
  teaching specific courses) and its compatibility to existing courses and
  standards
- What incentives are offered to teachers for attending and whether
  attendance is compulsory or voluntary

- What constraints against change exist within schools and departments and what provision is there for ongoing follow-up and support of inservice participants
- What links exist between professional development and teacher evaluation

To meaningfully evaluate the effects of training, school context, and personal/professional readiness for change, an evaluation might include a few selective interviews or some items on a questionnaire. If such questions are not to be asked, the assumptions for doing so should be specified—for example, "School context and incentive for change are similar enough for all teachers so that they may be disregarded as a source of differential or negative effects on training impact."

Examples of Professional Development Programs

The following examples illustrate the range of training options currently available.

Experience-based Models of Professional Training.   These programs link training activities directly to classroom practices.
    National Writing Project model.   This model, aimed at teachers at all levels, includes a unique set of features:

- Using the best teachers of composition as "experts" who lead training sessions for other teachers
- Allowing teachers of writing to learn by doing—by writing for their peers
- Encouraging teachers to draw upon the resources of university, but in a teacher-centered exchange
- Drawing upon the foremost knowledge of composition research and practice as part of the content
- Developing a new sense of professionalism that regards teachers as leaders, authors, and classroom researchers
- Matching the content of individual inservice programs to local needs, while making presentations on a "core curriculum" of important topics

The model uses summer institutes to train outstanding composition teachers, who then lead inservice programs and professional development activities for other composition teachers during the academic year.

Models of Training Approach

Training accompanying development of writing curricula. Two California school district projects—Fairfax Expressive Writing (grades K-6) and Vista Project Write (grades 10-12)—illustrate another inservice training as an accompaniment to the development of a specific writing curriculum (including materials and teaching strategies). The staff in each project tried out materials in class (and in Fairfax, observed lessons taught by teacher trainers), then met regularly to give formative feedback. This adjunct training or supplementary inservice is given to staff while they are in the midst of their regular teaching responsibilities.

Faculty and staff development programs at the college level. These offer great variations in content and process of training, since each has developed in response to a unique set of campus needs and resources. In general, they combine experience-based training with some unique delivery methods to offer both preservice and inservice training. (For complete descriptions of several programs, see Neel, 1978.)

Training experiences for college-level composition teachers include:

- Graduate-level courses in linguistics, rhetoric, composition, or some other related subject
- Preservice training—workshops of short duration held before a course begins
- Adjunct courses for teaching assistants, often run as workshops or seminars where teaching assistants discuss common problems and approaches
- Periodic workshops on common problems, such as standards for marking papers
- Apprenticeship programs in which teaching assistants take courses before teaching
- Team teaching, where less experienced faculty work with older or more experienced faculty

Many of these training experiences occur in conjunction with teaching duties, so that they provide support for ongoing improvement of teaching skills. In addition, some programs include counseling and supervision, where teaching assistants work under the observation and advice of a more experienced faculty member. Indiana University offers a systematic plan for structured classroom observation and feedback: interviewing faculty, making a descriptive observation of their classroom, and holding a follow-up interview for discussion of classroom events, particularly those with which the instructor is dissatisfied. These observations may be repeated as the instructor desires (Flanigan, 1979).

Many colleges and university composition programs use additional means to structure their composition courses and provide guidance for inexperienced teachers. These include:

- Required or recommended textbooks with orientation sessions in which course requirements are discussed
- A specific syllabus that includes materials to be used and a schedule to be followed (often accompanied by some orientation)
- Specified goals including quantity and type of writing to be completed
- A shared style-sheet or marking guide to use with student essays
- A standardized student-evaluation form for the course

These college training programs have most often been designed for graduate assistants and faculty from other disciplines.

Information-based Models of Inservice.   These are the more traditional types of professional development training, based upon the assumption that all that is necessary is the delivery of appropriate information to the teacher.

- "Teacher-proof" curriculum materials are designed to be used with a teacher's manual or to be self-explanatory (Obenchain, 1979)
- Traditional teacher institutes and courses typically involve presentation of materials through lectures and other types of more formal presentations. The model of the teacher is one who can be improved by passively absorbing appropriate knowledge (e.g., National Defense Education Act Summer Institutes)
- The models approach (Joyce and Weil, 1980) encourages teachers to learn about successful instructional models including those which focus on social interactions, information processing, personal development, and behavior modification and to incorporate the model strategies into their teaching repertoire whenever appropriate
- Supplements to experience and training (such as audiovisual programs, professional publications, and conferences) are used to complement regular teaching experience and/or training. These often occur during the school year under the sponsorship of the local school, district or some other agency such as university extension (e.g., National Televised Models of Teaching Writing, NCTE publications and conferences).

As with composition programs, actual training programs often consist of hybrid mixtures of different approaches and training procedures. For example, one training program developed by Winterowd and others (Huntington Beach School District in California) was both information- and experience-based. Teachers were introduced to the most pertinent developments in composition research and rhetorical theory and then encouraged to develop curricula and train other composition instructors.

3

Aspects of an Evaluation

The focus of an evaluation will usually be one or more of the eleven general components listed in this section: student writing performance, student attitudes and beliefs about writing, other student indicators, the process of teaching writing, teacher attitudes and beliefs about writing, teacher professional activities, training activities, program administration, cost analysis, side effects, or replications.

These components form the core of evaluation. For each component, we describe why it is important to examine it, how it can be measured, its strengths and weaknesses as so measured. We also offer some practical suggestions and guidelines and, where appropriate, present some case study examples from school districts, colleges, and universities. Throughout, we refer to books, articles, and other resources for readers desiring additional information.

Not all these components will be applicable to every evaluation. We present them here to cover the range of possibilities in examining the functioning and effectiveness of composition instruction.

3-1 ■ Student Writing Performance

Regardless of the nature, scope, or format of a composition program, its primary goal is to improve student writing. This section explores ways in which student writing performance can be evaluated. We first discuss purposes for such evaluations, and then the strengths and weaknesses of general measures of writing performance. Next, we examine six main data sources that can be tapped to provide information about student writing performance. These are:

- "Found" test data, available from tests that are routinely administered in a school, college, or university
- Student grades in composition courses
- Data from research instruments or commercially available tests of student writing
- Data from locally developed tests, typically calling for a writing sample
- "Naturally occurring" writing samples, usually teacher assignments
- Judgments from students made during self- and peer-evaluation of writing performance

Preliminary Considerations

Purposes of Evaluating Student Writing. An evaluation of students' writing performance can be conducted for a number of different purposes:

- A teacher wants to determine students' writing capabilities so that an appropriate instructional program can be planned.
- An institution wants to identify which students should enroll in remedial courses and which students are ready for more advanced work.
- Students want to know the strengths and weaknesses of their writing so they can improve their skills.
- An administrator wants to identify and remedy, if possible, problem areas in a department's composition instruction.
- A funding agency is interested in the overall effectiveness of a composition program.

The specific methods used to measure students' writing performance will be influenced in part by the purposes of the evaluation. For example, students concerned about the strengths and weaknesses of their own writing will be most interested in evaluation methods that provide diagnostic, analytic information. Funding agencies and top administrators who must decide whether to adopt a composition program may only want holistic information on student writing from a number of data sources.

Despite these links, no direct one-to-one correspondence exists between the purpose for evaluating student writing and a particular data source. Nor is there one best way to evaluate student writing performance. This section describes several useful procedures that can be adapted to various situations. We advocate using multiple measures and methods so that the effects of composition instruction can be more confidently assessed.

Measures for Evaluating Student Writing Performance. Two basic strategies can be used, either individually or in tandem, to measure student writing: direct and indirect assessments. *Direct* assessments involve examining an actual sample of student writing. The sample can be from class assignments or an essay written during a teacher-developed or commercially published timed test. Writing samples provide the best evidence of students' ability to write and should be part of the evaluation of composition instruction whenever possible. (See Spandel and Stiggins, 1980, for a general discussion of the issues and applications of direct assessments.)

Indirect assessments include objective or multiple-choice tests, either teacher-developed or commercially produced. Objective tests can be scored more consistently than essay tests, and many more skills can be measured by an indirect test than is possible in an essay test. The chief problem with indirect tests is their lack of credibility in measuring what many feel are the essential components of writing: organization, skills in composing appropriate prose for a particular audience, selecting content, and so on. Objective tests have been criticized by Purves and associates (1975), Cooper and Odell (1977), and Stibbs (1979), among others, for measuring editing or proofreading skills rather than composing skills. These researchers argue that objective tests involve selecting the best sentence, or recognizing correct usage, rather than producing or composing sentences and paragraphs.

A good resource for understanding the strengths and weaknesses of objective tests is *Common Sense and Testing in English* (1975), published by the National Council of Teachers of English (NCTE) and written by Purves and others. They identify several aspects of writing that can be successfully measured by objective tests: grammar and language skills, editing, proofing, and reading skills. So far, objective tests are not—they argue—as successful as direct assessments for measuring organization of ideas, appreciation of good writing, or ability to use language to express thoughts and feelings. But tests are faster and cheaper to use than essays. Researchers have examined the relationship between students' scores on multiple-choice tests and direct writing assessments (Breland and Gaynor, 1979; Hogan and Mishler, 1980; Bamberg, 1982; Breland, 1983; and Cooper, 1984). The results of these kinds of studies vary, but the correlation between direct and indirect assessments is usually .50 (White, 1985).

The choice of indirect or direct assessments (or both) depends on a number of factors including issues of validity and reliability (discussed in a later section), the purposes of the evaluation, and credibility. Whenever possible, given the budget and expertise available, direct assessments of student writing should be collected and properly analyzed. They may make it easier to explain to the students and their parents or counselors what needs to be improved (formative analytic evaluation); and direct assessments, when properly developed, administered, and scored, provide the best indicators of a program's effects on student writing.

Standards of Writing Performance. Whatever the purpose for assessing student writing or the evaluation method used, judgments must be made about the quality of student writing. These judgments can involve at least four general kinds of comparisons. First, student performance can be compared to some ideal standard, perhaps the most common way writing is evaluated. A teacher looks at a student's work and makes judgments on its merit according to some implicit or explicit standards. A second kind of standard is a publisher's norm. Commercially produced tests have developed norms that describe the average or typical performance of students on their test. Student test performance is then compared to publisher's norms, which means viewing students' performance against what other students have achieved on that published test.

A third type of comparison examines a student's writing level against his or her own past performance. How has this student's writing changed over time? This method means collecting two or more comparable kinds of student writing over a set period of time, typically a semester or academic year. A pretest measures the student's performance before the instructional period and a posttest measures performance after the course or program. In order for this to be a sound basis for conclusions, certain conditions must be met: for example, the comparability of the writing tasks must be established, and safeguards need to be provided against "teaching to the test."

Finally, the performance of students in one kind of writing program or course can be compared to the performance of other students in another innovative or traditional type of writing program. This method requires detailed planning: one must ensure the comparability of students in each of the programs, devise a test that is fair to both programs, and the like. Comparison groups allow one to obtain some indication of how much the students' skills might have improved without the special program or instruction.

An evaluation can use more than one of these methods. For example, administering a test to two groups of students at two different times (at the beginning and the end of the course) could involve all four comparisons.

Each of these comparisons requires early and careful planning in developing scoring standards (if teacher-developed tests are used), in collecting preprogram (baseline) data, or in establishing an appropriate comparison group. Which method is selected depends on the resources available for the evaluation, the audiences for the evaluation and their questions of interest, and the measures selected for the evaluation.

Regardless of the nature of the comparison made (to teacher's standard, to publisher's norms, to student's previous performance, or comparison-group performance), it is important to identify what specifically should be measured—that is, the features, skills or aspects of writing that one is interested in assessing.

Identifying the specific desirable features that characterize good writing can be problematic. Although there may be general agreement on some matters, such as the rules for punctuation, sentence structure, and grammar, as noted in Chapter 2, describing other characteristics of good writing (rhythm, style, coherence) is quite difficult. Nevertheless, the evaluator must identify the qualities that will be examined in judging student writing performance. One way to begin identifying these criteria is to examine past efforts at categorizing the components of effective writing (see Chapter 2 and the Additional Reading section). Criteria can also be developed through group efforts, with program staff, faculty, and audiences for the evaluation coming to some agreement on what is important to measure. Delbecq and associates (1971) and Chickering and associates (1977) offer general techniques for achieving group consensus.

General Criteria for Measures of Student Writing Performance. Whatever measure is being considered, direct or indirect, teacher-developed or commercially produced, the concepts of validity and reliability play an important role in selecting or constructing tests.

Validity is the extent to which a test or evaluation procedure measures what it is supposed to measure. We say, for example, "This test is a valid measure of spelling." There are two main types of validity. *Content validity* concerns the adequacy of test items as a sampling of the outcomes of the program or course. For example, a test that consists of 30 grammatical errors to be corrected would not be a valid measure for a program that taught spelling. To determine content validity, the test content is judged against the program content.

Criterion validity concerns the relationship between the test and a given desired outcome. For example, if student scores on a multiple-choice test of literary analysis fall in the same order as do their grades on essays analyzing literary selections, then the test can be called a valid indicator of achievement in literary analysis (example adapted from Purves et al., 1975). See Gronlund (1981) or Morris and Fitz-Gibbon (1978) for a general discussion of validity.

A prerequisite for validity is *reliability*, the extent to which a procedure is consistent in measuring whatever it does measure. Unreliability in measurement usually enters from one of three sources (Reilly, 1975). First, the test itself may be unreliable. For example, the task for students may not be well defined or of equal difficulty in pre- and posttesting or the test administration procedures may be vague and unclear. A second major component contributing to errors in measurement lies within the student. Shifts in mood, fatigue, anxiety level, or motivation are some of the factors that can cause a student's performance to differ from time to time regardless of his or her actual knowledge or competence. Finally, in those situations where the work is to be scored by a judge, as in an essay test, the rater can be a source of error. Each judge brings to the task his or her own set of attitudes and preferences. Although all these components can never be entirely eliminated as sources of error in a test situation, they can be minimized through careful test development, administration, and scoring.

As with validity, one may speak of several different types of reliability. *Internal consistency* is the extent to which items on a test are related or correlated with one another, which would imply that the instrument is measuring a common content, skill, or behavior. Test-retest reliability involves looking at the closeness of correspondence between results from taking the same form of a test at different times under conditions where one would expect no differences in performance levels (i.e., where no special instructional effort is made and the duration between time 1 and time 2 is too short to expect maturation effects). Do students who take the test at time 1 score the same when they take the test at time 2? Commercially produced tests report reliability figures in their technical manuals. Issues of reliability in tests of writing performance are discussed in Breland (1977). Procedures for calculating reliabilities for locally developed instruments are described in Gronlund (1981) or Mehrens and Lehmann (1979); for a small-scale evaluation, this can be done informally.

When readers are grading or scoring writing samples, *rater reliability* becomes important. Because perceptions fluctuate, two people reading the same essay may rate it differently, and the same person reading the same essay at different times may give it different ratings. For a test to be reliable, the extent of agreement among independent judges should be high. Training procedures and discussions of the scoring of sample papers can increase inter-reader reliability. Diederich (1974) and Morris and Fitz-Gibbon (1978) describe procedures for assessing and interpreting inter-reader reliability, and again this can be done informally for a small-scale evaluation effort.

Evaluators or teachers developing their own instruments need to be sensitive to issues of validity and reliability. Although using commercial tests solves the reliability problem, the available tests may not be valid for a particular purpose.

Besides the technical characteristics of reliability and validity, there are other prerequisites for selecting or developing measures to evaluate student writing performance. These include careful identification of the purposes for the evaluation, the intended audiences or uses of evaluation data, the potential effects of one measure over another, and the constraints (financial, logistical, political, and so forth) on the evaluation effort.

As we have stressed throughout, certain measures may be more appropriate for certain purposes. For example, if student writing performance is being assessed to select students for admission to a particular program, an objective standardized test might be the easiest and quickest to administer, provided certain conditions are met. If the evaluation is being conducted to give formative feedback to an instructor, then multiple measures (short objective test plus writing samples) would be useful to get a picture of the strengths and weaknesses of individual students. For a comprehensive summative evaluation of a composition program, measures that tap a variety of intended (and unintended) outcomes in a variety of ways (student assignments, objective tests, self-assessment, writing samples, and so forth) should be included.

Audience is another important consideration in selecting or developing evaluation measures. By audience, we mean the persons or groups who need, want, or will use the evaluation data. The audiences might include students, individual teachers, faculty colleagues, department chairs, school administrators, parents, or state departments of education. Note that the decision makers for the program and the audiences for the report will not always be the same people. No single evaluation can address the concerns of all the groups who might use the resulting information. Before beginning the evaluation it is important to consult with key individuals and groups who have a vested interest in the program or who are in a position to make decisions about its future and to identify their needs and concerns.

To collect student performance data without reference to the audiences and the various purposes to be served is likely to result in an evaluation that satisfies no one's information needs. In selecting or developing relevant measures, consider:

■ What kinds of evidence do decision makers or audiences regard as reliable and valid—that is, what is credible to them? For example, do they tend to be more persuaded by quantitative or qualitative data? Data from students or the opinions of highly respected teachers? Objective or essay tests?

■ What factors in student writing performance will be important in making a decision about the program? Test scores? Quality of writing? Variety of writing?

The potential effects of various measures on teachers and on the composition program itself should be considered before selecting a specific test. For example, one of the strongest arguments for developing one's own essay test rather than purchasing a commercially available instrument is the beneficial side effects on teachers of developing the test. The process of designing questions and agreeing upon scoring criteria can be a productive faculty development activity.

Finally, other constraints will affect the nature and format of measures selected. Availability and cost of commercially developed instruments, logistical factors in collecting student assignments, political feasibility of conducting a writing assessment, resources for analyzing writing samples—all might influence the choice of one measure over another.

In summary, although there is no single preferred way of assessing student writing, certain general considerations guide the selection or development of measures. These include the notions of reliability and validity, the purposes for the evaluation, audience and decision-maker concerns, and the constraints under which the evaluation will operate. Whenever possible, evaluators should employ multiple measures so that the fullest picture of student writing performance is presented.

Potential Problems in Evaluating Student Writing Performance.
One of the intents of a formative or summative evaluation is to determine whether a particular program makes a difference in student writing performance. This means looking at two or more samples or tests of student writing taken before or at the beginning of the course or program and then again at the end. Many other factors besides instruction can "explain" changes in student writing. In this section, we outline some of these factors and alternative explanations.

Different students taking the pre- and posttests. This is a problem when testing spans more than one academic term. For example, in school districts it is customary to administer tests once a year in the spring. Sometimes these tests are used for program evaluation, with the scores of one year (as a pretest) compared to scores of the following year (posttest). Without some assurances that the same students are taking the pretest and posttest, an alternative explanation for any improvement could be a change in the student population. Investigations of changes in student performance should, in general, involve only those students who took both the pre- and posttest.

Variations in the way the test is administered.   If the instructions to students are changed from pre- to posttest or different examiners give the test under different conditions, then changes in student performance may be attributable to these factors rather than to the program. Testing conditions must remain standard, whether one is using a commercially developed or locally designed test.

Variations in characteristics of the test.   Typically this is a concern with locally developed tests, where the pretest may inadvertently be made easier or more difficult than the posttest. A change in test difficulty could be the explanation for an observed improvement or decline in student writing, rather than the program itself. Less common, but also harmful, are tests that differ in the kinds of thinking or writing they elicit, so that the skills being measured are not similar from pre- to posttesting. One way to overcome this problem is to create a pool of items. To control for differences in item difficulty, specifically, the pool could be scrambled so that the pretest and the posttest are administered at the same time. Half the class takes the pretest and half the class takes the posttest at time 1. At time 2 those who the pretest now take the posttest. Similarly those who took the posttest at time 1 now take the pretest at time 2.

Practice effects.   One might hope to avoid variations in the test by using the same exam for both the pretest and posttest. However, any observed change could then be explained as the result of practice effects. It may be that students perform better on the posttest because they "practiced" on the test when it was administered as a pretest, or they perform worse because of boredom from taking the same test. This may be less of a problem in comparison-group studies, where both groups get equal practice, or in essay tests that ask students to write on general topics ("favorite object" or "favorite person"), which allows them to choose different subjects at each test period.

Teaching to the test.   This is particularly a problem for objective tests. Instructors, unconsciously, may direct their efforts toward those areas covered by the test. Clearly this would cloud the interpretation of test results. Was it the program itself that made the difference or the teacher's narrowly focused efforts in preparing students for the test? For those essay tests that use very general topics and sound scoring, it is hoped that teachers *will* "teach to" the test, since they will then teach writing. (If students know the specific topic in advance, there is also the danger that a student might simply bring to the test an essay written by someone else.) If it is not possible to keep the teacher unaware of the *specific* test items, because the teacher is also the evaluator, consider mixing pre and post items as described above, or having a colleague draw the posttest items out of a hat just before the test.

Variations in scoring procedures. If the standards for scoring the instrument change from pre- to posttest, then changes in student performance will be difficult to interpret. Although this is unlikely for objective tests, it often happens with essay exams. A blind scoring procedure can eliminate this potential alternative explanation. For example, the pretests are coded for authorship and date by someone who will not be scoring the tests and are held until the posttests are administered. The scorers then review the whole set of tests, pre and post, without knowing which is which.

Changes in the students themselves. Here we refer to changes independent of the program. For example, students mature and gain related experiences over an academic year or semester. This change itself, regardless of the nature of the program, could affect their writing performance. An estimate of expected natural changes can be obtained by administering the pre- and posttests to a comparison group of students similar to the program students. Identifying appropriate comparison groups is no easy task, but it can be critical to interpreting evaluation results. When using comparison groups it is important to describe their instructional program to determine in what ways, if any, it differs from the one under evaluation. This can aid in interpreting the outcomes of tests of writing performance. Options in selecting a comparison group and analyzing data from two groups are described in Fitz-Gibbon and Morris (1978) for beginning evaluators and Cook and Campbell (1979) for advanced researchers. Keech (1979a) discusses evaluation designs for comparison-group studies.

Differences in the initial skill levels of the program and comparison groups. If the groups are initially similar, posttest differences are relatively easy to interpret. The best way to ensure that the groups are initially equivalent is to randomly assign students to groups and use groups that are relatively large. When this is not possible, pretest performance should be examined to see whether the groups are similar or different. If they are different to begin with, a statistician should be consulted prior to analyzing posttest scores.

The preceding list is not exhaustive, but it does indicate the kind of care that must be taken to eliminate rival explanations before data collection begins.

"Found" Test Data

Description. By "found" test data, we mean tests that are routinely administered, usually annually. They are not designed to evaluate any specific educational program or course, but under certain conditions they may provide useful information about the functioning and effectiveness of composition instruction. School districts and some colleges and universities may routinely administer verbal or language arts tests as part of their ongoing assessment of student performance. In some school districts, such tests as the *Comprehensive Test of Basic Skills* (CTBS) or the *Stanford Achievement Test* are given yearly to measure student progress in verbal and quantitative areas. In addition, many school districts administer state assessment tests or proficiency exams covering writing and language arts skills.

At the postsecondary level, many institutions administer entrance or placement tests of writing skills to new students. Some institutions also administer *comprehensives*, tests given in the sophomore or junior year to diagnose individual student deficiencies and prescribe remedies (formative evaluation). Administered in the senior year, these tests serve as graduation requirements (summative evaluation). Comprehensives can be locally developed, as at Hampshire College, the University of California, Santa Cruz, or at St. John's College, or they can make use of standardized tests. (See Wood and Davis, 1978, for a general discussion of comprehensives.) The Graduate Record Examination, the Undergraduate Program Area Tests, and the Sequential Tests of Educational Progress have been used as comprehensives. The College Level Examination Program in English composition is used to grant students credit for learning acquired elsewhere. These tests are described in detail in Buros (1985).

Advantages and Disadvantages. The chief advantage of this data source is its availability; these data are routinely collected by the institution. The evaluator must spend some effort in compiling relevant information, but few resources are expended in collecting it. The disadvantages of using found data are that the tests may not necessarily be appropriate for the program, or may not be given to sufficient numbers or to the right students. In addition, there may be legal restrictions on their use (particularly data on minors). But if an institution is routinely administering a test to most program students, the available data could be carefully scrutinized to see if they provide useful information.

Guidelines for Use.   While it is beyond the scope of this guide to discuss in detail found data, we can offer some general suggestions.

Compare test items to program content.   A first step is to determine the relationship between test items and program content or activities. Can the test provide useful information about student achievement? What skills and knowledge are being measured? If a test is a very poor match to program content, then a more relevant instrument may need to be selected or constructed.

Check sample size.   Next, it is important to determine how many of a program's students have taken or will take the test. If most students are not involved in the testing for one reason or another, the results may not be valid indicators of a program's effectiveness. If the test is a good match but only a few students take it, then alternative measures should be sought for the other students.

Link findings to program.   The key to relating test results to the program is to eliminate alternative explanations for the findings. Besides evaluating the test for validity, reliability, and other sources of interference in interpreting data, one must examine contextual factors that may be contributing to the effects. For example, a new administrator or department chair who boosts morale and increases attention to writing may have an impact on student performance independent of any particular program. Similarly, the influx of new materials or increased attention by non-English faculty may, in fact, be responsible for observed outcomes. Admittedly, these factors are difficult to track down, but it is important when using found data to explore all possible alternative explanations for the findings.

Suggestions for individual teachers.   Found data can be helpful in giving individual teachers a sense of the entry levels and skills of their students. For example, collecting CTBS scores or Scholastic Aptitude Test-Verbal scores of new students may help in planning the instructional level and activities of the course. Because these tests are typically administered only yearly, they are less helpful to teachers in a formative sense. Summatively, teachers can compare the pre and post administration of the test, keeping in mind the need to rule out alternative explanations. Guidelines for interpreting change have been developed by Tallmadge and Horst (1975), among others. They suggest that a meaningful change should reflect at least one-third of a standard deviation's growth from pre- to posttest. Smaller changes are not educationally significant. A teacher could compare his or her students to those students not in the program who also took the test if there is an initial equivalency between the two groups.

Suggestions for institutions. Trends over time can be monitored—that is, student scores can be plotted against yearly test administrations, and improvements and declines can be noted. In addition, the performance of students in a particular program can be compared to norms, if they are available. Some of the standardized tests used at the postsecondary level, such as the Undergraduate Program Area Tests, have norms that provide comparability from institution to institution.

Data will be useful only if they are in a format that can be readily interpreted. This means using appropriate summary statistics, like the mean and standard deviation and, even more helpful, graphs and bar charts.

Example. Serlin (1977) used found test data, standardized test scores, and Subject A scores, to assess the impact of composition instruction on Las Lomas (California) High School students. His report identifies some of the problems in using these kinds of data.

Student Grades in Composition Courses

Description. Since almost all teachers assign grades, grades would seem to provide one readily available indicator of student learning. Current grades might provide a sense of how well students learned the material. Subsequent grades in later composition or English classes could be one indicator of long-term effects of a composition program.

Advantages and Disadvantages. The advantage of using grades as an evaluative measure is that they are often relatively easy and inexpensive to collect (assuming school records and transcripts are accessible), and they require no disruption of ongoing instructional activities. However, grades are weak indicators of student performance. Course grades may be the result of factors other than learning achievement. They are also subject to instructor bias—some faculty are "hard" graders while others are "easy"—which makes comparisons across courses difficult to interpret.

Guidelines for Use. Grade information is useful for monitoring the grade distributions in innovative programs, especially in schools or on campuses where grading and grade inflation is a concern. But other measures like comparative performance on common tests offer more direct evidence of improvement or changes in student learning.

Published Tests and Research Instruments

Description.   One kind of commercially available test is the standardized test which is typically prepared by measurement experts. The term "standardized" does not imply that the test necessarily measures what should be taught or at what levels students should be achieving. Standardized tests simply define methods of obtaining samples of student behavior under uniform test administration and scoring conditions and provide comparative results. With standardized tests, the same fixed set of questions is administered with the same set of directions and time constraints. Normative data are available so that a person's performance can be interpreted by comparing it to others tested under the same conditions. Examples of standardized writing tests include the *Test of Standard Written English* and the *Basic Skills Assessment.*

Another source of published tests are research instruments, developed and refined by researchers in linguistics and composition instruction. These tests may lack comprehensive validity and reliability information but could be useful for some evaluation purposes.

Prepared tests may be indirect—objective (multiple-choice) tests; or direct—essay tests, requiring a student writing sample; or some combination. They may be norm-referenced or criterion-referenced. *Norm-referenced tests* are those for which test performance is interpreted in a relative manner: How does a student's score on the writing test compare with those of other students taking the same test? Scores on *criterion-referenced tests* are interpreted in an absolute manner: Did a student answer the questions with 80 percent accuracy or make fewer than one error per 100 words? Norm-referenced interpretation tells how a person's performance compares with a known reference group—for example, with other students in a class, in all classes in a school, a school system, state, region or national sampling of students. Criterion-referenced interpretation tells how a person's performance compares with a definite standard. The standard is usually a judgment about appropriate performance under certain conditions, but it may be based on empirical "criterion validity" studies.

It is difficult to distinguish a norm-referenced objective test from a criterion-referenced test merely by looking at it; the items may appear quite similar. The differences show up in the procedures for developing the test and in how the scores are interpreted. It is possible for a criterion-referenced test to be used in a norm-referenced way, but it is less likely for the reverse to be true. Scoring an essay test can be both norm-referenced, by ranking student papers, and criterion-referenced, by determining whether a student has achieved a desired level of proficiency.

Norm-referenced tests are most useful for gaining a sense of the overall performance of students or for selecting students for certain kinds of programs. They are less useful for identifying specific strengths and weaknesses of students' performance. The debate over the appropriateness of each kind of test is described in Gronlund (1981) and Morris and Fitz-Gibbon (1978). Most of the commercially available tests in the field of English are norm-referenced.

Advantages and Disadvantages. Commercially published tests are readily available, typically have high reliability, and may be more credible than teacher-developed tests for some audiences. They usually have norms against which student performance can be compared in an informative way. Against these advantages are two major drawbacks. First, these tests do not necessarily reflect the intent or functioning of the program or course under evaluation. They are designed to measure writing skill or achievement in a wide variety of situations, and the specific items or task(s) may not match the program under scrutiny. Second, most standardized tests do not include direct assessments.

Whether one chooses to use a published test depends on resources available for the testing effort, audiences for the data (some audiences place more importance on certain kinds of measures), and general match between proposed published test and program functioning. Whenever possible, however, existing measures should be considered first since their use can save time and effort.

Guidelines for Use
Resources for selecting published tests. There are several good sources for locating information about published tests measuring writing skills.

Buros, O.K. (Ed.) *Mental Measurements Yearbook.* Ninth Edition. Highland Park, New Jersey: Gryphon Press, 1985.
This book provides descriptive information on commercially available tests for measuring writing achievement and language arts skills. For each test, information is presented on the target population, availability of norms and manuals, time required to administer the test, scoring procedures, price, and publisher's address. In addition, some tests are reviewed by measurement experts regarding their strengths and weaknesses.
Buros, O.K. (Ed.) *English Tests and Reviews.* Highland Park, New Jersey: Gryphon Press, 1975.
A compilation of English tests and reviews that have appeared in

previous editions of the *Mental Measurements Yearbook* (1938–1972).

Hoepfner, R., et al. *The CSE Test Evaluation Series.* Los Angeles: Center for the Study of Evaluation, UCLA Graduate School of Education, 1971–1976.

A list of commercially available tests of student achievement and attitudes. Tests are organized according to many groupings, including subject. Tests are rated rather than described, and the ratings are somewhat controversial.

Grommon, A. (Ed.) *Reviews of Selected Published Tests in English.* Urbana, Illinois: National Council of Teachers of English, 1976.

The section on writing presents a detailed evaluative review of four tests. Includes information on their strengths, weaknesses, and applications.

Fagan, W. T., Cooper, C., and Jensen, J. *Measures for Research and Evaluation in the English Language Arts.* Urbana, Illinois: National Council of Teachers of English, 1975.

This book includes descriptions of fourteen measures of writing skills that are not available commercially. Information is provided on each measure's purpose, extent of reliability, and validity. Many of these measures are scoring systems for essay tasks rather than specific test instruments.

Faculty members and evaluators at postsecondary institutions may find tests of academic competencies useful in measuring student writing performance. The Academic Competence Test developed by Educational Testing Service (ETS) is designed to measure the competence of students in four areas: communication skills, analytic thinking, synthesizing ability, and awareness. The test requires students to write short answers to problems or questions. Similar tests of academic competence have been developed by the American College Testing Program (Forrest and Steel, 1977) and by a group of researchers associated with the Institute for Competence Assessment in Boston.

Other resources that may be useful in identifying published tests include *News on Tests*, a monthly periodical distributed by ETS (Princeton, New Jersey 08540) which describes recent tests, and ERIC, a computerized data base on tests, measurement, and evaluation. For further information on locating general test resources see Backer (1977).

Selecting a test. Many of the concerns already mentioned in connection with using found test data apply here as well. The test should be examined to see whether its content is relevant to the program and whether it is aimed at an appropriate level. Other factors to consider include: cost, copyright date (best to choose more recent tests), the adequacy of administration and scoring directions and procedures, reliability and validity data, and comparability of the norm group to the students being tested. Whenever possible, it is helpful to obtain specimen samples of the test and contact people who have used the test to identify any problems or weaknesses they have uncovered.

Using and interpreting test data. Published tests can be effectively used with other types of measures to assess student writing performance. For example, to demonstrate equivalency of groups in program comparisons, Diederich (1978) has suggested that it might be possible to use a published, objective type test as a premeasure and a writing task as a postmeasure. This is not appropriate if one is simply looking at growth in writing, since pretest *writing* performance will be missing. However, as a strategy for determining the equivalency of groups, this suggestion has two advantages: it decreases the cost of the evaluation effort, since objective tests are typically less expensive than writing assessments, and it reduces the possibilities of teaching to the test, practice effects, and so forth. Diederich's research has shown strong relationships between certain kinds of objective tests and writing tasks. The disadvantage of this strategy is the possible lack of credibility of an objective test for measuring writing skill, even though the posttest is an essay.

Another approach is to use an objective test and a writing sample in combination as both a pre- and posttest for formative or summative evaluation. The writing sample could be scored holistically and the objective test could track specific student errors. The combination might provide a fuller picture of student writing performance than either measure in isolation. Such a combination is also valuable in one-time diagnostic tests.

Results from published tests, particularly those with norms, should be interpreted cautiously. A *raw score* (usually the number of right answers) is generally not very meaningful. Derived scores are scores that have been converted from one scale (the raw score scale) to another scale (percentile ranks, grade equivalents, and so forth). Derived scores are obtained by reference to norms: the typical, average performance. Norms are aids or guides in the interpretation and application of test results. They are *not* to be regarded as "normative" in the sense of providing proper standards for each student to meet. Rather, they are guideposts that show where a student stands in comparison to other students taking the same tests.

Examples.   Several school districts in California have used standardized test data to evaluate the impact of their composition programs.

These include Santa Rosa School District and Castro Valley School District.

Locally Developed Tests

Description.   A locally developed instrument is just that—a test created for a specific purpose and situation, often by someone not expert in measurement techniques. Teachers develop tests on their own all the time and use them for evaluating students. If these tests are used to evaluate programs, careful attention must be paid to the content of the test, administration procedures, and scoring criteria. Typically, locally developed tests are essay tests rather than objective tests. Because objective multiple-choice tests are available from commercial publishers, we recommend that those sources be examined before such test development efforts are undertaken. Creating an objective test that is reliable and valid can be costly—it is preferable to use an instrument that has already been developed.

Essay tests—direct assessments—on the other hand, are not as widely available from commercial publishers and are more likely to be developed by a local evaluator or teacher. This section, then, will focus on general considerations in constructing and scoring essay tests. Those interested in learning more about developing objective tests are referred to Gronlund (1981), Mehrens and Lehmann (1979), or other standard tests and measurements textbooks.

Advantages and Disadvantages.   The chief advantage of constructing one's own test is that it is more likely to be relevant to the content of the course or instructional program than published tests. It can more accurately reflect what the program is intending to accomplish or may be accomplishing. In addition, if the test is a collaborative effort among program staff and evaluators, the side effects of developing the test may improve the program by encouraging faculty and staff to describe in detail what the program is about.

On the other hand, instrument development takes time and resources. Of course it is possible to hastily construct a few questions without considering how they will be scored, what they truly measure, and so on. Poorly conceived tests will not provide very good information about a program's or course's functioning.

Guidelines for Use.   It is beyond the scope of this guide to describe how to construct and administer a writing assessment. The interested reader is referred to White (1985) for a comprehensive discussion of methods. Here, we will simply discuss some important issues.

Topic options. There are five important questions to be answered before constructing or selecting a test topic.

1. What general type of performance is measured?

Writing samples can be classified according to two general types: impromptu or timed writing and writing with revision. Impromptu samples require students to complete their essays within a fixed period of time (usually 20 to 30 minutes) during which they may or may not have time to revise their work. Impromptu samples measure a student's ability to create and organize material under time pressure and are indicative of the kinds of writing students do in college and university test-taking situations and final exams.

Revised samples specifically include time for students to draft and rework their essays. Students may have 30 minutes to an hour to write on day 1 and the same amount of time on day 2 for revisions. These tasks measure students' more polished performance, their writing and revising abilities. Revised samples reflect the kind of work students have to do on take-home tests and term papers. To provide broader information about the effectiveness of composition instruction, a writing test may include both an impromptu essay and a revised essay.

2. What mode of discourse is being sampled?

Several kinds of writing can be assessed. Traditional categories are narrative, descriptive, expository, and persuasive. (See White, 1985, for another analysis of topic types.) In narrative writing, students tell a story about scenes, objects, or people. Descriptive writing calls for impressions of an object, scene, or characters. Expository writing asks students to explain, analyze, or state their opinions about an issue, concept, or experience. Expository writing is typical of the work older students are expected to do in school. In persuasive writing the student is usually given a specific hypothetical audience and the task of persuading them of some view or to take some action. The kind of writing to be assessed will influence the choice of topic. For a discussion of the appropriateness of different tasks for assessing each type of writing see Keech (1979c).

3. How many samples will be collected?

Student writers are unlikely to perform consistently from one time to the next, or from one kind of writing task to another (Godshalk and associates, 1966). To obtain a better estimate of a writer's typical performance one must collect more than one sample. Diederich (1974) recommends collecting two samples at different times of day on the same type of task. Another plan is to obtain two samples in the same sitting on different kinds of tasks. While this method does not give a reliable estimate of student performance on either task, the combined scores more clearly reveal a student's overall range of performance.

4. What will be the length of time for testing?

In part, this will depend on whether the test will be exclusively impromptu writing or will provide time for drafting and rewriting. Since class periods are ordinarily 50 minutes long, a 20-minute writing sample, which permits two topics a period, seems appropriate. A pilot study conducted by the Bay Area Writing Project Evaluation Unit compared student responses when given 20 and 40 minutes to write on a topic. No clear pattern emerged documenting the superiority of a 40-minute sample over a 20-minute sample for measuring group performance, although there was considerable individual variation in performance. The amount of time to be allotted will also depend on the nature of the topic. More time is needed for tasks involving a great deal of reading or complex assembling of information. Twenty minutes is the *minimum* time necessary to obtain a valid, reliable sample. While longer opportunities may increase reliability, the gain may not justify the increased expense (in student time, scoring, and so on). A 20-minute sample, however, is only a measure of general literacy and does not necessarily reveal particular writing or thinking skills.

The appropriate time limit also depends on the purpose for the assessment. Writing tasks to be used for diagnosis or assessing individual needs may require longer time periods to allow students to do their best.

The amount of time devoted to revision should be at least the same as allowed for the first writing. During the rewriting phase, students are permitted to use their customary resources including dictionaries and notes. But if there is a day between the first writing and the revision, some students may obtain outside help, which could weaken the validity of the test. If a composition program stresses revision and editing skills, it may be valuable to read and rate both drafts, or to use a scoring guide specially designed to identify and evaluate changes made from the first to the second draft.

5. What instructions are given to students regarding the purpose and nature of the task?

The seriousness with which students approach the test can affect the validity of the test. By informing them why they are taking the test, when they will receive the results, and whether the test will have an effect on their grade, students might be motivated to take the task seriously. The results of a formative or summative evaluation of the students are usually important enough to students themselves to provide some motivation.

Selecting or developing topics. Once decisions have been made about the preceding issues, a topic can be selected or developed. Whenever possible, existing topics and scoring procedures should be examined for their appropriateness before embarking on an extensive development effort.

Here are some sample writing topics from actual assessments.

ELEMENTARY AND JUNIOR HIGH SCHOOL

- Fourth grade—Complete the following with at least two sentences: "I wish I had . . ."
- Fifth grade—Write a story that has at least four sentences and begins: "One day I found a magic machine . . ."
- Sixth grade—Describe your favorite animal.
- Seventh grade—Write a paragraph about your favorite holiday and describe why it is your favorite. Write a paragraph that begins: "When I was younger . . ."
- Eighth grade—Write two paragraphs about your favorite season and describe why it is your favorite. Pick something of your very own that you have strong feelings about. Do not choose a person or a pet dog or cat or other animal. Then tell what it looks like so that a reader can picture it in his or her mind the way that you do.

HIGH SCHOOL

- Explain how to do something so that someone else could do it.
- All of us probably have a secret desire to be another person. Who would you be and why?
- Everybody has experienced fear. Write about a time when you were afraid.
- If you had to change places with someone for a day, who would it be and why? What would you do during the day?
- Describe a happy experience.
- Think about a change in your life that was important to you. In some detail describe this change and tell how it has made you a different person.
- We constantly hear that television is a bad influence on our lives. We hear that it teaches people to be violent and to commit crimes. We

hear that it tempts people to stay "glued to the boob tube" instead of talking to each other or reading. Yet most of us watch television and can undoubtedly see some good in it. Choose and discuss one or two ways in which you think that television is of benefit to individuals, to families, or to society. Use specific examples to support your ideas.

■ If you could follow someone around for a day, either in person or invisibly, whom would you choose? You might want to write about someone you admire, a friend, a famous person, a personality type, or someone with a particular job. You might want to think about these questions:

Why would you be interested in that person's activities?

What is that person like?

What would that person's day be like?

You may write a story about the day, a letter, an essay, a biographical sketch, or use some other form.

■ There are probably several places you would like to be right now rather than sitting in this room writing an essay. Choose one of these places and describe it vividly, so that your reader can understand why you would like to be there. You may include descriptions of your personal feelings in this situation. The place may be real or imaginary.

■ Explain what is wrong with the following argument: It's pretty clear that on the whole, women are superior to men. In terms of health, the best evidence is that women *live longer*, and by a substantial number of years, and women are virtually immune to several diseases that are fatal for many men. On the mental side, there is the simple fact that girls, on the average, do better at school than boys.

Ruth and Murphy (1986) have identified several pitfalls in selecting appropriate topics. Teachers have a tendency to overelaborate, encumbering the test topic with all sorts of instructions: "You are writing to . . . ;" "Tell about . . . ;" "Tell how. . . ." The directions may hamper opportunities for originality and creativity. Other traps include asking students to address unreal audiences or placing students in alien situations. Kirrie (1979) recommends that the test prompt (instructions) be as nondirective as possible, asking students to address the general, adult audience representing the actual readers of the essays. A good topic for a 20-minute writing sample can be made from any word, phrase, or brief statement that invites a variety of interpretations and responses. "Write an essay on what——means (suggests) to you" and a word of advice that examples may be helpful and that good writing will be appreciated are all that are needed, according to Kirrie.

Before using new topics in a formal assessment it is helpful to pilot test them with a small sample of students similar to those who will be taking the test. After the students have completed the task, they may be asked to provide additional information about any problems they had. Their papers would then be scored in the expected fashion to see how well the system works. By administering and scoring the test before it is used in a formal assessment, the test developer can identify and correct problem areas and flaws.

A topic is "successful" if it generates a range of student responses, can be completed within the time allotted, is clear and understandable to the students, and can be scored relatively easily, reliably, and validly. White (1985) describes the process for designing effective writing assignments and lists the four characteristics of a good writing topic: clarity, validity, reliability, and interest.

Administering the tests.   We have talked about using standardized instructions to students when administering the test. Examples of coordinating and administering an assessment in a school district can be found in reports from the Modesto School District (California) and the Santa Clara School District (California). These reports also describe procedures for coding student information so that data can be appropriately tabulated and analyzed by computer. It is important to consider analysis issues before data are collected so that procedures can be established in advance. For example, one wants to ensure that relevant student information is recorded in a way so as not to bias those who will be reading the essays. Also, one wants to retain the student identification codes so that differences in performance on pre- and posttests can be determined. For a description of how to handle these details see White (1985), Myers (1980), or Diederich (1974).

Scoring the tests.   Scoring procedures should be set up in advance of data collection. There are two critical issues: who will score the tests and how they will be rated.

As a rule of thumb, each essay should be read by two trained readers with another person available to give a third rating only when the first two are substantially different. All essays are independently scored in a single session or on successive days. No rater should know another's scores until all judges have finished.

There are several models for scoring essay tests. (See Spandel and Stiggins, 1980, or White, 1985, for an overview of scoring strategies.) Holistic scoring, as described by Cooper and Odell (1977) and others, involves reading an essay for a total impression of its quality rather than for individual aspects of writing skills such as organization, punctuation, diction, and so on. The standards by which compositions are judged are those that the readers have developed from their training and from their experiences with student writing. They may use a specific guide or rubric that describes characteristics of essays receiving different scores. Or a set of *anchors* or representative example papers may be selected before the reading and used to illustrate the quality of response typical of specific scores or ratings. One rationale often given for holistic scoring is that the effectiveness of a piece of writing is not reducible to the sum of its parts; writing is composed of many, often interactive, elements that resist the item-counting procedures typically used in analytic scoring. The effect of holistic scoring is to rank-order a set of student papers according to overall success in performing a given task. White (1985) discusses the development and uses of holistic scoring.

In holistic assessments, essays receive a single point score from each independent rater. The scales can be 1–4, 1–5, 1–6, all the way up to 1–9 points, depending on the length of the student essay, the experience and preferences of the readers, and the training procedures. A popular all-purpose scale is 1–6 points. (See Santa Clara School District, Modesto School District, and Manitoba School District for examples of holistic scoring.)

Although holistic ratings may be intuitively appealing and familiar to teachers who assign an overall grade, critics of the method argue that a piece of writing cannot be judged without acknowledging and describing its particular attributes (such as diction and organization). Holistic scoring does not measure or provide information about particular factors that might contribute to effective writing. Further, holistic scoring yields only limited information (a total point score) which is not very useful for formative purposes.

In contrast to holistic scoring, analytic methods identify key components of writing. Students receive subscores on each of several factors, such as organization, development, style, sentence structure, and word choice as well as spelling and punctuation. It is important to note that using an analytic model does not automatically make scoring less subjective. Judgments are still made on fuzzy categories, but key components are separated out for review. Typically, four to twelve features are identified for scoring. Longer lists tend to make the task difficult and reduce the likelihood that readers are rating independent features. Analytic scoring is, of course, more useful for formative evaluation, because it provides some information about which aspects of student writing require improvement or deserve praise. Analytic scoring may also reduce holistic bias—overreaction to some feature such as the use of colloquialism or poetic imagery. On the other hand, with analytic scoring there is a danger of numerically weighting one trait or another in a way that may not accurately reflect the relative role of that trait in the overall effectiveness of the paper. In addition, analytic scoring is much slower and consequently more expensive.

The Oakland and Modesto school districts in California have effectively used analytic scoring models. For more information on creating and using such methods, see Cooper and Odell (1977). Dent and others (1978) have collected examples of post-secondary students' essays scored analytically for structure, organization, and grammar.

While these are the two major scoring models, several other types are appropriate for particular purposes. T-units can be used to measure syntactic fluency or sophistication in writing. A T-unit (terminable unit) is the smallest group of words that could be punctuated as a sentence (Hunt, 1977). Primary trait scoring is a kind of analytic scoring that involves looking at traits unique to a particular topic. The scorer using a primary trait orientation is interested in whether the writing has certain characteristics, or primary traits, critical to its success within a given rhetorical task. (See Cooper and Odell, 1977). Other scoring methods are described in Cooper and Odell (1977), Spandel and Stiggins (1980), and White (1985).

In deciding which scoring method to use, consider the experience of the readers, the amount of time available for scoring, the resources available, and the intended uses of the scored data. For example, analytic scoring may be more useful to individual teachers (and students) interested in the strengths and weaknesses of a student's writing. Holistic scoring can be less expensive than analytic methods that may require a single reader to read a paper several times. Although holistic scoring enjoys widespread popularity, a combined holistic-analytic approach is gaining advocates. All papers are scored holistically, and then, as an adjunct, a sample is scored analytically. If resources permit, scoring a sample of papers using both methods provides the most information on the effectiveness of composition instruction.

After writing samples are holistically scored, they can be reread using analytic approaches to look for characteristics of writing at certain scoring ranges or grade levels. This postanalysis adds information about the qualities of individual papers that might have accounted for the holistic score and that is useful to teachers and students as formative evaluation. In addition, such postanalysis can provide a description of the particular weaknesses that characterize student papers at the various scoring levels. Such information is also valuable to evaluators in interpreting holistic scores. Keech and Thomas (1979) have noted that students may write more awkwardly for a period while they are attempting to master new strategies, and this might depress their holistic scores. An analytic reading could reveal the higher writing risks students are taking and their improvement on more specific skills.

Types of scoring errors. Research conducted on the consistency and accuracy with which raters make judgments has identified the following types of error (adapted from Reilly, 1975):

- Leniency or harshness error. Some raters tend to make judgments that are, on the average, much more favorable or more lenient than judgments made by other raters. Conversely, other raters may make judgments that are consistently more unfavorable than the judgments of others. This is the familiar phenomenon of easy and hard graders.
- Errors of central tendency. Many readers are reluctant to commit themselves one way or the other and as a consequence tend to make most ratings near the average or center of the scale.
- Halo effect. In situations where a student is being assessed in several different specific areas, a favorable overall impression may result in unjustifiably favorable judgments in all areas; a negative halo effect can also occur.
- Contrast effect. The quality of the previously rated essay will often affect judgment. An average essay may tend to receive lower-than-average ratings if the previous essay was outstanding and higher-than-average ratings if the previous work was poor.
- Fatigue effect. There may be a gradual drift up or down in the "baseline" while going through a large number of essays.

Although there is no way to eliminate these sources of error, they can be minimized by identifying specific standards for scoring essays: thorough training of raters before they begin their task, regular calibration or retraining during reading sessions, and the use of at least two judges for each writing sample so errors cancel each other out.

Using and interpreting results. Student scores obtained from writing samples can be treated like scores obtained from objective tests—that is, subjected to the same kind of analyses and summary statistics. It is important to look not only at changes in the group's average score at each test period, but also at changes in the *spread* or distribution of scores. For example, are students' scores spread out (from high to low) at the pretest but more closely bunched at the posttest? This could mean that composition instruction has decreased differences or variability among student writers. Keech (1979b) offers suggestions on how holistic assessments can be used for school district requirements for proficiency testing.

"Found" Writing Samples

Description. Students routinely complete writing assignments for their writing classes and their other courses: take-home essays, in-class writing tasks, term papers, anecdotal or reflective personal writing. These found assignments might provide a rich source of information on student writing achievement, if they can be collected into *portfolios* and tabulated in an appropriate manner. Uses of the portfolio system are described in Ford and Larkin (1978) at the postsecondary level and Blake and Tuttle (1979) at the secondary level.

Advantages and Disadvantages. As with any found data, an advantage of using student assignments to assess writing performance is that comparatively few resources are expended in collecting the data, since students routinely complete these assignments anyway. However, in this case some extra effort must be made to decide on selection procedures, methods of evaluating or judging the portfolios, and scoring criteria. These data also have the advantage of supplying more and different examples of student work than could be obtained under limited testing conditions. In addition, actual examples of student work are the ultimate criteria: Is composition instruction improving students' everyday writing performance? Further, students' motivation to write well may be increased if they know their work will be part of a comprehensive evaluation.

Despite these advantages, it is not easy to interpret and use these data. What is one to do with fourteen essays and assignments from each of 120 students on many different topics? Considerable planning is necessary before one decides to use portfolio methods of evaluation.

Guidelines for Use. Consistent with our emphasis on using multiple measures for multiple outcomes, we recommend the portfolio method as an adjunct to other data collection efforts.

Selecting writing samples. At the beginning of the term students are instructed that they will be expected to turn in some of their papers written for the composition program or other classes for review and rating. Whether the teacher plans to use them in computing student grades or only for program evaluation is up to the individual faculty member. It is helpful to include two kinds of papers in the portfolio: those that were written in class in one sitting, reflecting a student's ability to write an impromptu essay, and those that were written at home or over several days, reflecting revision and polishing. The number of papers in each category will depend on the portfolio's purpose. Some teachers prefer to include early drafts and final versions, while others choose only the final effort. The papers can be selected by the student or jointly by the student and teacher. Selections are made at the end of the semester or academic year. In general, those papers selected are the best of all that were written.

Interpreting data. The collected papers, with all identifying information removed, are then read by someone other than the teacher. The reader may offer a holistic impression of the work or make a more detailed analytic examination of various components of a student's writing. Scoring might emphasize writing skills (grammar, punctuation, diction, spelling) or rhetorical competencies: organization, logic, style, or support of thesis. Both in-class and out-of-class papers could be read for traces of particular kinds of instruction, effects of rewriting and prewriting, and increases in the amount or variety of writing. Or papers could be scored according to their purposes (to persuade, describe, instruct, and so forth). In the end, the portfolio as a whole can be given some kind of overall rating or the individual paper totals summed. Alternatively, the growth and final performance level of each student might be described qualitatively, perhaps according to a checklist or rating system.

Portfolio data cannot provide the precise judgments more easily obtained from writing assessments or objective tests. The quantity and diversity of data necessarily make synthesis difficult. Nevertheless, portfolio data can provide information on the breadth and depth of student writing performance not otherwise obtainable.

Variations in using portfolios. The procedures just described are appropriate for summative evaluation of student work. Portfolio data also lend themselves to formative assessments of both programs and students. Collecting a random sample of student work, which will include good and bad examples, midway through the course or program can provide insights into the strengths and weaknesses of student writing and suggestions for improvement. In this case, it may not be important to set up scoring criteria in advance, but instead allow raters to read for emerging themes and impressions. This method can also provide a useful context for the evaluator's understanding of what is occurring in the classroom.

Judgments by Students: Self- and Peer-Assessments

Description. All the methods we have discussed so far have used the teacher or outside expert as the evaluator of student writing performance. But students themselves—either rating their own strengths and weaknesses or commenting on the performance of their peers—may provide useful formative and even summative information on writing skills. Since they are knowledgeable about their past accomplishments, students are in a good position to comment on their own growth and satisfaction with their writing performance. In addition, the experiences of sharing their work with their peers offer students an opportunity to see how their writing can affect others. Self- and peer-assessments can be solicited informally through individual or small group interviews that focus on whether learning goals are being achieved. Somewhat more formally, students can keep a diary or log on their writing projects. Or a self- or peer-assessment can be conducted through written surveys, checklists, or questionnaires.

Advantages and Disadvantages.   Although this source of data would not be appropriate as the sole indicator of student writing performance, it may provide an added dimension regarding the effectiveness of a program or course. Students' comments on their own or others' writing can offer an anecdotal richness and understanding of a program's more subtle effects. The informal methods of self- and peer-assessment have the appeal of a certain flexibility and individuality lacking in other techniques. Self-appraisal may also spark motivation as students identify their weak areas. Using peers (and self) as critics is a sound pedagogical practice and has been successfully used in the Bay Area Writing Project (Healy, 1980) and in college writing programs (Hawkins, 1976).

The problem with this technique is its inherently subjective nature and lack of uniformity across classrooms or programs. The evaluator must set the proper climate and atmosphere so that students feel free to express their views in a constructive fashion. The success and utility of this procedure will depend on the effort that students and teachers expend on it and the amount of guidance the student receives in the process. It seems most useful as a formative strategy for evaluating students and the effects of instruction.

Guidelines for Use.   If self- or peer-assessment is to be successful, students must be given detailed guidelines for identifying criteria against which to judge their own or others' performance. One technique is to have students identify criteria for evaluating essays before they begin to write. They discuss these standards with the instructor and each other and then use the criteria in small groups to respond to each other's work. Another method has students holistically score other students' papers. This is useful as both a teaching and evaluation technique.

Self- and peer-assessments can reveal whether students are capable of criticizing their own and others' work. Do they have useful things to say in response to peer writing? Are they able to use critical responses from others to improve their writing? These skills are important to assess in programs that emphasize training students to evaluate their own and others' writing.

Examples. The use of peer- and self-evaluation techniques is described in Beavan (1977) and Blake and Tuttle (1979). They give some specific suggestions for making this method work successfully.

3-2 ■ Student Attitudes and Beliefs About Writing

Preliminary Considerations

In addition to measures of writing performance, other aspects of students' behavior such as writing frequency or beliefs about and attitudes toward writing may be worth study, for several reasons. First, these behaviors and attitudes may be more easily modified than quality of writing performance over short periods of time. As Loban (1976) has noted, growth in writing occurs slowly; changes are more noticeable at two- or four-year intervals than during the course of a semester. Further, attitude changes often precede improvement in skills and can be considered short-term indicators of possible future changes. Daly and Miller (1975) documented a negative version of this: high writing apprehension accompanied avoidance of courses and careers that were perceived as requiring regular writing activities. Measuring students' attitudes and beliefs about writing can also provide a richer understanding of a program's more subtle effects. Attitude measures thus allow us to take into account some important aspects of learning processes.

Description. It is useful to distinguish between beliefs, attitudes, and values, and how each might be used in evaluating composition instruction.

- *Attitude:* Predisposition to respond in a consistent manner with respect to a given object or experience based on one's values about that object or experience; attitudes often link mental events (beliefs) with behaviors. Sample item: "I look forward to writing my ideas down."
- *Belief:* Information held about an object, linking the object to some attribute. Sample item: "Studying grammar can help me improve my writing."

- *Value:* A belief about the worth, utility, or importance of an object. Sample item: "Expository writing is the most useful type to learn."
- *Behavioral intention:* A special type of belief about one's future behavior. Sample item: "I plan to take more writing courses if I can."
- *Behavioral description:* Self-observation of actual behavior. Sample item: "I avoid writing."

The first four terms are all *constructs*—created or constructed explanations of certain recurring human experiences. Such constructs are useful for explaining why people act as they do. Sensible use of these terms presumes that people's mental entities (beliefs and attitudes) cause or motivate behavior. An alternative and more cynical view is that mental entities are created to justify or rationalize behavior. Research by social psychologists has shown the relationships between beliefs, attitudes, and behaviors to be complex and interactive. Mental changes can seemingly bring about behavior change; alternatively, beliefs and attitudes can be influenced by behavior. (See Fishbein, 1975.)

The complex relationship raises several questions. First, what effect does information (a traditional educational tool) have upon beliefs or attitudes? What kind of input or "treatment" then might cause long-term change? It seems possible to present information that changes beliefs (including behavioral intentions) and values without producing lasting changes in behavior. A second question concerns consistency. How direct is the relationship between changes in mental entities and changes in behavior? A third issue arises from differing opinions about learning processes. Will changes in behavior necessarily result in improved skills? Some teachers believe that changes in behavior will eventually lead to growth in skills—that increased writing or practice of certain techniques or methods will make students better writers. Composition research suggests that increasing the quantity of writing *alone* does not significantly improve performance, but that practice in certain techniques can do so (Bamburg, 1978).

Most instruments developed for composition evaluation make little distinction among these different components of attitude–behavior relations; however, it seems important to be as conceptually clear as possible about what is being measured and why. For example, a composition program that stresses learning certain skills or methods (e.g., tagmemic analysis) might require an instrument with specific queries about relevant beliefs and behavior (e.g., "What questions do you find most valuable to ask in exploring a topic?"). These kinds of items might be inappropriate for other types of programs.

Problems in Measuring Attitudes. Despite the importance of monitoring attitudes and beliefs as components of the learning process, few instruments have been developed to measure attitudes and beliefs about writing, nor have they often been considered in evaluations. This oversight seems to be the result of several problems encountered in evaluating attitude and belief change.

First, it is often difficult to construct instruments with demonstrable validity. Only one of the composition attitude measures that we review even reports any efforts to establish validity. In part this may be due to the lack of resources for developing such instruments, but it is also the result of the intrinsic problems associated with documenting the validity of attitudinal measures.

Second, some attitudes are unstable—they seem very sensitive to daily mood, momentary success in a course, changes in a relationship with an instructor, and so on. In addition, a student's attitudes may fluctuate with the aspects of writing that are being considered. For example, a student might excel in one type of writing and fail utterly in another type; his "attitude toward writing" may depend upon which type of writing experience is most salient in his mind. Thus reliability of attitude measures is difficult to establish.

Third, because attitudes, beliefs, and behaviors are complexly related, a measured change in any one of the three does not necessarily imply that changes in the others will follow. Attitudes and beliefs offer only secondary indications of behavior change, present and future. Measures of behavior change also must be interpreted conservatively with regard to inferences about attitude and belief change. At best, these data should be collected in conjunction with other information to allow description of patterns of changes.

Attitudinal data can be gathered using a variety of procedures including collecting student self-report measures such as questionnaires and interviews, observations of students inside and outside of class, and review of program records and documents, such as voluntary writings of students, attendance records, counseling files, and subsequent enrollment patterns. The choice of the most appropriate instrument depends on the nature of the evaluation and the evaluand.

Self-Report Measures

Description. Whenever possible, it is useful to obtain data from students about their own beliefs and values regarding writing. These data

can take the form of written questionnaires, individual or group interviews, informal discussion strategies, logs, or journals.

Advantages and Disadvantages

Questionnaires. Questionnaires are often the most efficient means
of collecting data when items or characteristics to be measured can be
clearly specified. Once items have been developed, they are relatively
inexpensive to duplicate and intrude very little upon ongoing instruction.
However, the validity of the measures can be affected by limitations of
human memory, lack of awareness of one's own attitudes, and distortion
of responses out of a desire to please the investigators or oneself.
Respondents must be considered trustworthy (i.e., likely to give accurate and comprehensive reports), and this likelihood is increased by the
anonymity of response that questionnaires permit. Questionnaires require considerably less time to administer than interviews and can be
particularly efficient when large numbers of respondents must be questioned. In addition, their standardized format makes quantitative analysis of the data relatively easy.

Because response rates to take-home or mailed questionnaires are
often very low (15–30 percent), it is best to administer surveys during
class time to "captive" audiences. When that is not possible, evaluation
resources should provide for second mailings or telephone or postcard
reminders to participants. If these procedures are followed response
rates of 80 percent or better are not uncommon. We recommend working
for that level of return, in order to eliminate possible challenges to the
validity of the procedure. (Berdie and Anderson, 1974, describe ways to
increase response rates.) If students have been too engaged in instruction
to be very aware of their attitudes and beliefs, or if instructional
experiences are in the distant past and memories of them sketchy, or if it
is likely that students may bias their reports or be unable or unwilling to
provide information, then other sources of data should be gathered.

Interviews. This modified form of self-report makes use of an
interviewer, who works from a structured list of questions. Most often
questions are open-ended. However, other formats can also be employed
in interviews. Interviewers typically write down respondents' comments
rather than tape record them (due to the high cost of prerecording and
transcription); fewer questions can be posed in an oral interview compared to a written questionnaire. Interview items, however, can be more
flexible—designed to suit the purposes of a particular evaluation. They
can allow systematic exploration of complex topics such as motivational
strategies, which are hard to precode into a standard written checklist.

Identification of individual differences is easier, because an interviewer can press for further clarification on complicated questions as well as direct attention to questions considered particularly important in the evaluation. In addition, unexpected responses can be pursued and elaborated. The primary disadvantages of this method are the expense and time required for hiring and training an interviewer and eliciting the cooperation of the respondents. The reliability and validity problems inherent in self-report measures are not overcome, either; however, the presence of the interviewer does make possible more uniform responses, because the interviewee can be asked to explain or elaborate upon any answers that are incomplete. Also, the face-to-face contact is often an additional motivation to the respondent to provide more detailed, pertinent information. The danger, of course, is that the respondent may fabricate desired responses to please the interviewer.

Guidelines for Use.   It is beyond the scope of this guide to examine the many important topics involved in designing and conducting attitude surveys or interviews. Here we highlight some of the general issues. For further information the reader is referred to Sudman and Bradburn (1982), Henerson and associates (1978), Demaline and Quinn (1979), Berdie and Anderson (1974), and standard texts on survey methodology.

   Establishing validity and reliability.   In section 3-1 we discussed validity and reliability in the context of measuring student writing performance. These concepts also apply to measuring student attitudes. Reliability is somewhat easier to calculate than validity. At a common-sense level, one can eyeball the extent of agreement between two tests or two judges or two items to get a sense of consistency; however, an instrument can be reliable (consistent within itself and in the results it yields from one administration to the next) but not be valid.

   Validity is particularly difficult to establish for measures of attitude and belief. In the process of developing a measure, steps can be taken to establish its *content validity*. Does the instrument contain items regarding beliefs and attitudes appropriate to composition instruction? For example, students in a program that teaches the stages of the writing process might be asked whether they valued prewriting and revising activities, for what purposes they believed them to be most useful, and how they intended to use them in the future. A program concerned with changing student motivation to write might want to make use of the Writing Apprehension Scale (Daly and Miller, 1975) or to design a special instrument that measures attitudes about other aspects of writing. Appropriate items can be developed by discussing with program staff the nature of the composition activities, consulting with researchers and professionals about key practices in composition instruction, and examining past evaluation instruments. Questionnaire items can often be improved by constructing questions that allow respondents to describe both negative and positive effects, whether intended or unintended by the program.

Similar procedures can be used to establish *construct validity*. See Henerson and associates (1978) for details on calculating construct validity.

Design of instruments. Because the most frequently used instrument for measuring attitudes and beliefs is the questionnaire, we offer some guidelines for its design and use below. For a more complete discussion see Sudman and Bradburn (1982).

In decisions on the format and content of an instrument, the need for brevity and minimal disruption of program activities often seems in conflict with the desire to collect comprehensive, detailed information. Two guidelines for making design decisions are:

- Tie content of questionnaire as closely as possible to the method or program being offered and to other important, but possibly unanticipated outcomes of instructional experiences.
- Collect only information for which a definite need can be identified and for which specific plans for analysis and interpretation have been formulated.

Far too often evaluation staff are tempted to collect information because it might be "interesting"; little or no thought is given to its eventual purpose or use. Careful planning is essential to avoid such wasted effort.

The following tips and suggestions are helpful in designing questionnaires. For detailed guidelines see Berdie and Anderson (1974), the Questionnaire Brochure Series (1978), and Demaline and Quinn (1979).

- Try to avoid questions that are ambiguously worded or are "leading" (the answer you want students to make is obvious or given in the question).
- Choose vocabulary whose meaning is clear to respondents and be sure terms are used consistently or defined in the questionnaire (for example, "editing" can mean rewriting entirely or correction of grammar and punctuation).
- Supply sufficient context so that questions are clear. The three examples in Figure 3.1 illustrate sources of confusion that should be avoided. In the first example, the word pairs are not polar opposites, and responses may vary with the context the student has in mind. The same problem occurs in the second example: liking may vary with the context

FIGURE 3.1

Example 1

Rate the following word pairs along the scale of importance. If both constructs are equally important, place a check in the center space:

	Very Impt.	Impt.	No Diff.	Impt.	Very Impt.	
Own feelings	—	—	—	—	—	Community feelings
Graded papers	—	—	—	—	—	Ungraded papers

Example 2

Rate the following on a 1–5 scale:

	Dislike				Like Very Much
Writing a letter	1	2	3	4	5
Writing a poem	1	2	3	4	5

Example 3

Rate the following items in the blanks provided using a 1–5 point scale where 1 = strongly disagree, 2 = disagree, 3 = neither agree nor disagree, 4 = agree, and 5 = strongly agree:

___ (1) I am afraid of writing essays when I know they will be evaluated by the teacher.

___ (2) I am often helped by hearing what other students think of my writing.

supplied by the student. This problem may be avoided by providing some more detail or frame of reference, as in the third example.

■ Design of specific questions, choice of response mode (such as open-ended, where respondents write their comments freely, or forced-choice, which requires respondents to select options from a predetermined set), and the format of the questionnaire should be carefully considered and reviewed by someone experienced in questionnaire design.

In general, we recommend a combination of closed-ended and open-ended questions. Forced-choice questions are easier to analyze (and interpret, if carefully designed), but it takes longer to formulate and pilot test them. Open-ended questions generate data that take comparatively longer to process and often involve training coders and developing special coding procedures. It seems wise to include a few open-ended questions in any instrument despite their drawbacks. They allow respondents to identify concerns and outcomes that may not have been anticipated by questionnaire designers. They also make possible a more individualized response to major topics, a tactic that can work to persuade respondents that their opinions are important to express.

Examples.   Here we present a few examples of possible formats for questionnaires or interviews. For further information see Henerson and associates (1978), Morris and Fitz-Gibbon (1978), Questionnaire Brochure Series (1978), or Demaline and Quinn (1979).

Forced-questions choice. The questions in Figures 3.2 and 3.3 are examples of items that could be asked about writing processes. They are meant to suggest, not prescribe, some different response formats. They are categorized by whether they refer to behaviors, attitudes, or beliefs.

In Figure 3.2, the first two sets use a five-choice response format, with categories from "1 = strongly disagree" to "5 = strongly agree." The last set uses a two-choice format with an opportunity for an open-ended response. Notice that items should be phrased according to whether they measure behaviors, attitudes, or beliefs.

The item in Figure 3.3 calls for respondents to report aspects of their behavior. Note the numbers in parentheses to the right of the items: these are guide numbers for data entry so that the results can be analyzed by computer. We recommend computer analysis for response groups larger than 20 and urge design of the questionnaire so that data can be entered directly without any intermediary coding. This requires anticipating the kinds of responses for all questions and working out how many spaces to allow for data entry.

Topic items.   Some other dimensions to consider in student attitude questionnaires include:

- Attitudes and beliefs about types of writing assignments or experiences
- Attitudes and beliefs about personal achievements in writing
- Use of writing skills learned in other classes
- Skills improvement during course
- Class assignments: value, clarity, novelty, number completed
- Comparisons to other classes: amount of work and value

Attitude questionnaires about composition instruction and related topics include the Writing Apprehension Questionnaire, Daly and Miller (1975); the Emig-King Student Attitude Questionnaire (1978); and the Keech Student Questionnaire (1978).

One of the most difficult and provocative of tasks in the effective

FIGURE 3.2

Please use the following scale to rate each statement below:

	Strongly Disagree	Disagree	Neither Agree nor Disagree	Agree	Strongly Agree	Don't Know
(1) Description of writing *behaviors:*						
• In my own writing, pre-writing is an important first step to composing.	1	2	3	4	5	( )
• Revising has become easier because of this English course.	1	2	3	4	5	( )
(2) *Value/attitude* toward processes:						
• It is a joy to put feelings into words.	1	2	3	4	5	( )
• Expressing ideas through writing seems to be a waste of time.	1	2	3	4	5	( )

(3) *Beliefs* about processes:
Please agree or disagree with the following statements and explain why or give examples.

Agree   *Disagree*

_____ _____	Prewriting helps me focus my thoughts.
	Explanation or Example: _____
_____ _____	Writing makes me think more carefully about questions than does talking.
	Explanation or Example: _____
_____ _____	Revising is primarily for making changes in grammar and punctuation.
	Explanation or Example: _____

design of evaluation instruments is the choice of words and question formats most appropriate for the intended audience and purpose—the rhetoric of questionnaire design. These tasks call upon skills and sensitivities that many English-teaching professionals have devoted their lives to developing.

FIGURE 3.3

Please indicate how many times in the past month you have written for the following audiences:

Number of times	Audience	
_____	English teacher	(1–3)
_____	Students in English class	(4–6)
_____	Other students (including personal notes)	(7–9)
_____	Social studies teacher	(10–12)
_____	Math or science teacher	(13–15)
_____	Other teachers (please indicate their subjects)	(16–18)
	Subjects:	(19–21)
_____	School clerks or secretaries	(22–24)
_____	School principal or other administrators	(25–27)
_____	Adults in the community	(28–30)
_____	Adults outside the community	(31–33)

Observations

Description.   Because beliefs and attitudes are presumed to cause related behavior, they can be inferred from data gathered in behavioral observations made by someone other than the teacher or student. For example, if a composition program is aimed at developing in students the belief that prewriting activities can aid in clarifying their ideas, and the program encourages them to prewrite whenever appropriate, then observations about the frequency with which students voluntarily engage in such activities can provide useful information. Such conclusions must always be drawn with care, since some other explanation might be responsible for the behavior. For example, a teacher might be giving extra credit for all the prewriting students do, or might be weighting student portfolios on the basis of quantity rather than content. If these alternative explanations can be ruled out, however, then inferences about beliefs and attitudes based on behavioral observations can be quite plausible. Observations can be collected through a variety of methods including rating scales or checklists of student behaviors, anecdotal records, simulations, or sociometric techniques. See Henerson and associates (1978) for details on these observational methodologies.

Advantages and Disadvantages.   Although it is difficult to develop and apply observational techniques, they offer one important advantage. Observations take place in natural settings or in settings that simulate natural conditions, so that the information gathered may be more valid and reliable than that elicited by questionnaire methods. For example, if we are interested in how students write, we could certainly ask them to describe the process they go through, although some students might not be able to respond adequately. A better approach might be to structure a writing task and observe students as they undertake it. Through observation we can infer student attitudes about writing.

A number of pitfalls make observational techniques difficult to implement. First, these procedures tend to be expensive in terms of time and resources for training observers. Second, observational methods differ and are frequently not very reliable. Observers must separate relevant from irrelevant occurrences, guard against making generalizations from limited samplings of behaviors, and restrain their own biases and expectations when observing student behavior. Third, it may be difficult to synthesize and interpret large amounts of observational data. These problems have worked against the widespread use of observation for assessing student attitudes.

Guidelines for Use. Few standardized instruments have been developed for the observation of composition instruction or other writing activities. Many observation instruments, however, have been designed for use across subject areas and particular instructional techniques, such as questioning strategies (Simon and Boyer, 1974; Borich and Madden, 1977). Readers interested in using observation should consult existing instruments first, for possible adaption to composition instruction.

Using someone other than a student to report on composition activities can provide a reliability check on students' perceptions. In addition, information can be collected on aspects of instructional processes that students might not notice or be able to attend to, such as behaviors of students in small writing groups or in individualized instructional settings, or question-and-answer patterns in large group discussions. If observers are well trained and work according to systematic procedures, reliability problems can be minimized. In addition, observation can be designed to focus upon some particular aspects of instruction and allow intensive data collection in one area. Observation data can be useful adjuncts to other sources of information.

Review of Program Records

Description. Accounts of student behavior kept as part of program or school records may also provide evidence from which inferences about student attitudes and beliefs might be drawn. Inventories of quantity and type of student writing, particularly voluntary writing, can suggest the impact of composition instruction on beliefs and attitudes. Other school records such as attendance data and counseling and discipline referrals, as well as information about participation in extracurricular projects such as the school newspaper or literary magazine, can also provide useful data.

Advantages and Disadvantages. These data sometimes are easier and less expensive to collect than some of the other measures suggested in this section. They cause little or no interruption of ongoing instructional activities. If an evaluation takes place or continues after a project concludes, these data are often among the most accessible, although their validity decreases with age. Also, it may not always be possible to link these data with a particular composition program. For example, students may join the school newspaper not because they enjoy writing but because it gives them press privileges.

Guidelines for Use. There are no specific methods for collecting and interpreting these data. Care needs to be taken to prevent violations of confidentiality for certain data from school records. These data are best collected in conjunction with other, more direct assessments of student attitudes.

3-3 ■ Other Student Indicators

Surveys of Students' Writing Activities

Description. Britton and his coworkers at the University of London have demonstrated the value of surveying the types of writing done by students and the audiences for whom they write (Britton et al., 1975). They found that the amount and kind of writing actually done in the schools is often sharply at odds with what teachers claim to value. Their type of survey has since been replicated in England, Australia and the United States. Such a survey affords another kind of insight into student writing experiences and can greatly enrich the understanding of a program's impact.

These surveys have been used almost exclusively at the secondary level. In some cases, investigators have collected all the writing done in a school or class during a day or a week and classified it according to type, intended audience, location where writing was performed, and purpose. On other occasions, students, teachers, or school principals have been asked to supply this information in summary form in questionnaires or interviews. Britton has noted that it is as important to measure "inputs" (or instructional experiences) of writing programs as it is to measure "outputs" or quality of writing performance. The writing survey measures an important input for students—opportunity to practice writing.

Advantages and Disadvantages. This procedure is best used in conjunction with other sources of data about student writing. Its effectiveness will depend on the methods of data collection and analysis.

Most researchers recommend collecting data for a period longer than one day, because writing assignments may be given and then revised over several days' time. The cost of data collection and analysis, however, increases greatly with each additional day. The coding methods selected will also affect the outcomes. Somewhat arbitrary decisions will have to be made concerning criteria for length (e.g., how long "a page of writing" is) and purpose.

One drawback of using questionnaires or interviews is that students, teachers, and administrators may have a desire to please the investigator or to give data that conform to program goals. All may be forgetful of what has gone on in the more distant past or, in the case of a school principal or department chair, may not be well-informed on these matters. Thus, systematic collection and coding of writing by independent observers is more expensive but more reliable than interviewing key program personnel for their summary observations.

In spite of these potential problems, the information gathered can be useful for understanding some of the activities of writing instruction and whether these are consistent with participants' perceptions and reports. It does provide information on input (opportunities to write), process (the kinds of writing students do), and output. (See section 3-1 for a description of how naturally occurring writing samples can be used to judge student writing performance.) This method can be used to gather descriptive information about activities in a single class as well as comparative data about writing in several different classrooms or programs.

Guidelines for Use. If at all possible, student writing is best collected for periods longer than one day. If resources do not allow this, then statements from students and teachers should be gathered to discover whether the collection day is typical.

The evaluator may decide not to notify teachers until immediately preceding the collection day(s), so that they will not plan writing in addition to that which they might normally assign. Of course school administrators or English department chairs should be asked for approval in advance of the actual collection activities.

The coding system should be carefully described as part of the final report. It is best to have more than one coder so that raters can check one another's work for reliability (consistent use of the coding standards).

If students, teachers, or principals are used as sources of information, it is most desirable to gather the opinions of more than one group.

Examples.   Caldwell (1979) of the Bay Area Writing Project designed a form for teachers to use in summarizing the writing they collected over several days from a sample of their students. They were supposed to gather all the papers students had written, whether formally assigned or not; however, it was difficult to persuade most students that some kinds of writing, such as personal notes, should be submitted. This procedure, then, undoubtedly underestimated the amount of personal writing completed. The collected writing was coded for purpose and intended audience. This survey was used for formative evaluation and improvement of writing instruction.

Fillion (1979) of the Ontario Institute for Studies in Education conducted surveys of high school principals in Ontario, Canada, asking the following questions:

- How much writing do students do in this school? How frequently? In which subjects?
- How many teachers encourage expressive or exploratory writing (for new ideas/styles)?
- Is there a school newspaper or other activities that promote student writing?
- How often do students read and respond to each others' writing?
- What kind of responses do students typically receive to writing?
- How often do students revise or elaborate writing?

Data collected in response to these questions formed the basis of descriptive reports. See also Applebee (1986), Donlan (1974), and Gere (1977 and 1979) for examples of writing surveys and discussion of their uses.

Student Enrollments

Description.   In some cases it may be possible to collect information on students' subsequent enrollment in composition, English, or related classes. These data can be used as indicators of long-term impact of composition instruction.

Advantages and Disadvantages.   The advantage of using these data is that they are often relatively easy and inexpensive to collect (presuming school records are accessible), and they require no disruption of ongoing instructional activities. The disadvantage is that enrollment patterns reflect factors other than the composition program under evaluation and need to be reported and interpreted conservatively. For example, competing courses in vocational subject areas might draw enrollment away from English or composition classes at a time when jobs are hard to get, or certain requirements might be introduced that cause students to choose one course over another. Whether a student enrolls in a course may be influenced not only by the student's desire to do so but also by availability of other courses, scheduling considerations, degree requirements, and so on.

Guidelines for Use.   Data on course and enrollment patterns should be interpreted cautiously, in light of the problems cited above. At best, they give weak, secondary indications of the success of instruction. They are most useful when accompanied by a questionnaire that helps identify students' reasons for selecting subsequent composition courses.

Example.   Becker (1972) describes ways in which enrollment data have been collected and used in the evaluation of composition programs.

3-4 ■ The Process of Teaching Writing

Preliminary Considerations

Examining the processes or behaviors involved in teaching writing can be worthwhile for the following reasons:

- To provide information useful to teachers who wish to improve their teaching methods, coverage of particular topics, handouts, and so forth (formative evaluation of teaching; staff development)
- To determine how to improve (or whether to use) a specific approach or set of curriculum materials (product or method evaluation, formative or summative)
- To help interpret the outcomes of a program evaluation, and to obtain a good description of what is being taught and how so that evaluation results can be more clearly understood (summative program evaluation)
- To describe in what ways, if any, composition program activities

deviate from a particular approach (formative or summative evaluation for program replication)

■ To identify the impact of inservice training (formative or summative evaluation of inservice)

■ To decide upon hiring, promoting, or advancing to tenure a faculty member (summative teacher evaluation)

Most evaluations of teaching, however, particularly in recent years, have taken a very narrow view, examining changes in teaching behaviors or in the "products" or outcomes of the teaching process such as student test scores. Seldom has the current popular wisdom about measuring and rewarding writing processes extended to measuring and rewarding teaching processes. This narrow scope is unfortunate because it ignores the potential for evaluation procedures to serve as powerful tools in program improvment and staff development.

Other circumstances also work to make many faculty disinterested in evaluation or analytic description of teaching: the diversity of methods in the field (making clear-cut evaluation difficult), their own scant training for teaching composition, and perhaps their unsatisfactory experiences with past evaluation. For example, the typical pattern for teacher evaluation in secondary schools is one or two cursory classroom visits per year by an administrator.

The aims given above can be used to remind teachers and others involved in evaluating composition of the value of examining teaching processes and behaviors. The methods and instruments described in this section survey the wide array of tools available for evaluating different aspects of this process.

The need for designing evaluations meaningful to participating teachers must be balanced against the equally pressing need to minimize disruption of ongoing instruction and faculty conference time. Unless the data being collected are justified by the purpose of the evaluation *and* acceptable to the teacher in terms of time and effort required, there is little point in proceeding. Evaluators should select those instruments that are least burdensome to teachers in a specific instructional setting and most appropriate for evaluating a particular program.

Methodology Inventory

Description.   The method most frequently used in describing and evaluating the process of teaching writing has been the methodology inventory, a list of techniques and practices that might be included in the teaching of composition. Teachers report their use of the techniques, sometimes elaborating their responses with estimates of frequency of use and successfulness of impact. On occasion, the methodology inventory can be used as an observation scale, though this would require extended site visits and, in most cases, multiple observers.

Advantages and Disadvantages. This type of measure is usually inexpensive to develop and administer, can require minimal time for faculty to complete (though actual times range from fifteen minutes to over an hour), does not intrude on classroom activities, can yield quantifiable results, and can be designed to measure a particular content, instructional approach, or teaching strategy. Its disadvantages, however, are numerous.

First, it suffers from the same reliability and validity problems that all self-report measures do. Teacher's responses may not be accurate because of faulty memory or because answers are biased in favor of wishful thinking or efforts to please the investigator. There is little way to avoid these problems, other than by supplementing the methodology inventory with data collected from other sources (classroom observers or students). Careful briefing and a good feeling of cooperation can also increase reliability. Second, it is often difficult to devise a frequency scale that is meaningful and used consistently by all the respondents. For example, a technique such as "organization of writing by comparison and contrast" might be the focus of one lesson, receive passing attention in class discussions, and be available to students to use at their discretion. If a teacher is asked to indicate whether "organization of writing using comparison and contrast" is taught according to the following scale— "never, seldom, occasionally, or frequently"—the teacher may hesitate before answering. The technique is taught "frequently" in terms of all composition courses the teacher gives (i.e., in every course), but "occasionally" in the discussions of a particular class, and only "seldom" among the specific topics presented in formal instruction. And, of course, one teacher's "seldom" might equal another's "occasionally." Thus the inventory needs to be as specific as possible about the context respondents should use for the items and the frequency measures should be less subjective; for example, "once a week," "five times a semester," or "formal presentation," "informal discussion."

Third, composition teachers are only beginning to develop a standard terminology. For example, "expressive writing" can refer to clarifying ideas (Britton, 1975) or creating literary products such as poetry. Clearly, this absence of common definitions can hinder interpretations of the results. Finally, methodology inventories can describe the use and frequency of single techniques but provide little information on *how* (and in particular, how *well)* they are organized and employed in the instructional sequence.

Guidelines for Use.   Whenever possible it is best to combine methodology inventories with other sources of information about classroom activities, as a reliability check. Careful attention needs to be paid to the format of the questions so that respondents will be using the same frames of reference and the same definitions of key words. Pilot testing the form is one way to identify potential sources of difficulty. For example, what might be a significant change for one teacher (beginning to use peer response groups for all writing assignments) might be coded in the same category as a minor change for another teacher (awarding numerical scores or points to assignments rather than letter grades). Both might respond "yes" to the question, "Have there been changes in your procedures for evaluating or responding to student writing this term?" However, the first change would be of a quite different magnitude than the second, involving a shift from a teacher-centered response approach to a peer-centered response approach.

The interpretation of inventories is a haphazard art. Most researchers merely report the techniques in terms of summary levels of use (and significant differences when pre–post designs are used). Other researchers have attempted to group items into related clusters, such as "techniques for teaching prewriting," which allows for more general comparisons. For example, teachers may not all be using the same specific techniques, but may be emphasizing a general approach, such as the use of prewriting activities to clarify ideas. Such interpretations must be strictly qualified, for often there is the assumption that "more is better"— that more check marks mean more conscientious or improved teaching. (For examples of procedures for interpreting results from methodology inventories see Donlan, 1979, and Thomas, 1978.)

Examples.   These examples are derived from studies of composition instruction primarily at the secondary and postsecondary levels. Any of them could easily be adapted for elementary instruction.

Donlan (1979) of the Inland Area Writing Project and University of California at Riverside has developed a methodology inventory that contains the following categories and items:

- Stimuli for writing (12 items)
- Prewriting techniques (10 items)
- Writing (9 items)
- Revising/editing (6 items)

- Evaluation (19 items)
- Language development (103 items)
- Varieties of discourse (6 items)
- Publications (4 items)

He administered the form prior to and following inservice training and also developed procedures for grouping data and interpreting the results.

Koziol (1979) of the University of Pittsburgh has designed a detailed form (called PCRP Assessment Survey II) that incorporates the above groupings and includes the following additional categories:

- Frequency of written composition assignments
- Philosophy of language and composition learning
- Audiences for student writing
- Publication practices
- Teacher support for written composition program

Other inventories can be found in Keech and Thomas (1979), who list and describe numerous promising practices in composition, and in Thompson (1978), who gives extended discussion to the impact of inservice training on the classroom practices of sixteen teachers, grades 2 through 16.

Composition Questionnaires

Description.   A composition questionnaire is a more elaborate checklist than a methodology inventory. It is used to collect data about such topics as a teacher's education and preparation, professional activities, and philosophy of teaching composition as well as about methods and techniques. Usually it combines the frequency-of-use rating scales included in methodology inventories with multiple-choice and free-response questions. Such data can be useful for interpreting student outcomes as well as for understanding instructional processes.

Advantages and Disadvantages.   Collecting such specific information permits more detailed descriptions of teaching activities and allows more refined interpretation of student assessment data. Such detail may be quite useful in discovering whether, for example, two teachers claiming to be using the same technique are using it very differently, due to contrasting philosophies of composition or dissimilar training. Because these data are subject to the same reliability limitations of all self-report measures, however, they must be interpreted with caution.

Guidelines for Use. The issues discussed and suggestions made about the design and use of questionnaires apply here as well.

The most frequent source of problems in the design and use of these questionnaires is the collection of too much data. Overly long questionnaires not only waste teachers' and evaluators' time but can cause ill will between evaluators and teachers. Collect only those data that will serve explicit evaluation purposes.

Examples. Questions can be asked about a wide variety of topics including education, teaching load, past teaching experience, special support services in teaching, professional development training, and so on. Material discussed throughout this section and the next can be used to generate appropriate topics. For specific examples of questionnaires see NCTE (1972) or Koziol (1979).

Structured Interviews

Description. Structured interviews, a modified form of self-report, allow respondents to report aloud to an interviewer who works from a "structured" or established list of questions. (See section 3-2 for more complete discussions about designing and carrying out interviews.)

Advantages and Disadvantages. The expense of employing and training an interviewer for large numbers of teachers cannot be justified in most evaluations. The few cases where it might prove advantageous include: evaluation of the impact of inservice training in which teachers attended different versions of a program and the degree of variation in the versions is unknown, or as a preliminary and follow-up phase to classroom visits made for the purpose of evaluating teachers. At other times, selective interviews with a sample of prospective respondents can prove valuable for developing items to appear on written survey questionnaires.

Guidelines for Use. The issues discussed for written questionnaires apply to the design and administration of interviews and analysis and interpretation of their outcomes. (See Gorden (1975) for strategies and suggestions regarding interviewing.) With more than one interviewer, special provisions are needed to train the interviewers to ask questions in a similar fashion. Periodic conferences held throughout the interviewing process can help identify potential inconsistencies and improve reliability.

Examples. Thompson of the Arizona Writing Project (1978) used structured interviews and some other data sources to identify crucial aspects of teacher belief, attitude, and behavior that might affect the impact of staff development training. She included questions such as:

- What is your ideal image of a writing teacher for the grade level you teach?
- Have any changes taken place in your expectations of students' writing?
- What have you learned about teaching writing this semester?
- What learning outcomes do you expect students to accomplish in your class? Why are they important?

Nold (1979) asked teachers to keep writing portfolios for all students. At the end of the school term researchers selected folders of a highly skilled student writer, an average student writer, and a minimally skilled student writer and interviewed teachers concerning their teaching strategies, assignments, and responses to these individual students.

Graves (1979) recommends that teachers keep portfolios of assignments for each of their students. Teachers can then be interviewed about selected portfolios; they can sort the papers from highest to lowest quality and explain their judgments. Students can complete the same exercise, responding to questions such as, "Which do you think the teacher likes best? Least? Why?" This provides a record of different perceptions of the teacher's evaluation practices.

The evaluation unit of the Bay Area Writing Project used structured interviews covering teachers' professional activities, approaches to teaching composition, classroom activities, grading and response practices, and descriptions of their English department. See Thomas (1979) for the complete interview form.

Classroom Observations

Description. Few instruments have been designed for the observation of composition classes or instruction. Though instruments developed for other observation purposes can be adapted for use in composition instruction, the complexity and variations of teaching approaches require that such efforts proceed with caution.

Advantages and Disadvantages. The expense of employing and training an observer cannot be justified for most evaluation budgets. Situations in which it might prove advantageous include monitoring replications or evaluating the impact of different versions of a staff development program.

Guidelines for Use.   The lack of observation instruments can be turned into an advantage by engaging the teachers themselves in the process of developing measurement tools. Under certain conditions, costs can be minimized by training faculty to observe one another. In the process they may become more sensitive to aspects of composition instruction that they themselves have deemed important. This approach seems particularly appropriate to formative evaluation and program development. Of course this suggestion presumes a high degree of cooperation and mutual support among faculty as well as sufficient time for such activities. At the elementary and secondary level the procedure could be placed in the realm of staff development activities for which there seems to be increased funding and support in some locations. *Mirrors for Behavior* (Simon and Boyer, 1974) describes 99 instruments that could be adapted for classroom observation of composition instruction. The Conference on College Communication and Composition (CCCC) Committee on Teaching and Its Evaluation in Composition (Larson and associates, 1983) has developed a list of 20 questions to serve as a guide to developing observation instruments. Suggested topics include:

- Classroom procedures
- Appropriateness of instructional techniques for the specific students
- Response to students
- Techniques used in teaching writing skills
- Content of writing instruction
- Relationship of writing to the other language arts
- Response to student writing

The committee recommends that more than one visit be made during a school term and that the goals and emphases be clarified beforehand "so that the visit will seem to be not a police action but a positive effort to assist the teacher's professional improvement."

Decisions about which aspects of classroom activities to observe, what background knowledge or skills an observer needs, what coding procedures to use (anecdotal comments versus precoded rating scales), what data sampling plan to employ, and how to analyze the data and report results, should be made in light of evaluation goals and constraints. (See Henerson and associates, 1978, for a description of options and alternatives.)

Examples.   Indiana University began a formal program of observation for composition instructors in 1973–1974. Under this program teachers explain their goals to observers, who then give them detailed observations and discuss whether their behavior seemed consistent with their goals. The procedure includes a preobservation interview, classroom observation, and a follow-up conference. In the classroom, observers focus on specific aspects of the instructional processes that the instructor wants them to attend to, as well as on:

- Student-teacher behavior before the class begins
- The process of beginning the class
- Patterns of talk and discussion
- Classroom movement
- Eye contact
- Voice and mannerisms of the teacher
- End-of-class procedures

The program has been used for over 150 instructors, including new graduate student teaching assistants and experienced faculty (some with up to 20 years of classroom instruction). For a detailed description, see Flanigan (1979).

Educational Testing Service (Alloway, 1978), as part of the evaluation of the New Jersey Writing Project (Rutgers), adapted a classroom observation form, adding a checklist of composition instruction techniques to measures of:

- Classroom organization
- Instructional organization
- Classroom activities (student movement, activity change, conversation, leaving the classroom)
- Classroom procedures
- Student-teacher interaction
- Teacher behavior and personality
- Student behavior

Students' Perceptions of Teaching

Description.   Student description and evaluation of teaching can take a variety of forms. Typically, students are asked to describe methods and practices involved in teaching composition and rate the effectiveness of various aspects of instruction. Few standardized forms have been developed specifically for composition instruction; many more are available that evaluate teaching effectiveness in general.

Students are the most knowledgeable observers in any classroom for certain dimensions of teaching, but many researchers have been rather reluctant to solicit students' views. The reluctance is often rationalized in terms of students' immaturity, effects that are probably less serious than in the case of a principal making evaluation ratings after one or two visits. Student opinions are increasingly being sought, especially at the college level, and especially as one component of multimeasure evaluation designs. At least one study suggests that student ratings may be a useful check on self-perceptions of composition teachers (Hoetker and Brossell, 1979).

Advantages and Disadvantages.   These measures can provide valuable information from knowledgeable sources. Often this information allows insights into the process of instruction that are difficult to infer from students' writing performance.

McKeachie (1979) has ably summarized the uses for student evaluations of teaching: to improve teaching, to provide data relevant to judgments about teaching effectiveness, and to stimulate students to think about their education. He notes that ratings are not automatically valid and useful for these purposes; they require careful design and preparation, and confidence on the part of both students and faculty that good use will be made of the information.

Guidelines for Use.   Student perceptions of teaching are best used in conjunction with other sources of information on teaching effectiveness. It is also important to limit the nature of the items on the questionnaire to areas in which students can reasonably be expected to have some knowledge. For example, students should not be asked to rate the adequacy or quality of the content covered. Those judgments are best made by someone expert in the area, such as a faculty colleague. If students are informed of the purposes of the data collection effort, and if data collection procedures guarantee anonymity of response (particularly in any feedback to the teacher), the reliability of the measure can be increased. Guidelines on constructing or selecting instruments, administering questionnaires, and reporting and interpreting results can be found in Borich and Madden (1977) or Kowalski (1978) for precollege teaching, and Centra (1979) for college teaching.

Examples.   *English Journal* (October, 1979) published a survey of students' descriptions of their writing instruction including measures of writing frequency, type, and instructional techniques used. This is an example of a descriptive survey; no effort was made to gather students' evaluations of the value of the instruction they received.

The CCCC Committee on Teaching and Its Evaluation in Composition (Larson et al., 1983) has developed an extensive list of questions that might be used in evaluating instructional experiences. Included are items that measure:

- Skills, attitudes, and instruction prior to instruction
- Course activities and their effects on students
- Changes in skills and attitudes after instruction

Students' perceptions of teaching and of its effectiveness are also included.

Collections of sample instruments can be found in Kowalski (1978) and Centra (1979).

Evaluation of Writing Assignment Topics

Description. This method involves independent raters judging the quality and appropriateness of teachers' composition assignments. This kind of assessment might be valuable in formative or summative evaluation of an individual teacher or in collecting comparative information about the activities of several teachers.

Advantages and Disadvantages. This method does not intrude upon ongoing instructional activities; one need only collect the assignments given to students. However, the reliability and validity of the ratings could easily be questioned, especially if raters are not carefully trained to assess assignments systematically, or if raters are in some way associated with the composition program. Even under the best of conditions, this measure gives only limited clues concerning instructional processes and outcomes—the validation of the raters' judgments is mostly informal.

Guidelines for Use. This measure is most useful in conjunction with other methods of evaluating the processes and outcomes of composition instruction. Careful attention should be given to training raters, and interrater reliability checks should be made periodically.

Although this method has been developed for summative evaluation purposes, individual composition teachers might find this technique useful in developing or refining their own assignments.

Examples.   The CCCC Committee on Teaching and Its Evaluation in Composition has identified useful questions for assessing the appropriateness of a teacher's assignments in composition courses. Information is provided on content; there are no guidelines for question format or data collection. The CCCC Committee suggests that the following aspects of assignments be considered in any rating activity:

- Format of the assignment (written or verbal explanation)
- Clarity of directions
- Relationship to other class assignments
- Audience for the composition (and specification)
- Purpose and context
- Related materials and substance for prewriting
- Opportunities for discussion of assignment with teachers
- Opportunities for class time spent in writing
- Adequacy of time provided to complete the assignment.

To this list we might add such items as whether grading criteria are made known to students and whether the teacher has tried writing the assignment, either prior to or while students are completing it. (Some inservice projects stress that teachers of writing must write—though not necessarily with students on every assignment.) Note that all these dimensions are descriptive, simply requiring collection of information about current practices. Values assigned to the responses (judgments of appropriateness or merit) must be locally determined, on the basis of needs and program context, and evidence about actual results. This method would not be likely to provide a sound basis for personnel decisions.

Standardized Measures of Teaching Expertise

Description.   Some measures assess teachers' beliefs about and attitudes toward aspects of language and composition instruction. These measures offer lists of important aspects of composition instruction. As such, they could provide the starting point for identification of differences in opinion and belief.

Advantages and Disadvantages.   Because widespread dispute exists among professionals in the field of composition instruction, these measures might elicit a number of different, yet equally defensible answers. No reports have been made of validity or reliability estimates, so at this point these measures might be most effectively used for descriptive purposes only. Further, these measures carry with them the disadvantages of all self-report methods.

Guidelines for Use. Given the above disadvantages, these measures seem best used to generate descriptive information about differences in philosophy and belief. They might be helpful in formative feedback or in program development.

Examples. The *NCTE Composition Opinionaire* (1972) contains 55 statements about writing and language instruction that are rated according to whether the respondent strongly agrees, agrees, disagrees, strongly disagrees, or has no opinion. Here are sample items:

- "Grades are the most effective way of evaluating compositions."
- "Assignments during the last two years of high school should require primarily expository writing."
- "Every good paragraph should have a concluding sentence or clincher."
- "Students should have freedom in selecting the topics for their composition."

The *Froegner Language Inquiry Test* (1979) consists of 100 statements about writing and language instruction, using rating criteria similar to those on the *NCTE Opinionaire*.

- "Linguists now know the characteristics that the English language should have."
- "Standard English allows for no choices in language forms."
- "Splitting the infinitive may sometimes enable the writer to express his ideas with greater clarity and force than otherwise."

The *Illinois Tests in the Teaching of English*, "Attitude and Knowledge in Written Composition," by Evans and Jacobs (1972) describes classroom settings, composition assignments, and student writing samples. Respondents are presented with an instructional scenario and then asked multiple-choice questions about the appropriateness of the assignment, the quality of student writing, and so forth.

3-5 ■ Teachers' Attitudes and Beliefs About Writing

Description. Teachers' attitudes and beliefs can be assessed using self-report measures (questionnaires and interviews) or reports of others.

These data can serve several purposes. First, attitudes and beliefs are an important aspect of teaching and learning experiences and can help provide a more complete description of the functioning of the program. Second, because attitude change often precedes behavior change, these data can be useful indicators of future improvement or growth. This is particularly important in short-term evaluations, where a teacher may have little opportunity to change behavior, but may experience important alterations in attitude and belief. Third, data on attitude can aid in identifying and understanding how or why one teacher's behavior differs from another's. For example, two teachers might use the same technique very differently because of contrasting attitudes or beliefs about composition instruction. Finally, generating and collecting information on teachers' attitudes toward writing could serve as the basis for faculty discussions and program development efforts.

Advantages and Disadvantages.   Few instruments measuring the attitudes and beliefs of composition teachers have been developed either locally or for commercial distribution. Although identifying important and widespread beliefs in a field marked by such diversity of approach and method is quite difficult, the value of these data make assessment of attitudes an important evaluation component.

Guidelines for Use.   Some suggestions for choosing or developing appropriate measures, for deciding how and when to administer them, and how to analyze the results, are given in section 3-2. Items from this area can be combined with topics mentioned in section 3-4, particularly composition questionnaires and structural interviews. In addition to such general references as Henerson and associates (1978) and Demaline and Quinn (1979), the following examples illustrate the kinds of instruments that might be used.

Examples

Questionnaires.   Blake (1976) describes a procedure to develop a questionnaire regarding teachers' attitudes and beliefs for measuring changes in participants in an inservice training course. The following categories and kinds of items are included:

- Skills of writing: "The ideas in writing are important, not the kinds of sentences in which they are used." (belief)
- Varieties of writing: "I almost never write letters." (behavior description)
- Kinds of writers: "I admire writers of fiction." (value/attitude)

Emig and King (1978) of the Rutgers-New Jersey Writing Project developed a teacher questionnaire to assess the impact of inservice training. It contains 50 statements about the teaching of writing which respondents rate according to a five-point scale (ranging from "almost never" to "almost always"). The scale includes the following categories and sample items:

- Evaluation of own language skills: "I write better than I speak."
- Preference for writing activities: "When I have free time, I prefer writing to reading."
- General beliefs/attitudes about language/language instruction: "Communicating with others is more important than expressing oneself."
- General attitudes/beliefs about writing/writing instruction: "Poorer student writers don't spend as much time on writing as good students."
- Teaching practices: "If a paper has many misspellings, I give it a low grade."
- Writing behaviors of the teacher: "I revise what I write."

Several measures described in section 3-4 under "Standardized Measures of Teaching Expertise" may also be appropriate for assessing teachers' attitudes and beliefs. These include the *NCTE Composition Opinionaire* (1972), the *PCRP* (Koziol, 1982), and the *Illinois Tests in the Teaching of Composition* (Evans and Jacobs). More extended discussion of issues involved in measuring attitudes toward language use and language change can be found in Gere and Smith (1979) and Schuessler et al. (1982).

Interviews and observations. There are no readily available interview formats or observation scales for specifically measuring teachers' attitudes and beliefs about writing. Specific content for interview formats and observation scales can be modified from questionnaire items presented in this section and earlier. Relevant beliefs and attitudes concerning the process of teaching writing might also be reflected in faculty activities outside the classroom, including participation in various professional activities, tutorial work with students, or participation in student publishing programs. Data about these activities could be collected through observation or faculty self-report.

Standardized measures. Commercially or professionally developed measures of attitudes or personality dimensions might also be considered. See Henerson and associates (1978) for some general examples.

3-6 ■ Teachers' Professional Activities and Leadership Roles

Description.   Measures of teachers' behavior outside the classroom may provide useful descriptive information about the functioning of a program or the impact of staff development activities. Areas to examine include teachers' cocurricular and professional activities and leadership roles.

Advantages and Disadvantages.   These measures can provide supplementary descriptions of teachers' behaviors, including unanticipated side effects of the program. They carry with them all the disadvantages of self-report techniques. In some cases, it may be difficult to establish consistent and meaningful relationships between numbers or types of professional activities and their qualitative contributions to an instructor's professional growth or to the program being evaluated. Choosing to measure these behaviors can be quite valuable, however, in acknowledging their important role in the continuing development of faculty skill and expertise. It can also provide an incentive to faculty to engage in such activities, one valuable side effect of evaluation.

Guidelines for Use.   For guidelines on choosing and developing questionnaires and observation measures and interpreting their results, see sections 3-2 and 3-4. Instruments for assessing teacher behavior outside the classroom can be treated similarly, with the following examples illustrating some dimensions that might be considered.

Examples
   Questionnaires on professional activities.   The National Writing Project model identifies the most successful composition teachers in a summer institute who then become trainers of other teachers and leaders in professional improvement efforts such as curriculum reform and design of writing assessment programs. As part of the evaluation of the Bay Area Writing Project, the following checklist of professional activities was developed as a postmeasure of change (Roark, 1978). Respondents used a five-point scale—from "no change" to "greatly increased"—to rate each item. (If the questionnaire is to be administered twice, as a measure of change, other response categories should be used; for example, specific frequencies might be listed—e.g., "daily," "weekly," etc.) The checklist evaluates changes in professional activities resulting from Writing Project Training:

■ Discussions with fellow teachers on the teaching of writing

- Collaborative activities with other teachers and team teaching
- Taking a leadership role in the planning of school or district writing programs
- Taking a leadership role in the planning of English proficiency standards or proficiency test content
- Giving presentations at inservice or professional meetings
- Organizing or coordinating inservice activities
- Other professional activities related to the teaching of writing

Observations. Donlan (1979) asked Inland Writing Project leaders to rate participants' leadership skills. A special form was developed for the assessment and used to measure change over the course of the project.

3-7 ■ Training Activities

Professional development activities—preservice/inservice training, faculty development, conference attendance, professional journal reading—may be an important component or effect of a composition program. (For ease of reference throughout this section they will be referred to as training activities.) These efforts contribute to teachers' knowledge or teaching skills and may require special evaluation strategies beyond those already discussed.

Formative Evaluation by Participants

Description. The goal of formative evaluation is to give program staff information about the immediate impact of the training so that they can make changes in future sessions as necessary. Research on staff development demonstrates that ongoing formative evaluation is important to the success of training programs (Berman and McLaughlin, 1978). Some of the most frequently used methods are described below. Of course, other data collection procedures could be employed, such as interviews or observations by nonparticipants. These methods are more expensive, however, and may not be necessary for formative purposes.

Participant logs. In some training courses, participants take turns writing brief, anecdotal summaries of each training session, with evaluative comments added when appropriate. These are then duplicated and distributed to all participants so that by the end of the training period all participants possess a record of the events of each session. Training leaders and program staff can use these diaries and the discussion they generate for the purposes of formative feedback.

Thompson Methodology Inventory. Thompson (1978) has developed a standardized measure that can be used to obtain participants' evaluations of methods or approaches demonstrated in training sessions. Participants are asked to rate the usefulness of a particular method, the likelihood that they might try it, its appropriateness for their students and current composition program, its probable value to other teachers, and the overall quality of a specific presentation.

Brief questionnaires. A number of training programs use brief questionnaires that ask participants to rate a particular presentation on several dimensions as well as to make more general comments or to raise questions or issues about the training for future discussions. These forms ar usually completed (anonymously) at the end of each training session.

Index cards. A variation of the brief questionnaire is to give participants blank index cards and request that they write down their comments, questions, or suggestions. The cards are turned in at the end or middle of the session and reviewed by the staff. These can be completed anonymously if participants wish.

Advantages and Disadvantages

Participant logs. Logs give an individualized and often humorous or colorful history of the sessions. They do not reveal the overall group response to each presentation or session, nor is it easy to quantify these logs into summary statistics. A special benefit of logs is to encourage teachers to write and respond to one another's writing—a valuable experience in development of faculty expertise. Logs may take more time than some of the other response measures, but depending on the size and length of the training sessions, each participant may only have to prepare one entry. The time required to read and analyze them depends on the amount of information program staff want to extract.

The Thompson Methodology Inventory. Use of this measure provides detailed information on each individual presentation, thus allowing comparisons among different offerings. Because the inventory gathers information about the perceived effectiveness of specific techniques, it permits investigation of factors that influence teachers' performance. It requires little time to complete, perhaps five minutes, and is relatively easy to summarize.

Brief questionnaires. Like an inventory, questionnaires can provide systematic data from each participant on all the training sessions. Questionnaires are more flexible, allowing opportunities for individual comments or specific questions. Depending on how many comments participants write, questionnaires may take only a few minutes to complete. Multiple-choice responses can be quickly tallied and summarized; open-ended responses may take longer to read and analyze.

Index cards. These allow for more individualized responses since participants are free to comment or not on any aspect of the training. They are less obtrusive than questionnaires or an inventory; the time required for reading and analysis depends on how much participants write. Their chief advantage is to provide fast indications of problem areas or questions regarding the progress of the sessions.

Guidelines for Use. The choice of measures for formative feedback depends upon several factors: the time program staff wish to take from ongoing training activities for evaluation purposes, the kind and amount of information they wish to collect, and the time they wish to devote to reading and analyzing the results. Regardless of the instrument or procedure chosen, one can encourage participants to respond more effectively by adhering to some general guidelines. Anonymity should be preserved; participants who wish to can identify themselves, but most often, anonymity facilitates honest, critical responses. It is best if participants see that their suggestions and criticisms are thoughtfully received; requested changes should be effected as appropriate or reasons for not altering the program should be discussed. Flexibility in use of these measures is encouraged; they are designed to serve the needs of the program staff for information on the progress of the training activities.

Examples. The Bay Area Writing Project (UC Berkeley) and the Northern Virginia Writing Project (George Mason University) are among many programs using participant logs. Sample entries may be requested directly from them.

The Thompson Methodology Inventory (Thompson, 1978) includes some of the following items:

- "How compatible is this method with others you use now?"
- "How appropriate is this method to use with students at your grade level?"
- "How likely are you to try this method?"
- "How likely would students using this method improve their quality of writing?"

The Bay Area Writing Project (UC Berkeley) has developed a one-page evaluation form that participants complete at the end of each session. They are asked to rate the speaker's topic, delivery, and organization of the presentation on a 1-to-7 point scale and explain their ratings. They also answer the following open-ended questions, if they wish:

- "What, if anything, would have made last week's presentation more effective for you?"
- "As a result of your experiences in the inservice so far, what specific suggestions do you have, if any, for topics/activities/procedures?"
- "What questions do you have about the general process of writing?"

Data from these questions are useful to program planners in shaping content to meet participants' needs and in identifying ineffective aspects of the training.

Summative Evaluation by Participants

Description.   Summative evaluation by participants can take different forms. If evaluators want to measure the immediate value of training to the participants, they might administer questionnaires or interviews as close to the completion of training as possible. If evaluators want to assess the effects of training on classroom performance, summative responses can be collected after three to six months. A few evaluations have included both immediate and delayed responses, as well as pretraining assessments, to identify implementation patterns over a longer time span.

The procedures for gathering data depend on the evaluation's purpose, the type of training, and resources available. Some projects have used lengthy questionnaires or intensive personal interviews. A variety of formats, including multiple-choice and short-answer questions and rating scales, allow inquiry about such dimensions of program content as value of presentations, quality of program organization and management, appropriateness of content for participants' writing skills, expected impact on teachers' teaching and writing behaviors, and so on. Many of the measures discussed earlier in this chapter can be adapted to identify specific kinds of training impact. Regardless of the type of procedure chosen, it seems essential to find some way to question participants, because they are in the best position to assess the relevance of the training to their particular needs.

Advantages and Disadvantages.   The relative strengths and weaknesses of questionnaires and interviews are discussed earlier in this chapter. In general, interviews are preferable to written questionnaires if training experiences are complex or if probing is necessary to explore subtle impacts of the program. If important outcomes of the training seem to elude clear identification, interviews can assist in isolating important issues and topics that can be refined into a written questionnaire for broader distribution.

Guidelines for Use. Examples of instruments and sample items for assessing the process of teaching writing, teachers' attitudes, and professional activities are offered earlier in this chapter, along with advice about related measurement issues such as validity, reliability, and effective instrument design. Certain concerns and questions make some measures and items more appropriate than others for summative evaluations of professional training. Obviously, items should be relevant to the content and purpose of the training and its possible unintended effects. But there is an additional consideration: What might make the evaluation experience most rewarding and least burdensome for the participants? Answers to this question must be balanced with details of the evaluation context: Who is sponsoring the evaluation? Who is the client? What is the purpose of the evaluation? Does it allow for evaluation to be a staff development activity? And finally, what type of evidence will be most convincing to the client? Consideration of these practical aspects of the evaluation helps shape its design.

If scheduling allows, participants might benefit from renewing acquaintances with one another as part of the evaluation activities. In that case, group interviews might be combined with questionnaires. If participants might benefit from a chance to reflect on their experiences, then open-ended questions, preferably administered in a personal interview or on the telephone, would encourage the most complete responses. For practical reasons, evaluators must consider the human rewards that can be built into the designs.

Examples. The California State Department of Education funded the development of a naturalistic approach for evaluating training which draws upon information gathered in interviews with school personnel. Teachers and administrators are asked to describe useful training experiences, resulting changes in educational practices or programs, and the general climate for professional development within the district. Pilot testing of this approach has illustrated its usefulness in identifying the impact of state-funded programs on an entire district as well as on individual teachers and administrators (Joyce and associates, 1982).

The following list of items can be used in self-report measures (questionnaires and interviews) or modified for use in observations and the collection of other behavioral data.

Overall rating of inservice.   It is often useful to gather summative ratings of the training and its components. This can be accomplished by listing each component of the program and asking respondents to rate the overall value of each, as shown in Figure 3.4. A variation is to list the components and have participants rate each one with a letter grade, A–F, and add open-ended comments as they wish.

Ratings of separate components.   It may be useful to ask more specific questions about various components. Individual speakers can be rated separately, either for overall value or for more detailed aspects of their contribution such as content, organization, and manner of delivery. Program activities, administration, and logistics can also be assessed individually. The following examples are from a form which asked participants to rate each item using a five-point scale (1 = "strongly disagree" to 5 = "strongly agree").

- "The needs of district teachers were adequately reflected in the initial planning of this program."
- "The coordinator has given effective leadership to this inservice program."
- "I had a problem because of insufficient information about forthcoming meeting dates, speakers and/or topics."
- "The participants of this inservice have functioned effectively as a group, contributing to one another's experience."

Suggested improvements.   Suggestions for changes or additions to the program can also be solicited. Most simply, open-ended questions like the following might be asked: "Do you have any criticisms or suggestions for improvement of this training program? If so, please give them in the space below." Often program planners and evaluators find participants'

FIGURE 3.4

	No Value		Some Value		Great Value
a) Training as a whole + other components	1	2	3	4	5
b) Speakers	1	2	3	4	5
c) Presentations by participants	1	2	3	4	5
d) Writing assignments	1	2	3	4	5
e) Logistics and organization	1	2	3	4	5

open-ended comments the most useful in making modifications in context, format or structures.

Future activities.   In some cases, it is useful to include a specific list of follow-up activities of possible interest to teachers and inquire about their participation in future offerings. This is especially valuable for those programs that can provide follow-up support to teachers. For example, in the evaluation of the Bay Area Writing Project, participants used a five-point scale (1 = "no interest" to 5 = "great interest") to indicate their interest in the following activities:

- "A follow-up workshop, before next fall, at which participants could consult with one or two BAWP speakers about plans for next year's courses"
- "Release time to visit demonstration classrooms where BAWP ideas are being carried out"
- "A chance to see movies or videotapes of the classrooms of BAWP teacher consultants"
- "Visits by BAWP consultants to your classroom, with individual consultation as desired"

Impact of the training.   Participants' ratings of the impact of the training on their own teaching behavior and on their other professional activities, and their estimates of its impact on their students, can also provide useful information about a program's effectiveness. The following examples are from questionnaires developed by the Bay Area Writing Project Evaluation, administered as post-only surveys. (The format would have to be changed for a pre-post administration.) In this set of questions, participants rate each item from 1 ("not at all") to 5 ("very much").

- "Were you using any BAWP ideas in your classroom before this inservice began?"
- "Has the inservice caused you to plan to carry out any new BAWP ideas in your teaching so far?"
- "Do BAWP ideas seem suitable to the realities of your classroom and school?"
- "As a result of participation in the training, has there been any change in your thinking about the goals and objectives of instruction in composition?"

In the set of questions in Figure 3.5, participants indicated the degree of impact that BAWP training has had, in general, on their students' attitudes and skills.

FIGURE 3.5

	Greatly Decreased		No Change		Greatly Increased	Don't Know
a. Students' valuing of writing	1	2	3	4	5	( )
b. Students' enjoyment of writing	1	2	3	4	5	( )
c. Students' confidence in their writing ability	1	2	3	4	5	( )
d. Students' overall writing skill	1	2	3	4	5	( )
e. Other student effects (please describe)	1	2	3	4	5	( )

Evaluation of Training by Nonparticipant Evaluators

Description. Training can also be evaluated by using the perceptions of individuals who are not participants in the program. These observers can report periodically to project staff so that improvements can be made during the training. Observers can also record activities and reactions over the course of the training in order to make a final summative report. A variation of this approach allows observers to participate in some of the training and write descriptive logs or reports.

Advantages and Disadvantages. The reliability of the data can be questioned if systematic observation procedures are not used and if an observer's past experience with teaching or training has been too limited to allow for sensible judgments. This procedure is relatively expensive, requiring a skilled observer. Further, there may be credibility or validity problems, depending on who is selected as an observer. Caution should be exercised in using faculty colleagues (Centra, 1979). Observers without background or experience in composition instruction pose another set of problems, including their acceptability to program staff. Given these constraints, use of an outside observer should be considered cautiously.

Guidelines for Use. The selection and training of observers is quite important. (See section 3-2 for guidelines in using observers.) Situations in which this type of data collection might prove useful include:

- Process-based training where participants may be so busy with training activities that they are unable to provide comprehensive evaluation data
- Training programs with complex content that might require extensive description from an independent observer
- Training programs whose content varies so widely that an independent observer is needed to report on the range of variations

Examples. The following topic areas were derived from an observation form used to evaluate inservice training programs of the Bay Area Writing Project. Space was left after each item for the observer's comments (Roark, 1978).

- *Description of training coordinator's role.* Rapport with teachers; amount of interaction; efficiency and organization; timing; physical arrangements.
- *Presentation.* Method of presentation; manner of speaker; handouts: number, quality, use in program; other materials; interaction with audience: level of audience interest and attention, kinds of questions asked; usefulness; theoretical and research references; value of content; speaker's main points.
- *Participants' activities.* Nature of activity and relation to speaker's presentation; materials; level of interest and participation; clarity of focus; usefulness; overall value of activity.
- *Opinions* of the meeting expressed by coordinator, speaker, or participants.
- *Summary points.* Comparison with other inservice meetings: teacher morale and attitude, quality of presentation, value of participatory activity, general organization; principal strengths; principal weaknesses; suggestions.

Evaluation of the Impact of Professional Development Activities

Clearly, data obtained from the participants or from an independent observer are only one component of the evaluation of an inservice program. The most important benefits of training may be the long-term effects on teaching behaviors and professional activities, on student writing performance, and on the nature and functioning of the writing curriculum. The other evaluation components discussed in this book can be usefully applied to the evaluation of professional development programs. The reader is encouraged to review those sections for evaluation ideas and suggestions.

3-8 ■ Program Administration

Preliminary Considerations

Administrative decisions and procedures affect every aspect of a program's functioning, from initial design or adoption phases to reporting final outcomes. Yet although administrative guidance, support, and facilitation—or restriction and opposition—can significantly affect the success of a program, it is difficult to identify evaluation measures and procedures that are sensitive only to administrative activities because the responsibilities for program functioning are rarely so clear-cut that blame or praise can be given to administrators alone.

Nevertheless, it seems important to include at least brief consideration of the possible influence of administrative policies and procedures as part of *all* evaluations, regardless of their scale, whether the evaluation is of a single technique being used in one composition course or of a large-scale project. Identifying the dimensions of administrative functioning often brings important descriptive insights about how an educational program actually functions. Also, describing key characteristics permits more meaningful interpretation of student and teacher performance. A third reason for examining program administration occurs in the special case of *replication projects*, in which a technique or an entire course or program is duplicated at a site different from its origin. Of course, adoption of techniques or approaches occurs all the time. Replication evaluation is concerned with the case in which claims of success at the adoption site are based on the strength of the original project's success. Here the major concern is whether the administration is adequately monitoring the replication effort so that fidelity to the original model or approach can be clearly established. We discuss this situation in detail in section 3-11.

Evaluators of administrative functioning most often have used a checklist. From those already in existence we have constructed a summary of the topics which seem most important to consider. The relative importance of each item must be decided locally and will probably vary from site to site. For a discussion of administrative concerns influencing composition instruction at the college level, see Hairston (1979) and Lindemann (1979).

Key Dimensions

The topics listed below are the kinds of questions to be asked about administrative influences on the educational environment.

Educational and Institutional Context of the Program

- What resources are available to the program? Consider direct financial allocations and indirect support.
- What constraints limit the program's content and functioning? Institutional policies and practices may sometimes contradict official program goals or interests.

Administrative Responsibilities

- What planning activities do administrators undertake? Consider who is consulted and how planning proceeds.
- What program development activities can be observed? Successful projects provide systematic opportunities for faculty to exchange information and upgrade their skills.
- How effectively do administrators manage the internal affairs of the program? By this we mean the type and amount of support provided to faculty, the equitable scheduling of courses and workloads, and the efficient uses of resources, facilities and equipment.
- How effectively do administrators manage the external affairs of the program? Here consider the ways in which the program is portrayed to the public and to policy-makers.
- Are record-keeping procedures effective? Successful programs have in place systematic procedures for gathering information about students, faculty and program activities.
- Has the program established formative and summative evaluation procedures? Projects need to develop ways to monitor and assess their own effectiveness. If they depend on external sources of funding, they may also be required to develop reasonable summative evaluation plans.

For detailed checklists of administrative dimensions see Joyce (1982), Scriven (1975), or Lindemann (1979).

Guidelines for Use

Selecting Features to Evaluate. The evaluation's purpose and its audience in part determine the administrative activities to be described and monitored. If information is needed to help interpret the results of student writing assessments or to understand constraints on teaching processes, then the investigation into administrative functioning will be more limited in scope. If administrative functioning is viewed as part of an overall program evaluation, then a larger number of dimensions will be included and data should be collected from as many different sources as resources allow. In this latter case it may be most efficient for evaluators to identify the critical features of composition instruction and then collect data about how administrators might be facilitating or inhibiting their effectiveness. Data about the more general educational context in which the program operates are useful for most evaluations of program administration, because the resources and constraints of the community and institution set limits on what any administrator can do.

Developing an Evaluation Plan.   A variety of methods and measures can be considered. Self-report (interviews or questionnaires) can be used with administrators, faculty, students, and support staff. Observations can be made of ongoing department activities such as staff meetings, or of daily events such as administrator-faculty conferences and activities in faculty work areas. Evaluators can also review departmental records and publications such as program policy statements, memos, faculty or student files, publicity bulletins, course outlines or program descriptions. The choices of which data to collect, what sampling or collection plan to use, and how to interpret the results depend upon the features of the program being evaluated as well as the aims of and audiences for the evaluation. Before making these decisions, it may be wise to review important program documents and perhaps conduct a few selective individual or group interviews with key program personnel. In these interviews, which might take only an hour each, general questions could be asked about the program's functioning and administrative duties. From the information gathered at that time, more detailed data collection forms and procedures could be developed, including a more systematic sampling of project records and reports, interviews or questionnaires, and observations. (For an extended description of procedures and instruments to use to evaluate program administration, see Morris and Fitz-Gibbon, 1978.)

Illustrations.   In the mid-1960s, NCTE staff members and other professionals conducted an extensive, three-year study of the teaching of English in 158 high schools in 45 states. The research staff administered checklists and questionnaires to students, faculty, counselors, librarians, and administrators. Classroom observations were made during a two-day site visit to each school, and a sample of student papers from each school was read. Most of the schools had been selected because they had outstanding English programs. An extensive written report detailed the findings of the study (Squire and Applebee, 1968). Among the factors which seemed to account for general program excellence were:

- Well-prepared, active, ever-learning teachers
- Principals' interest in academic values
- Favorable climate for teaching; cooperation among teachers; slightly lower than average teacher load
- Excellent department heads, with time and inclination to supervise teaching and to lead in curriculum planning

These results suggest that administrative functioning strongly influences program quality. Another one of their findings—that the least successful program often existed in schools where no one seemed "in control" and where teachers felt powerless to improve conditions—reinforces this point.

As part of an extensive evaluation of inservice training programs offered by the Bay Area Writing Project, a sample of program sessions was observed and training coordinators were interviewed. From that information questionnaires were developed for both coordinators and inservice participants to identify how well the program was functioning. On the basis of these data, recommendations were made to program staff regarding ways of strengthening logistical and organizational aspects of the project (Roark, 1978).

3-9 ■ Costs

Description.   Cost analysis is or should be an important component of almost every evaluation. The thoroughness with which it is conducted will depend on the resources available for the evaluation and evaluator expertise, but certain points should be included whenever possible. Just as evaluation of composition instruction cannot be solely equated with measurement of student writing performance, so cost analysis cannot be solely equated with accounting and quantitative analysis. *True* (or actual) costs (and benefits) remain among the most elusive aspects of any program to quantify.

The most appropriate definition of cost is *all negative effects* (monetary and nonmonetary). Identifying and calculating these effects may be quite challenging because they are often differential and relative. The real questions are: Costs—to whom? Benefits—for whom? Within what time frame? Calculated according to what accounting and estimating principles? Answering each of these questions involves judgments and clear reasoning about true costs and benefits. The best cost analyses address the conceptual issues that we describe in this section and clearly document what was included and why. The worst merely offer a bottom-line figure (usually dollar cost per student) without any indication of what features went into the calculation. After defining four common types of cost analyses, we will give some general suggestions of procedures to follow.

Major Types of Cost Analysis.   Cost analyses vary in their purposes, procedures, and type of data considered. Detailed descriptions are too complex to present here and are readily available elsewhere (see Levin, 1983; Rossi and Freeman, 1985; and Haggerty, 1978.) It is important, however, to note some important distinctions in their purposes and some essential, shared procedures.

   Cost feasibility analysis.   This procedure is the most limited in scope and tries only to answer the question, Do the total costs of a program alternative being considered exceed available resources? No effort is made to formally determine benefits or effects of the proposed alternative.

   Cost benefit analysis.   This procedure involves converting total or major costs and benefits to monetary terms in order to determine whether costs exceed benefits. A common rating standard using monetary units allows comparison among different alternatives but it is often impossible to apply.

   Cost effectiveness analysis.   When benefits cannot be converted to a monetary figure, some of them may be described by a standard measure of effectiveness such as test scores. In this case, costs are described in monetary figures; only those benefits that can be converted to an effectiveness standard are calculated. This procedure allows comparisons between different alternatives but does not directly answer the question, Is a single program worth its costs? Nor does it include nonmonetary costs.

   Cost utility analysis.   When different effectiveness measures are to be used (such as reading and writing scores) and when minimal effectiveness data are available, cost utility analysis can be used to estimate a final cost-utility ratio. This procedure should not be attempted without expert assistance.

   Despite their differences, all these analyses aim to produce some *bottom-line figure* or statements of costs and resources or benefits (Figure 3.6). They all involve comparisons (within or between program alternatives). They all depend upon establishment of some common denominator(s), as shown in Figure 3.7. (For a complete description and examples, see Levin, 1983.)

FIGURE 3.6

Comparisons Made in Different Cost Analyses

Type of Analysis	Comparison(s) Made
Cost Feasibility	Total costs compared to available budget and other resources
Cost Benefit	Total costs compared to total benefits
Cost Effectiveness	Costs of different program alternatives are compared; effectiveness measures (e.g., writing assessment scores) of alternatives compared
Cost Utility	Utility, likelihood that utility will occur and costs of different alternatives are compared

FIGURE 3.7

Common Denominators Used in each Analysis

Type of Analysis	Data Collected	Common Denominator
Cost Feasibility	a) Financially calculable costs and resources	a) money
	b) Costs and resources not easily converted to monetary figures	b) descriptive lists
Cost Benefit	a) Total (or major) costs and total (or major benefits	a) money
	b) Costs and resources not easily converted to monetary figures	b) descriptive lists
Cost Effectiveness	a) Total (or major) costs	a) money
	b) Total (or major program outcomes	b) effectiveness standards (e.g., test scores)
	c) Costs and resources not easily converted to monetary figures	c) descriptive lists
Cost Utility	a) Total (or major) costs	a) money
	b) Total (or major) program outcomes	b) arbitrary standard for total (or major) program outcomes of utility + likelihood of occurrence (given in probability estimates)
	c) Costs and resources not easily converted to monetary figures	c) descriptive lists

Guidelines for Conducting Cost Analyses

Identifying costs and benefits. Most cost analyses flounder in the selection of costs and benefits to include and in the process of converting them to some common denominator. We urge evaluators to place major emphasis on this stage of the analysis. A commonsense approach can aid in identifying and selecting which costs and benefits to include in the analysis. Some typical monetary costs include:

- Personnel costs (salaries, fringe benefits, and so forth, for all professional and support staff)
- Facilities (acquisition, rental or maintenance, and so forth)
- Materials and equipment (books, supplies, and so forth)
- Participant expenses (tuition, supplies, transportation, and so forth)

Even this brief list makes clear one of the problems in identifying costs. The first three costs are paid by the educational organization sponsoring the program. The fourth cost is borne by program participants, which illustrates the importance of the question, Costs–to whom? Even if the total cost of a program is within the total available resources of a department or school, it is also necessary to identify who will bear the costs and whether they are capable of doing so. For example, there may be adequate money in the personnel budget, but no money in the facilities budget to ensure safe upkeep of meeting areas. Or the institution may be able to bear the total costs, but only at the price of charging tuition so high that prospective students would not be able to afford the instruction.

The list given above identifies only the most specific and direct *outlay* or *cash flow costs*—that is, those that will be incurred directly and can be easily quantified. If a longer timeline is considered, there may be other *indirect costs* (or overhead) such as depreciation, taxes, and insurance. A program may involve differential *life cycle costs;* design, acquisition or start-up, and maintenance or follow-up costs all may need to be specified. (Some of these may be very long term and hard to calculate— for example, an increased demand for composition electives might require hiring new faculty two or three years after a program begins.) Costs incurred in the future may need to be treated separately as *discountable costs* and adjusted to current equivalent figures. Calculating some of these costs can be quite complex and may require the assistance of someone skilled in costing procedures. The evaluator's major responsibility here is to identify those costs that will be important over time.

All the above costs are quantifiable in monetary terms, though some might be easier to calculate than others. Some of the most important costs of a project, however, are not quantifiable. Great *psychological costs* may overshadow all direct costs: changing to new curriculum materials without adequate preparation of the teaching staff may result in hostility or misunderstandings about how to use the materials, which could lead to a far less effective program. However, the psychological cost of not making some curriculum changes, even if they are flawed in design, may be severely damaging to morale in other situations. Even more difficult to calculate may be the *opportunity cost* of an alternative program, which would be forgone once an option is chosen. Every course of action entails opportunity costs: the time and effort spent that could be devoted to other activities. These *intangible costs* cannot be easily converted to monetary terms, but at the very least these kinds of costs can be identified in descriptive lists, so that decision makers and audiences of the evaluation report are aware of them.

Benefits must be given as thorough consideration as costs (unless only a cost feasibility analysis is being performed). Benefits are even more difficult if not impossible to quantify in monetary terms. For example, some studies have shown that individuals with higher writing anxiety tend to avoid courses and even careers which they perceive to require extensive writing activities. If a composition program successfully reduced writing anxiety in such individuals, with the long-term benefit of changing their course and career options, it would be important to include this in the description of potential benefits. Yet how could that be calculated in terms of the numbers affected or the dollar benefit? We recommend the commonsense approach: *all potential benefits* should be identified, as best as possible. The most important ones and those most likely to occur should be pursued in some detail to present a clear descriptive picture of possible outcomes. Choice of a time frame can help limit parameters. Decision makers for an individual program may want to consider only those benefits (and costs) that occur while students participate in the program, or during the period when financial costs will actually be incurred, the *payback period*.

Compiling a complete list of costs and benefits. Obviously a complete cost and benefit identification could take considerable time and effort. The main concern of an evaluator is to identify all *major* costs and benefits. We recommend what is known as the *ingredients approach:* itemizing all that goes into acquiring or developing and maintaining a program alternative (i.e., its total ingredients) and then identifying associated costs and benefits. This information can be collected by reviewing program plans or documents, questioning key program personnel, and observing the program alternative in operation, if possible. Some other data sources can also be consulted, including individuals who are not participating directly in the program. For example, by questioning those in the business office or upper administrative levels, an evaluator may discover old rivalries among different departments or schools that might be eased in the professional development activities that have been proposed. (This might become an important positive side effect, once the program begins.) Or, discussions with members of the buildings and grounds crews might reveal some economies of scale that would be upset by a new program. In fact, cost inquiries often turn up unexpected side effects and thus can serve a double purpose.

Choosing common denominators.   Once a complete list of the major costs and benefits has been compiled, the next task is to decide which are the most important to include in the analysis. Those costs and benefits deemed "less important" and to be excluded from the major analysis could still be listed somewhere in the final report, because a decision maker might weigh their significance differently. Also, if the project or alternative being analyzed is going to be replicated, potential replicators would need to have as complete a list as possible. It may be necessary to separate important quantifiable items from those that cannot be quantified either in monetary terms or such standards of effectiveness as test scores.

When calculating quantitative entries one must be sensitive to the consequences of calculating and reporting items. For example, costs averaged over a long time period may disguise some prohibitively large initial outlays. Average incremental gain in student performance measures may disguise the differential effects a program might have: Students who begin with high initial skill levels might benefit a great deal from one proposed program alternative; remedial students might gain far more from another one. These differences should be identified as part of the analysis, with the final effectiveness judgments reported for different student groups. It is best to consult experts before engaging in extended quantitative analyses or calculations. (See Levin, 1983, for dicussions of several examples.) However, many of the expert's decisions will have to be made in consultation with the evaluator and program officials. The most important aspects of cost analyses depend on clear conceptual distinctions and not on sophisticated numerical calculations.

A difficult task in cost analysis is the reconciling of disparities that inevitably occur. Sometimes these result from differences in the times when benefits and costs occur. Often an evaluator must balance a ledger where long-run benefits (e.g., learning to use writing as a tool for thinking more clearly) are posed against minimal short-run costs (e.g., purchase price of a computer) and unknown long-run psychological costs (e.g., teachers with no option to buy or use the computer may lose motivation). Other times there may be differential benefits to various groups of students, as noted above. Our suggestion is to find some way to report all effects that seem important, even if they cannot be easily quantified or allow a single bottom-line figure. Evaluation recommendations can be made upon a mixture of qualitative and quantitative evidence. (See Morris and Fitz-Gibbon, 1978, for suggestions about constructing a program index that allows comparison of seemingly disparate data on a uniform scale of importance.)

Reporting results. A variety of procedures and formats can be used to report results. The fault of many cost analyses, which makes their use limited, is their lack of completeness. Cost analyses are most useful if all major costs and benefits are reported. Items that cannot be quantified should appear in descriptive lists. Completeness in reporting is especially crucial because costs and benefits may vary in importance or monetary equivalent from one site to another, or from one time period to another.

All procedures for converting costs and benefits to monetary terms or to some other standard need to be fully explained. This makes clear any subjective decisions and allows reanalysis of the raw data, should someone care to use a different method of computation.

Example. As one component of the Bay Area Writing Project (BAWP) evaluation, general costs were examined. Several decisions had to be made in order to plan the level of analysis to be used. BAWP not only conducted local inservice programs but also acted as the coordinating and administrative leader of the National Writing Project sites. The BAWP central staff was quite small, considering the scope of their activities, and each staff member carried out both local and national responsibilities. Because the benefits of local inservice training had been widely studied using observations, interviews, and questionnaire surveys of inservice participants and staff as well as assessment of some participants' students' writing performance, it was decided that the local inservice would be the focal point of the cost investigation. Interviews were conducted in two districts to identify additional or hidden costs of inservice training incurred by the districts beyond the standard training fee they paid to BAWP. In addition, it seemed important to describe as carefully as possible the activities of the central staff, to gain a better understanding of what it "cost" them to administer local inservice programs. This part of the study resembled a cost-benefit analysis.

In addition to data collected on local inservices, two other areas were investigated. The leadership activities of the BAWP central staff as they related to the National Writing Project were described. Because of limited evaluation resources it was not possible to collect data on benefits from each of the National Writing Project sites. Benefits could only be characterized as services offered to the sites by the BAWP staff. These were compiled in descriptive lists. The calculation of the costs of these services also had to be limited to data readily available; in this case it consisted of the salaries and other ongoing expenses required for maintenance of the central staff. A final portion of the study was devoted to reporting rough cost figures for some comparable inservice and curriculum development programs: a local development project for teaching composition skills in kindergarten through eighth grade and some nationwide science projects sponsored by the National Science Foundation. (There was no comparable national project in composition or in the other language arts.)

Because BAWP is a large-scale project and because evaluation resources were limited, the strategy of devoting the most resources to the data readily available—involving careful cost accounting for local programs and the central staff, supplemented by more general comparisons with other programs when possible—seemed the wisest. A chart summarizing the costs of a local inservice to BAWP and to the sponsoring district and the details of this cost analysis can be found in Stahlecher (1979).

3-10 ■ Side Effects

Description.   Side effects are the unintended good and bad effects of the instructional program or course being evaluated. In evaluating composition instruction we are primarily interested in whether students improve their writing performance (the intended outcome), but we also want to identify good and bad unintended effects of the instruction. Is enrollment in social sciences electives dropping because of the new composition program? Does participation in peer feedback groups lead to stronger social interactions among the students and hence less attention to academic tests? Has the special writing skills center made English teachers feel less responsibility for teaching writing?

The search for side effects underscores the importance of looking at what a program has actually done, not what it has intended. Many evaluations restrict themselves to looking at whether the goals of the program have been met. Certainly it's important for the staff to find out whether they have succeeded in what they have been trying to do. But goals shouldn't be the sole focus of an evaluation. They may be too vague, too specific, too hard, or too easy to attain. The focus of an evaluation should be on what the program accomplished, whether intended or not.

It is not possible to offer a single comprehensive list of side effects that might occur in all evaluations of composition instruction. Instead we offer a process for identifying side effects, tips, and techniques we have found useful in ferreting out and validating unintended outcomes. We also describe a case example of some side effects in the evaluation of the Bay Area Writing Project and its national replications (National Writing Project Network).

Process for Identifying Side Effects. Most often the search for side effects occurs simultaneously with ongoing evaluation activities. Observations are made and data are reviewed with an eye toward unexpected outcomes. Identification and verification of side effects is an iterative process. A passing comment picked up in an interview with an administrator can be pursued with other administrators and teachers.

There are five general ways of identifying side effects. At the beginning of a project as the evaluation design is being conceptualized, it is useful to brainstorm possible unintended outcomes on key participants and nonparticipants (students, teachers, administrators, and so forth). Cognitive, affective, and behavioral effects that might occur as a result of composition instruction can be identified. These notes are maintained as a running list of potential side effects or areas to explore. Several times during the course of the evaluation, additional brainstorming sessions can be held to identify new possibilities, augment existing areas, and eliminate those that turn out to be irrelevant, inappropriate, or unverified.

Also, at the beginning of a project, a special attempt is made to review the published literature as well as unpublished or fugitive evaluation reports of similar projects. When possible, it may be useful to contact the evaluators or authors of the reports for additional contextual information. Reviewing the literature and evaluation reports is a good practice not only for identifying side effects but also for getting ideas about successful and unsuccessful evaluation designs and instruments.

A third way to identify side effects involves reviewing collected data to look for trends, comments or peculiarities that may indicate unintended effects. (It is helpful for interview questions to include some "fishing" for unexpected outcomes.) For example, in the course of interviewing faculty members regarding their teaching practices, one evaluator discovered that they felt the increased emphasis on writing had created a split between composition and literature. They were concerned that this might give students the false impression that the two areas are independent and isolated. This unintended effect could be explored by reviewing information from other sources: student questionnaires, administrator interviews, or composition and literature experts. If it becomes a documented effect, the program staff might want to take steps to remedy the perceived schism.

If not already part of data collection efforts, side effects can be identified through observation of instructional activities and examination of materials. One can look at what is happening in the project, what is being taught beyond the stated goals or ignored as a result of time spent on the project. There are always opportunity costs for participants in a project (what else could they be doing instead of participating in this program?). Some of these may turn into noteworthy side effects.

In evaluating large-scale composition projects it may also be helpful to contact recognized leaders in the field of composition instruction or prominent experts at the federal and state levels or affiliated with professional associations. These people can be useful sources of information on the ripple effects of a large-scale effort (national impact), its projected long-term effects, or its reputation.

The search for side effects is an iterative process. The interpretations and reflections of a single person may form the initial impetus for more intensive investigation. It is often valuable, if time and resources permit, to interview, selectively, those working in the institution or community but not directly related to the project or program. Maintenance staff, clerical and support workers, and classroom paraprofessionals may all be able to offer insights different from those of the participants.

As side effects are identified, they are verified from other data sources and refined. For example, if it is suspected that there is more "writing across the curriculum" as a result of publicity about a new composition program and a presentation at a faculty meeting, this possibility can be explored through interviews and discussions with science and math teachers or by reviewing assignments in those classes.

Data on side effects may be difficult to synthesize. It is useful to conceptualize them into positive and negative effects, at different levels of possible impact, on various groups (participating and nonparticipating students, teachers, programs, schools and institutions, and so forth). These data become an additional component in the evaluation and are treated like other dimensions.

Example.   Using the process described above, we identified a number of side effects during our evaluation of the Bay Area Writing Project (BAWP). Samples of these are presented here to illustrate some unintended outcomes. These, of course, would not be relevant to all kinds of composition programs since unintended effects are specific to a particular context and situation (Stahlecher, 1979).

- *Increased professionalism and status of teachers of writing.* The emphasis on writing gave participating composition teachers an opportunity to discuss conceptual issues and ideas, which led to feelings of renewed professional identification and sense of accomplishment. Collegiality increased and teachers collaborated more freely on assignments, curriculum planning, and student problems. (Data obtained from teacher interviews and discussions with leaders of professional associations.)
- *Perceived separation of writing from other disciplines.* The visibility of the training programs focused a great deal of attention on writing instruction. Faculty members in other disciplines felt that they were not obligated to teach or be concerned about their students' writing since the English faculty were so active in composition instruction. They abdicated their responsibilities in developing students' writing skills. (Data obtained from nonparticipant teacher interviews.)
- *Shift in conceptualization of teacher's role.* As a result of the way writing was taught in the inservice program, teachers tended to change their views of their roles. Previously, teachers saw themselves as judges and arbitrators and emphasized the product of writing: the final version of the paper. Now, they tend to view writing as a process with stages of prewriting, composing, and rewriting. In each phase teachers serve as diagnosticians and trainers who help students refine and perfect their writing skills. More teachers are learning to analyze writing processes and to look for the causes of student errors. (Data obtained from teacher interviews and review of the literature.)
- *Increased collaboration among school districts and postsecondary institutions.* The BAWP model is based on close association of universities and local schools. The nature of the program has led to new opportunities for articulation and closer cooperation between local schools and colleges on issues related to teaching writing. This collaboration has increased sensitivity and empathy among both groups of faculty to their respective teaching obligations. (Data obtained from interviews with precollege and college faculty.)
- *Better accountability procedures and monitoring of student outcomes.* Some of the evaluation procedures have been incorporated into the ongoing functioning of the program. This has led to better checks on the effectiveness of program operations. (Data collected from administrator interviews and observations.)
- *Use of the BAWP model in other disciplines.* The BAWP ap-

proach of teaching composition has been adapted to the teaching of mathematics. (Data obtained from interviews with university math faculty members and high school math teachers.)

Unintended outcomes can provide a richer understanding of the strengths and weaknesses of composition instruction and may lead to major modifications of evaluative judgments. Uncovering side effects may well be one of the most important components of an evaluation.

3-11 ■ Replications

Description. *Replication* means repeating or doing again what has previously been done. For example, a teacher has effectively used prewriting to improve the quality of students' final drafts. Another teacher would like to adopt the technique and replicate the first teacher's instructional strategy and results. Or, an entire composition program in one school district or university might be replicated at another location. Exact duplication of a program, curriculum, or instructional technique is nearly impossible because modifications typically must be made in personnel to suit the new environment. Nevertheless, a chief concern of an evaluator looking at a multiple-site program is the extent and amount of replication of the original model in another setting.

Key Issues. Depending on the focus of the evaluation, the methods described earlier in the chapter may be appropriate for the evaluation of replications or the evaluation of a program for replicability. A program that is based on a theoretical model or adapted from an existing project may be usefully evaluated by collecting data on students' writing performance and attitude, teachers' attitudes and indicators, side effects, cost, and so on. Evaluating a program specifically set up to replicate an existing project (sometimes called a spin-off) requires data on the components already mentioned as well as investigation of the relationship between the replications and the original model.

It is important to identify the nature and type of variations between the original model and the replication. If the replication varies too greatly in methods, procedures, or instructional strategies, it will not be a replication at all, but rather a program in its own right. In that case it is useful to understand why the original model was not or could not be replicated. This information could be important for future decisions regarding the dissemination of the composition approach. If the replication is similar to the model, and common data are collected from all replications, generalizations could be made about which features are consistently effective and which are a function of certain circumstances or situations. This would be useful information for further dissemination of the model.

A good strategy in evaluating replications is to develop a checklist of essential components of the original model and then gather data through observations, interviews, or questionnaires to see how many or what proportion are retained in the replications. Essential components can include such items as type and amount of content covered, staffing patterns, structure and function of the program, and so on.

The amount of contact between the staff of the replication and the staff of the original model is important to determine. If the purpose of the evaluation is to see whether the approach is generalizable, one would hope for little communication. This would indicate how the model might work without support from the original developers, which will most often be the case in widely disseminated innovations. Typically, one finds differences in the level of enthusiasm of staff. People working on the development of a new approach or new composition program are frequently committed to the project and spend extra time and effort to ensure its success. The replication's staff may lack the original's missionary zeal, possibly affecting the amount and nature of change.

In synthesizing the findings from the evaluations of a number of replications, special statistical techniques may be useful in determining the overall effectiveness of a composition model. For example, the amount of change in students' writing performance might vary from replication to replication. Some students might show a great deal of improvement, others very little. If the evaluator is interested in an overall picture of the model's impact on students' writing skills, advanced statistical procedures may be appropriate to integrate these findings. Techniques like metaanalysis (Glass, McGraw, and Smith, 1981) involve looking at the size of effects across different studies. These strategies and other methods of research integration require expert consultation but can be useful in understanding the overall effects of composition instruction and its replications.

Example. Evaluating replications of the Bay Area Writing Project posed a problem because the model being disseminated specified the process to be used in training composition teachers far more specifically than the content. In fact, the model involved offering districts and their teachers a long list of the most promising practices currently available in composition instruction and letting them choose those that seemed most suited to their needs. This characteristic made the model flexible and likely to be used in very different kinds of school settings, but it meant that content could vary widely in the replications.

Several strategies were used to identify the degree to which content was consistent across the replications.

- The content of a few inservice programs and participants' logs were collected and analyzed according to types of presentations made. Those appearing most frequently were compiled into a summary list, which was used in a questionnaire administered to local teachers and to national directors to identify similarities in program content across different replications. In addition, individual techniques or strategies concerned with the same general aspect of teaching writing, such as prewriting or rewriting, were grouped together to identify broad similarities in the program content. (See Thomas, 1978, and Donlan, 1979, for an explanation of this technique.) Through interviews with program staff and administrators, replications were rated on whether they included presentations related to these broader categories.

- Key staff members and some participants were interviewed to identify unique characteristics at some replication sites.

- Some inservice programs were observed extensively and visits were made to a sample of others to determine the degree of consistency of presentations and activities, such as the frequency with which teachers wrote as part of their training.

- Case studies of inservice training programs and their impact were conducted in three local school districts to determine the range of training variations and their related effects in dissimilar educational environments.

4

Assembling Evaluation Components

We began this book with some vignettes that illustrate the kinds of problems that make evaluation a necessity. In this chapter, we repeat these vignettes and give a brief indication of ways to handle those problems, in terms of assembling the evaluation components. Then we do the same with a larger case study.

4-1 ■ Vignettes

Vignette A. *Several teachers have designed and tried out a new writing program. They are enthusiastic about its effects, reporting great success in improving student writing performance. The school principal is pleased with the program but finds the pressures of accountability too great to ignore. The program is to be evaluated.*

■ *Question A1: Can the principal or teachers use state (or district) test data to evaluate success?* State or district data are difficult to use for a number of reasons: (a) typically the tests are not closely matched to the aims of most composition programs; (b) in particular, there are no samples of essay writing in most such tests (Colorado and California are exceptions); (c) even though the multiple-choice tests may give a fair indication of certain aspects of writing ability (for summative purposes), they provide little chance for identifying student subskills that require improvement (formative use)—a deficiency that will tend to alienate the teachers who are mostly interested in the formative role; (d) the time of year at which the tests are given may not be at the moment of peak performance—end of the spring term—so the effectiveness of the program may be underestimated; (e) furthermore, such annual tests never determine students' performance level at the beginning of instruction (first week of fall term, for fall or year-long classes, or of spring term for spring-only classes), so they cannot directly measure growth during the time the teacher is working with these students. The only pretest they provide is on a different set of students—the ones who were at that same grade level in the previous year. Because those students may not be comparable to this year's group, one might get a decline in scores between the two years even though the new program was in fact a success and brought its students along much further than the previous program would have.

In spite of all these drawbacks, which understandably make many schools anxious to abandon the use of such data, they are not entirely useless. If the school demographics (type of neighborhood and student population) remain fairly constant, and if no other major change occurred in the school that might affect everyone's writing, and if the teachers are the same as last year, then the scores will give a general indication of changes. Now, those conditions are quite often met, and since it is of the greatest importance to have some general sense of how writing skills are progressing, we do not want to overlook or belittle state (or district) assessment. But it's usually not enough (develop your own writing tests too, or obtain fall and spring test data); and it must be used cautiously.

■ *Question A2: How can teachers and the principal be sure that observed outcomes are due to the program and not to other factors?* Of course, the best way to put such doubts to rest is to find or set up a control or comparison group. Since only some of the teachers are involved in the new program, one might think to use the other teachers' classes for a very rough comparison. But the teachers who decide to start up a new program are likely to be different—for example, in enthusiasm—from those who don't, so this is risky. A better design would have the innovators randomly pick one of their classes to continue receiving the old program. This is still a risky design, because the enthusiasm or even the program content may spill over into those classes; or the teachers might make less than their best effort with those classes in order to artificially widen the gap in favor of the innovation. But monitoring for this, plus extremely thorough discussion of the need for the comparison group, and a careful design, should limit these sources of trouble.

Also, a search should be made for alternative possible causes of improvement, such as extra paraprofessionals from special funds.

Vignette B. *College administrators compared a new way of teaching the first composition course with a traditional course, using a standard-*

ized test of editing skills and easily collected information including comparative performance records of each group of students in subsequent composition classes. On the basis of these data, they found no apparent differences between students enrolled in the innovative course and those enrolled in the traditional offering. They decided to discontinue the innovative course because of its cost (it involves tutorial assistance for students). The faculty who developed the innovative course protest, requesting one more trial to teach and evaluate the course. The administration agrees but provides no financial support for the evaluation.

■ *Question B1: Who should be involved in conducting the evaluation?* The best solution would be an evaluation team or even advisory committee. The team must include representatives of the faculty as well as the administration. (It cannot simply consist of faculty, since that would give it no credibility with the administration. The administration now has a stake in the outcome—they have made a preliminary negative decision on the course and could be suspected of rationalizing that decision by "cooking" the data if they alone conducted the evaluation.) The tasks of the evaluation advisory committee are to approve the design, check the field work and data synthesis, identify those who are to do the data gathering, and so forth. Students might be involved as well, because they take a great deal more interest in school when they have something to say in what happens, and because they often come up with good suggestions. It might also be a good idea to include community and taxpayer representatives—especially, in the case of composition, prospective employers.

■ *Question B2: What kinds of measures might best reflect differences between the two programs?* The measures that have been used in the earlier evaluation are rather simple and—in the case of the "subsequent performance" measure—insensitive. That is, it would take a very powerful program to show a significant difference in performance in later courses.

It would be quite easy to point out differences between the two programs by focusing on content and testing only those things that are in the new program and not in the old. Of course, this would give a biased result, since there are presumably things in the old program that are not in the new. (This is one good reason for having representatives of both teacher/supporters and administrator/opponents of the program on the evaluation design team.) All we really know about the innovative program is that it involves tutorial assistance to students, and we need to look a little more closely at what those tutors are doing. Identifying appropriate measures for the evaluation begins with a clear understanding of the nature of the program.

■ *Question B3: How can evaluation costs be kept low?* The costs can be kept low by using faculty members and administrators, possibly working as pairs, to do the data gathering and planning, either as part of their regular load or with a small allowance of released time. In some cases, graduate students might also be involved in the evaluation. Some expert advice might be time-saving and could be obtained quite inexpensively on specific issues such as available tests; it might save the time involved in the construction and pilot testing of a test that in fact duplicates one already available. This is a typical in-house evaluation that can still have very good credibility if the two parties are represented at each point. But if a difference does show up this time it may just be due to enthusiasm and not the merit of the course.

Vignette C. *An urban school district is offering inservice training in composition. Participation is voluntary, and about 30 percent of the teachers enroll. During their inservice training, teachers request a district-wide assessment of student writing performance to determine the strengths and weaknesses of their new teaching strategies. Teachers who did not enroll in the program object. Some are afraid they might be compared unfavorably to teachers who have had inservice training. Others object to giving the administration yet another accountability measure.*

■ *Question C1: Which types of evaluation methods are likely to give teachers the most useful information regarding student writing performance?* Vignette C is in many respects like Vignette B. Volunteers are involved in both cases, and hence one cannot be sure that superior performance by the group with the special training—should such superiority manifest itself—is due to the special training or to the enthusiasm and prior professional commitment and extra training of those teachers. One needs to be very careful in advance to "walk through" the possible outcomes and legitimate interpretations of them. The difference is mainly that in Vignette C the teachers are requesting not an overall (holistic) evaluation of the new approach but a "strengths and weaknesses" evaluation—that is, an analytical evaluation. This requires more sophisticated testing and should involve comparing participating and nonparticipating teachers and their students in order to find out the ways in which the new training has worked better than before (a strength) or worse (a weakness). However, one is going to have to use writing tests that focus not on holistic performance, but on analytical performance, and preferably remedially oriented analytical evaluation. For example, one might use the traditional set of categories—mechanics, structure, ideas, sentence construction, and so forth. Or one might use one of the currently more popular categorizations of student performance by mode skills. It would be even better to be able to identify components or aspects of student writing that can be easily tied to remedial programs.

■ *Question C2: How can the anxieties of the nonparticipant teachers be reduced?* The anxieties of the nonparticipants might be reduced by focusing on comparisons between students and not between classes, by focusing on remediation and not on absolute levels of performance, and by ensuring anonymity of the teachers who taught the students. Anxieties can also be reduced by giving teachers clear explanations of why the evaluation is being conducted and what it can and cannot do; disclosing the benefits or payoffs for participation (e.g., data on their own students' performance); and involving a representative of the nonparticipating teachers on the evaluation team or advisory committee.

■ *Question C3: Can the results of this student writing evaluation be used for evaluating teachers?* These measures cannot be used for teacher evaluation, because they have been explicitly designed to avoid the possibility of evaluating teachers! Indeed, if even one or two measures were adopted, it would be essentially impossible to make any inferences about the relative merit of individual teachers. Evaluating teachers is a complex undertaking and requires more detailed information than the results of student writing performance.

Vignette D. *A large state now has several National Writing Project sites. The Higher Education Commission is currently considering a proposal to fund an evaluation of these writing projects. The aim of the projects is to improve student writing performance by improving their teachers' attitudes and practices. The projects do not offer a single recipe for teaching writing, but rely on a process of making teachers aware of a wide variety of teaching practices.*

■ *Question D1: What types of evaluation instruments could measure changes in the teachers' attitudes, beliefs, and practices?* Sample instruments and methods for measuring changes in teachers are described in sections 3-5, 3-6, and 3-7.

■ *Question D2: How might an evaluator relate findings about change in teachers to improvement in student writing?* This is the crucial and most difficult evaluation question for teacher-oriented approaches to student writing. Ideally one would have a recipe book that shows that certain changes in teachers' behavior and attitudes reliably produce certain improvements in students' writing. We have some hints as to what works but no indisputable causes.

A serious evaluation of any inservice teacher approach must investigate direct measurement of changes in student writing. One could pool all the sites and all their teachers, and simply look to see whether students of the participating teachers improve faster than similar students of nonparticipating teachers. But such a holistic evaluation approach does not allow one to identify which teacher practices lead to student improvement. An analytical approach would require the additional cost of making a profile of each teacher's practice repertoire and correlating profiles and student performance. There are grave difficulties about approaching this question in any practical school context, unless one has a considerable period of time, complete support from teachers and school administrators, and substantial resources of expertise and money, an uncommon situation at the district level but perhaps feasible at the state level.

■ *Question D3: Can a program's impact on participating teachers and their students be usefully assessed without reference to changes in the nonparticipating teachers?*   The impact on the participating teachers and the students can be usefully assessed without reference to change in nonparticipant teachers, but the results are likely to be less useful for some purposes than comparative results. In fact, some kind of comparison will have to be made because we need to have an estimate of how well the students would have done had they not been involved in the project. To do so, one could look at how students of other teachers do during the same time period or at how students of these same teachers (the participating teachers) did during a previous time period. But comparing students of other teachers raises the issue of differences between teachers—as we discussed in Vignettes A and B. Comparing prior students of the same teachers raises the possibility of other changes having occurred in the school environment, or of the general ability or motivation level of the students having changed. Still, neither approach is useless, and a combination of the two—where possible—makes a strong evaluation design. (The ideal design would involve a random allocation of teachers, something that can be arranged among volunteers.) If one does not have data from the previous year for students of participating teachers, then one can only make the simultaneous comparison with nonparticipating teachers. If the evaluation covers two or three years, then, in the first year one can collect "baseline data" on change in the students whose teachers will receive training in the following year (or in the intervening summer), and then in the second year see how the students of those teachers perform.

Of course, if a summative evaluation is not necessary, informal methods can provide useful information. For example, one can identify the impact on teachers by asking them about changes in their teaching style—or, more expensively, by observing them across the two-year period. And one can do the same with respect to students—ask them about impact and compare reported impact in the classes of participating versus nonparticipating teachers.

The major difficulty with any short-term study, even one covering two or three years, is to avoid confusion of program effect with Hawthorne effect. It is also difficult to get some sense of the durability of the program and its long-term effects on students. Whatever the design, a five-year downstream check with employers or graduate schools should be made to see whether any composition instruction has had a significant long-term impact.

Vignette E.   A classroom teacher returns from a professional conference eager to try a new approach for teaching expository writing. It will involve dropping some required readings from the department course syllabus and substituting new materials that she will prepare. She decides—and gets permission—to try out the new approach in two of her four classes. She picks the two for which she feels it is most suited—the classes in which student motivation and achievement are currently highest.

■ *Question E1: If the new curriculum seems to the teacher to be an improvement, what claims can be made about its generalizable effectiveness?* Almost no generalization is plausible in this case. Not only are we unable to generalize to (some) other teachers, we cannot even plausibly generalize to other classes taught by this teacher, because she herself picked nontypical classes for the experimental treatment. Of course, generalizing to other schools or districts would be even more hazardous. However, one should never simply dismiss the instincts of an experienced teacher. If, knowing all the above, she still feels the new approach is a real improvement, we should strongly encourage her to find other teachers willing to try the new approach on *their* high-achievement classes.

■ *Question E2: What data could be inexpensively collected to determine whether the new approach works better with one type of student rather than another?* "Found" data—term paper grades and state assessment—could be analyzed. The teacher may need to supplement this with some tests created by and marked by others. But the teacher would not need analytical evaluation—only holistic and matrix sampling.

■ *Question E3: What are the best evidence and arguments with which to persuade the department chair and school principal that the new approach should be continued as an option beyond the trial period?* To establish credibility, it's best to have someone else certify the results. It is also useful to consult with the principal beforehand to discover what he or she would consider most persuasive. The evaluation of the trade-offs of dropping some materials from the department syllabus is difficult. Are the gains so large as to make it a sensible trade? One must focus directly on the obvious and at least partly legitimate concerns of administrators for preserving a common core program.

4-2 ■ Case Study: An Evaluation Plan for the Program "Training College Faculty Across Disciplines to Teach Writing"

We have discussed a number of different instruments, methods, and procedures for evaluating composition instruction and applied them to the vignettes. To place our major points in context, we offer now a larger case study, a description of an evaluation plan for a faculty development program at a state college.

Description of the Program

Recently, State College adopted a requirement that students must complete two upper-division "Advanced Study" courses, in subject-matter departments, each requiring them to write at least 5000 words during a semester. The intent of these courses is to "improve students' abilities to reason logically and to write clearly."

To help the instructors of these courses to incorporate writing components, a series of voluntary workshops were developed by faculty members from the English department. These workshops, offered during the semester in which the faculty member taught his or her Advanced Study course, covered such topics as: (1) using writing as a way of learning in various disciplines, (2) diagnosing student writing problems and developing methods to address them, (3) designing and presenting writing assignments to students, (4) writing exam questions that stimulate critical thinking, (5) responding constructively to student writing (i.e., styles of marking), and (6) referring students to appropriate tutoring and other kinds of assistance. The workshops were led by three experienced writing teachers who also met individually with faculty member participants throughout the semester. During these consultations, the writing teachers focused particularly on designing specific assignment topics and on ways of criticizing student work, and they shared hints and shortcuts for improving student writing.

In addition to the group workshops and individual consultations, a third feature of the program provided student reader assistance for the faculty participants. Readers (graduate students in English) were responsible for marking student papers (in pencil only) to free up the faculty member to look at a complete set of papers in terms of more general questions: Did the assignment achieve its learning purpose? Was it clear to the students what they were to do? What degree of success did the students have with the assignment?

The project director recognized the problems of depending upon outside readers but felt some inducement was necessary to get faculty members to participate in the workshops and consultations, since these would require at least two hours per week.

Purposes of the Evaluation

The purpose of the evaluation was to provide information about the impact of the program to campus administrators who had to decide whether the workshops would be continued during the following academic year. In addition to this summative concern, the evaluation was designed to collect formative data for use by the workshop leaders and project director in modifying and refining aspects of the workshops and consultations, should they be continued. The evaluation was explicitly directed to the following audiences:

- The funding administrator
- The project director and workshop leaders
- Other State College administrators (central office administrators, deans, and English department chairpersons)
- State College faculty participants
- Program developers at other campuses considering such intervention efforts
- Evaluators

Focus of the Evaluation

Through discussions with the client for the evaluation (the funding authority), the project director and workshop leaders, and an examination of course materials and the original proposal, the evaluators narrowed the focus of the evaluation to the following questions:

■ What is the nature of the program? What are its activities and purposes? Those unfamiliar with the program needed to know as clearly as possible what was actually being evaluated. This included a description of selection procedures for faculty participants, an overview of the curriculum and the instructional methods, examples of assignments and activities, narrative portrayal of a "typical" workshop or consultation session, and so on. Data to characterize the program came from site visit observations, survey questionnaires, interviews, review of program materials, and other sources.

■ What is the impact of the program on faculty skills in teaching composition, for those instructors coming from disciplines outside English? Faculty participants in the program were interviewed, surveyed, and observed to determine the impact of the program on their teaching techniques and approaches.

In order to understand more clearly the effects of the program, three groups of faculty members provided data: current workshop participants, former workshop participants (to determine whether the effects of the project were sustained when faculty members taught on their own without support of consultants and readers), and a comparison group of faculty members who were eligible to participate in the workshop but declined the invitation, or who expressed no interest in the project but already had substantial writing components in their courses.

Data gathered on current participants helped identify the immediate impacts on teaching skills, while information on former participants suggested types of longer-term impact. Reports from nonparticipants who emphasized writing provided impressions as to the impact of different techniques on the same population of students. This group also provided information useful in formative evaluation of advertising for the training workshops.

■ What is the impact of the program on student composition skills? Changes in students' performance were measured in several ways:

Pre- and posttests of student writing performance, using an expository or persuasive writing task

Portfolio analysis: collecting and judging samples of students' writing for course assignments using both holistic and analytic assessment

"Found" data analysis: investigating the impact of the project on student performance on the campus-wide junior proficiency exam. This design could be strengthened by using a comparison group of students, perhaps those students of the comparison faculty members.

■ What is the impact of the program on students' beliefs or attitudes about writing? Although changes in current students' writing performance were of major interest, students' self-report about their attitudes toward writing were also investigated. Attitude changes may precede improvements in skills and can be considered indicators of possible future improvements or they may warn of coming declines. A brief pre- and posttest questionnaire provided useful information on alterations of spontaneous writing practices and attitudes toward writing. Both current and former students were surveyed.

■ What is the impact of the program on the campus's environment? Reactions of key campus administrators and a sample of faculty members were investigated to identify the broader effects of the program. The intent was to determine whether a need existed for this type of program, how well known the workshops were to the campus community, whether other site resources could provide similar services (critical competitors), and the prospects for institutionalizing the workshop offerings.

■ What are the costs of the program? Here the evaluation was concerned with how much the program cost compared to other alternatives—its relative cost-effectiveness. Those funding the program indicated that cost data might be most compelling in making a decision about expanding or discontinuing this project. Information about monetary and opportunity costs were gathered from faculty participants and their students.

Areas Omitted from the Evaluation

Additional aspects or areas the evaluation might have examined include the effects of the program on the graduate student readers, the generalizability of the program to other campuses, the relative effectiveness of various program components, shifts in general attitude to school. In this case, these areas were deemed less critical after thorough discussions with the funding agent, campus administrators, and program staff.

Methodology of the Evaluation

To answer the evaluation questions, data were collected from a number of different groups:

Current faculty participants. During the first weeks of instruction faculty members participating in the workshops during the current semester completed a pretest questionnaire designed to assess attitudes toward writing, current writing practices, previous experience giving writing assignments, perceptions of student writing problems, and expectations for the workshops. See Exhibit 1 later in this chapter for a sample questionnaire. (This and subsequent questionnaires were developed by Davis and Wood, 1981. Because of space limitations, this and all subsequent questionnaires have been compressed.) A parallel questionnaire, which also assessed faculty reaction to the project and its components, was administered as a posttest (see Exhibit 2) at the end of the semester. In addition, a task was given to faculty members, in order to identify the impact of the program on their ability to judge and respond to student writing. Prior to beginning the workshops, faculty participants were asked to mark and grade a student paper as they normally do. The task was repeated at the end of the semester using a comparable student paper. These data provided additional information about the effectiveness of the workshops in refining faculty members' skills. A sample student writing assignment for faculty members to grade is shown as Exhibit 3.

   Former faculty participants.   Former participants were interviewed to assess their reactions to the workshops and the impact of the experience on their subsequent courses (Exhibit 4).

   Comparison group of faculty.   A sample of faculty members eligible to participate in the workshops but who declined were surveyed to assess their reasons (see Exhibit 5). Their views about this type of intervention and their knowledge of alternatives were also probed.

   Students of current participants.   A pretest questionnaire (see Exhibit 6) was administered at the beginning of the semester to assess students' attitudes toward writing and their views about their needs and their own strengths and weaknesses. A parallel questionnaire was administered at the end of the semester (see Exhibit 7) which also asked for students' reactions to the course and any changes they observed in their instructor's teaching. To assess improvements in student writing performance, students were to be asked to complete an essay task—an impromptu writing assignment at the beginning and end of the semester. However, faculty strongly resisted taking class time for this evaluation activity. Instead student portfolios were collected as an indication of changes that might have occurred in writing skills. These portfolios were examined for global improvements and trends such as a decrease in certain kinds of errors or increased fluency and coherence. "Found" proficiency test data were also used. State College requires that all students pass a test of writing skills in their junior year. Those students who completed the Advanced Study requirement were identified and data collected to determine if their passing rate on the proficiency exam was higher than the rate of a comparable group of students who had not taken Advanced Study courses. Despite difficulties in "matching" students, a rough look was possible.

To follow up on a potential side effect of the program, a survey of the dropouts of these classes was conducted. If the increased writing load seemed too burdensome for some students, there could be a higher attrition rate with the introduction of these courses. Student dropouts of faculty participants were surveyed to determine if their leaving the class was related directly to the writing component (see Exhibit 8). Again, because a random matched control group was not available, only preliminary conclusions were attempted.

Students of former participants. Class lists were obtained from faculty members who had previously participated in the workshops. Their students were sent a brief questionnaire (see Exhibit 9) to determine their reactions to the course and whether any of the writing emphasis "spilled over" into their work in other classes (another possible side effect).

Comparison student group. Comparison students were selected to match (roughly) students of faculty participants. They were administered a version of the attitude questionnaire given to participating students (Exhibit 6).

Campus faculty and administrators. A sample of faculty members and key campus administrators were interviewed in person or on the telephone to determine their familiarity with and reaction to the program (see Exhibit 10). Data were collected on their perceptions of the need for the project; their knowledge of faculty participants' reaction to the course or its impact on faculty and students; their own reaction to the program; and their views of problems with institutionalizing the project on the State College campus. Members of the Educational Policy Committee and the Course Committee were interviewed, as well as the Dean of Academic Affairs, to obtain the administrative perspective.

Similar programs elsewhere. Telephone interviews were conducted with staffs of similar courses or programs at other colleges and universities in the state. The purpose of these interviews was to identify alternative models for improving faculty skills in teaching composition and to provide a context for understanding the amount of change (in faculty and students) that might be expected with these interventions. Additionally, evaluation information was gathered about their successes and problems, so that factors contributing to the effectiveness of these programs could be identified and pursued at State College.

Project director and workshop leaders. The project instructors were periodically interviewed about the workshops and their estimates of faculty progress. In addition, they were observed teaching the workshops, holding consultations, and making presentations in classrooms. To document the costs of the program they were asked to keep a brief log of the time they spent on the workshops.

Other information. Information was gathered on enrollment patterns and rates of attrition for these new courses; grade distributions; fiscal costs of conducting the workshops; and time estimates from students and faculty members.

Figure 4.1 summarizes the major evaluation activities.

FIGURE 4.1

Summary of Evaluation Design

Evaluation Question	Instrument/ Data Source	Sample	Data Collection
What is the nature of the project?	■ Examination of materials ■ Observation ■ Interview	■ Current participants ■ Site visits	Ongoing
What is the impact of the project on current faculty participants' attitudes?	■ Questionnaire	■ All current participants ■ Sample of comparison faculty	Pretest-Posttest
What is the impact of the project on current faculty participants' skills?	■ Grading task	■ All current participants ■ Sample of comparison faculty	Pretest-Posttest
What is the reaction of current faculty participants to the project?	■ Questionnaire	■ All current participants	Posttest

FIGURE 4.1 (Continued)

Summary of Evaluation Design

Evaluation Question	Instrument/ Data Source	Sample	Data Collection
What are the long-term effects of the project on faculty?	■ Interview	■ All former participants	Mid-semester
What is the impact of the project on students' attitudes?	■ Questionnaire	■ Sample of current students	Pretest-Posttest
What is the impact of the project on students' writing skills?	■ Portfolio analysis ■ Judgment of faculty participants ■ Student self-report	■ Sample of current students	Pretest-Posttest
What is the reaction of students of former participants?	■ Questionnaire	■ Sample of former students	Mid-semester
What is the impact of the program on campus?	■ Questionnaire ■ Interview ■ Attrition data ■ Grade distributions	■ Dropouts of course ■ Key campus administrators ■ Campus records	Ongoing
What are possible funding options for program?	■ Interview ■ Cost data	■ Key campus administrators	Ongoing
What are key features of similar projects, common problems, and alternative models?	■ Interview	■ Staff of similar programs	Ongoing

Comments on the Evaluation Design

The design described here is complex, comprehensive, and most likely beyond the resources of typical evaluators. It does indicate, however, a range of components that might be examined and from which an evaluation design might be developed.

As part of designing an evaluation, it is useful to speculate on a "What-if" basis regarding possible outcomes. This often reveals potential loopholes before the evaluation gets underway.

It is also helpful to have someone else metaevaluate the design before data are gathered. Such metaevaluation can identify problem areas and suggest improvements that will enhance an evaluation's validity and credibility. For example, a metaevaluator might point out that most of the data are being collected from participants (and hence advocates) of the program. This imbalance might affect the credibility of the results and the validity of the evaluation as well. Incorporating critics, either in providing data, or as part of the evaluation team, could strengthen this design. A metaevaluator might also comment on the length and complexity of the evaluation instruments and suggest that some be eliminated or shortened.

Exhibit 1

Faculty Questionnaire—Pretest

As part of the evalution of the Writing Workshops, we are interested in your expectations and your candid assessments of students' writing skills. Your answers will be kept confidential and only summary results will be reported.

Name _____
Course _____ (1-2)

1. What are the chief reasons you proposed a course for Advanced Study?
2. What knowledge and skills do you hope to acquire as a result of participating in these workshops?
3. How helpful do you think each workshop component will be to you in teaching your Advanced Study course?

	Not at all helpful			Very helpful		
a. consultation with workshop leaders	1	2	3	4	5	(3)
b. opportunity to have workshops leaders provide instruction directly to students in your class	1	2	3	4	5	
c. reader assistance	1	2	3	4	5	
d. summaries of student problems prepared by readers	1	2	3	4	5	
e. workshop sessions	1	2	3	4	5	
f. workshop handouts	1	2	3	4	5	
g. opportunity to learn how other faculty members teach writing	1	2	3	4	5	(9)

4. Approximately how many *different* courses have you taught at this college? _____ (10-12)

5. In how many of these courses have you required students to do the following?

   a. write a research or term paper; in ____ courses (13-14)
   b. write two or more short papers, essays, or reports; in ____ courses (15-16)
   c. write lab reports; in ____ courses (17-18)
   d. keep a journal; in ____ courses (19-20)
   e. write stories, poems or plays; in ____ courses (21-22)

6. In the past, how often have you employed the following techniques?

	Never	Infre-quently	Some-times	Fre-quently	Always	
a. students work together in small groups to help each other with writing	1	2	3	4	5	(23)
b. students evaluate each others' writing	1	2	3	4	5	
c. students engage in pre-writing activities	1	2	3	4	5	
d. students are required to revise their writing	1	2	3	4	5	

e. students submit first drafts for comments or grading	1	2	3	4	5
f. students write assignments in class (other than midterms and exams)	1	2	3	4	5
g. examples of student writing are discussed in class	1	2	3	4	5 (29)

7. How descriptive of the way you mark students' papers is each of the following?

	Not At All Descriptive		Somewhat Descriptive		Very Descriptive	
a. write only general comments, either at the beginning or end of the paper	1	2	3	4	5	(30)
b. write comments throughout referring to specific aspects of the paper	1	2	3	4	5	
c. rewrite parts of student papers to show them how they might have written a phrase, sentence or paragraph more effectively	1	2	3	4	5	
d. try to balance positive and negative comments on each student's writing	1	2	3	4	5	
e. limit comments primarily to what the student has done well	1	2	3	4	5	
f. limit comments primarily to the errors or problems in student's writing	1	2	3	4	5	
g. indicate mechanical errors (spelling, grammar) and correct them	1	2	3	4	5	
h. indicate mechanical errors without correcting them	1	2	3	4	5	
i. comment on lapses in logic or organization	1	2	3	4	5	
j. suggest ways to improve the style of writing	1	2	3	4	5	
k. assign a single grade representing a combined evaluation of content and form (mechanics and usage)	1	2	3	4	5	
l. assign a split grade: one for content, one for form	1	2	3	4	5	(41)

8. How much of a problem is each of the following for students in your courses?

	Not a Problem	Somewhat a Problem	A Major Problem	Don't Know	
a. selecting a topic	1	2	3	4	5 ( ) (42)
b. doing research and taking notes	1	2	3	4	5 ( )
c. thinking through their ideas before writing	1	2	3	4	5 ( )
d. actually sitting down to write	1	2	3	4	5 ( )
e. deciding who is the audience	1	2	3	4	5 ( )
f. using correct grammar and punctuation	1	2	3	4	5 ( )
g. spelling	1	2	3	4	5 ( )
h. editing and rewriting drafts	1	2	3	4	5 ( )
i. style and originality	1	2	3	4	5 ( )

j. logic and organization	1	2	3	4	5	( )
k. getting papers in on time	1	2	3	4	5	( ) (52)

9. Everyone has his or her pet peeves about the quality of student writing. What are yours? What aspects of writing do you think are especially critical?

10. Based on your experience with students on this campus, how would you rate the overall quality of student writing?

Extremely Poor				**Excellent**
1	2	3	4	5 (53)

11. Below are some topics which could be covered in these workshops. For each one, please candidly assess your skill in that area.

	Not At All Skilled			Very Skilled	
a. giving constructive feedback to students	1	2	3	4	5 (54)
b. writing essay test questions	1	2	3	4	5
c. diagnosing student writing problems	1	2	3	4	5
d. designing writing assignments	1	2	3	4	5
e. evaluating student writing holistically	1	2	3	4	5
f. motivating students to write	1	2	3	4	5
g. knowing when and where to refer students for tutoring	1	2	3	4	5
h. avoiding plagiarism	1	2	3	4	5
i. helping students structure and organize their papers	1	2	3	4	5
j. convincing students to edit and rewirte their papers	1	2	3	4	5
k. grading students' writing	1	2	3	4	5 (64)

Now, go back to question 11 and place a checkmark next to those topics you would especially like to see covered in the workshop. List any others in the space below.

12. How would you rate your own:

	Very Low			Very High	
a. fluency or productivity as a writer	1	2	3	4	5 (65)
b. confidence in teaching writing	1	2	3	4	5
c. enjoyment of writing	1	2	3	4	5 (67)

13. Have you ever attended any other workshops to teach writing?

    ____ (1) no
    ____ (2) yes (please describe salient features or components of
          those workshops) (68)

14. How much time outside of class do you expect your students to devote to each of the following in this course?

    a. reading: ____ hours per week outside of class (69-70)

b. other research: ____ hours per week outside of class (71-72)
c. writing: ____ hours per week outside of class (73-74)

15. Please try to estimate the extent of student attrition in this course in the past (percentage of students who do not complete the course) ____% (75-76)

Exhibit 2

Faculty Questionnaire—Posttest

As part of the evaluation of the Writing Workshops, we are interested in your reaction to the sessions and your candid assessments of changes in students' writing skills. Your answers will be kept confidential and only summary results will be reported.

Name _____ (1-2)
Course _____

1. How would you rate the usefulness of the program in assisting you to incorporate a writing component into your Advanced Study course? Please explain your rating.

Of little use				Very useful	
1	2	3	4	5	(3)

2. Overall, how helpful was each workshop component?

	Not at all helpful			Very helpful	
a. consultation with workshop leaders	1 2 3 4 5				(4)
b. opportunity to have workshop leaders provide instruction directly to students in your class	1 2 3 4 5				
c. reader assistance	1 2 3 4 5				
d. summaries of student problems prepared by readers	1 2 3 4 5				
e. workshop sessions overall	1 2 3 4 5				
f. workshop handouts in general	1 2 3 4 5				
g. opportunity to learn how other faculty members teach writing	1 2 3 4 5				(10)
h. other (please describe)	1 2 3 4 5				

3. Did the workshops cover everything you expected? (11)
____ (1) yes   ____ no (please explain)

4. Approximately how many of the sessions did you attend? (12)
____ (1) 1 or 2   ____ (2) 3 or 4   ____ (3) 5 or 6   ____ (4) 7 or 8

5. As a result of your participation in the program, how often did you use any of the following techniques?

172

	Never	Infre-quently	Some-times	Fre-quently	Always	
a. students work together in small groups to help each other with writing	1	2	3	4	5	(13)
b. students evaluate each others' writing	1	2	3	4	5	
c. students engage in prewriting activities	1	2	3	4	5	
d. students are required to revise their writing	1	2	3	4	5	
e. students submit first drafts for comments or grading	1	2	3	4	5	
f. students write assignments in class (other than midterms and exams)	1	2	3	4	5	
g. examples of student writing are discussed in class	1	2	3	4	5	

6. In the future, when you mark student papers, how likely are you to:

	Not at all likely				Very likely	
a. write only general comments, either at the beginning or end of the paper	1	2	3	4	5	(20)
b. write comments throughout referring to specific aspects of the paper	1	2	3	4	5	
c. rewrite parts of student papers to show them how they might have written a phrase, sentence or paragraph more effectively	1	2	3	4	5	
d. try to balance positive and negative comments on each student's writing	1	2	3	4	5	
e. limit comments primarily to what the student has done well	1	2	3	4	5	
f. limit comments primarily to the errors or problems in student's writing	1	2	3	4	5	
g. indicate mechanical errors (spelling, grammar) and correct them	1	2	3	4	5	
h. indicate mechanical errors without correcting them	1	2	3	4	5	
i. comment on lapses in logic or organization	1	2	3	4	5	
j. suggest ways to improve the style of writing	1	2	3	4	5	
k. assign a single grade representing a combined evaluation of content and form (mechanics and usage)	1	2	3	4	5	
l. assign a split grade: one for content, one for form	1	2	3	4	5	(31)

7. Based on your experiences this semester, how much of a problem is each of the following for students in your Advanced Study course?

	Not a Problem		Somewhat a Problem	A Major Problem		Don't Know	
a. selecting a topic	1	2	3	4	5	( )	(32)
b. doing research and taking notes	1	2	3	4	5	( )	
c. thinking through their ideas before writing	1	2	3	4	5	( )	

d. actually sitting down to write	1	2	3	4	5	( )	
e. deciding who is the audience	1	2	3	4	5	( )	
f. using correct grammar and punctuation	1	2	3	4	5	( )	
g. spelling	1	2	3	4	5	( )	
h. editing and rewriting drafts	1	2	3	4	5	( )	
i. style and originality	1	2	3	4	5	( )	
j. logic and organization	1	2	3	4	5	( )	
k. getting papers in on time	1	2	3	4	5	( )	(42)

8. Have your pet peeves about the quality of student writing changed as a result of participating in this program? What aspects of writing do you now think are especially critical?

9. How would you rate the overall quality of student writing in your Advanced Study course?

	Extremely Poor				Excellent	
a. at the *beginning* of this semester	1	2	3	4	5	(43)
b. at the *end* of this semester	1	2	3	4	5	(44)

10. Please indicate the changes, if any, in your students':

	Greatly Decreased		No Change	Greatly Increased	Don't Know		
a. enjoyment of writing	1	2	3	4	5	( )	(45)
b. confidence in writing	1	2	3	4	5	( )	
c. fluency or productivity in writing	1	2	3	4	5	( )	(47)

11. Compared with other classes you teach, how much time do you think students have spent on your Advanced Study course?

_____ (1) much more time   _____ (2) somewhat more time   (48)
_____ (3) same amount of time   _____ (4) somewhat less time
_____ (5) much less time   _____ (6) don't know

12. At the present time, how would you rate yourself in the following areas?

	Not At All Skilled				Very Skilled	
a. giving constructive feedback to students	1	2	3	4	5	(49)
b. writing essay test questions	1	2	3	4	5	
c. diagnosing student writing problems	1	2	3	4	5	
d. designing writing assignments	1	2	3	4	5	
e. evaluating student writing holistically	1	2	3	4	5	
f. motivating students to write	1	2	3	4	5	
g. knowing when and where to refer students for tutoring	1	2	3	4	5	
h. avoiding plagiarism	1	2	3	4	5	
i. helping students structure and organize their papers	1	2	3	4	5	
j. convincing students to edit and rewrite their papers	1	2	3	4	5	
k. grading students' writing	1	2	3	4	5	(59)

13. At the present time, how would you rate your own:

	Very Low				Very High	
a. confidence in teaching writing	1	2	3	4	5	(60)
b. enjoyment of teaching writing	1	2	3	4	5	(61)

14. If you use any of the techniques or ideas from the workshop in any of your *other* courses, please describe specifically which techniques.

15. Would you recommend the workshop to other faculty members? (62)

    ____ (1) yes
    ____ (2) not sure (what reservations do you have?)
    ____ (3) no (why not?)

16. What aspects of the program could be improved or changed (e.g., workshops, topic sessions, activities, readers)?

17. Would you have participated in these workshops if you were *not* given:

	No	Not Sure	Yes	
a. assigned time	1	2	3	(63)
b. reader assistance	1	2	3	(64)

18. If changes were to be made in the workshop activities, how would you feel about the following modifications?

	Poor Idea			Excellent Idea		No Opinion	
a. offer some workshop for faculty prior to their teaching Advanced Study courses	1	2	3	4	5	( )	(65)
b. eliminate readers	1	2	3	4	5	( )	
c. assign each faculty member a specific reader	1	2	3	4	5	( )	
d. reduce the number of workshops sessions	1	2	3	4	5	( )	
e. increase the number of workshops sessions	1	2	3	4	5	( )	(69)
f. other (please describe)							

19. How do you feel about the Advanced Study requirement? What advice, suggestions or recommendations would you like to pass on regarding these courses?

20. Any other comments about the workshops or the evaluation?

Exhibit 3

Sample Student Assignment

Please read the following assignment and sample student letter and mark and grade the paper as you normally would do.

Assignment: A local professional association is sponsoring an awards program called "Orchids and Onions." The purpose of the competition is to recognize buildings in the area that exemplify the "best" and "worst" practices of design and architecture. Select a building with which you are familiar and write a letter to the association nominating it for either an orchid (best practices) or an onion (worst practices) and describe your reasons for doing so.

Sample Student Letter:

Dear Sir:

Thank you for your recent informative letter regarding the activities of the XXX Professional Association. At your suggestion, I would like to come up with a proposal for an entry in the upcoming "Orchids and Onions" award competition.

To someone who is used to see the golden arches of Mc. Donalds, Me& Me restaurant in Berkeley could be the ultimate image of a fast food chain restaurant. Situated on the corner of Parker and Telegraph Ave., it greets the passer-by with a fragmented facade which hides a dull box with an open courtyard at one end. The stucco covered concrete fragments were meant to be part of a continuous wall, parallel to the actual building, which would have created a dead corridor in the struggle of the architect to bring to this area a glimpse of Middle Eastern character. The ghosts of Mies van der Rohe and of the De Stijl movement were hunting the Architect, but the site, its location and the local atmosphere made him content with only a Mexican-Arabic image of a building which tells us of ruins propping up a box, as if to prevent it from the final disagreement with the laws of structure.

Not only was the intent of the Architect and his peers to use fragments as a sign of temporary, but they relied onto arches as well, which begin at one end, continue through the little building and come out at the other end, all tired and contorted fromthe process of creating additional layers, to parallel the fragmented delineation of the property and glazed wall main street facade.

Speaking of the main street, Telegraph Ave. gives its building an uncomfortable location, because of the troubled years of the 1960's and of the continuous deterioration of of the store front into a no-body's alley. To pull his building out of the surrounding and its own mediocrity, the Architect uses a daring pink color scheme which spills on the inside aswell, with its unchallenged hues.

The interior brings an amosphere of relaxation and quiet thoughts among customers, who are scaterred between tables and booths, under the blessings of color images of Mediterranean food, hanging green plants and subdued lights. The open courtyard, surrounded by a "transparent" fence, offers additional sitting area, with tables and chairs as light brown spots on the palette of pink.

Me & Me stands for Who & Who in Yidish, but,for me, it becomes a "concrete" representation of the sheep call. Looked upon from the distance, it reminds me of dunes of sand and of palm trees, which, one day, might bring some shadow over this oasis of asphalt and cars. Through its controversial image, the restaurant surpasses the preceding schemes of the fast food chain business. It stands aloof from the rest of the neighborhood and time alone could make it successful, with the fall of stucco and the abundance of graffiti.

And, since the Architect was careful enough to provide a place for medals, I would say that his fragments would be somewhat enhanced with onions hanging on.

Sincerely,

Exhibit 4

Interview Protocol for Former
Faculty Workshop Participants

1. What are the chief reasons you proposed a course for Advanced Study?

2. What made you decide to participate in the program?

3. Approximately how many of the sessions did you attend?
   1 or 2 _____
   3 or 4 _____
   5 or 6 _____
   7 or 8 _____

4. How would you describe your level of participation in the workshops? (active withdrawal, passive attendance, enthusiastic participation)

5. What do you think you learned the most about (what made the biggest impression on you) from the workshops?

6. As a result of the workshop have you changed
   • the kinds of writing assignments you give (describe: types, lengths, instructions given)
   • the techniques you use to teach writing (describe)
     - students evaluate each other's writing
     - use of prewriting
     - use of revision
     - students submit first drafts for comments or grading
     - students write assignments in class (other than tests)
     - examples of student writing are discussed in class
   • the way you mark student papers (describe)
     - write only general comments at beginning or end
     - write comments throughout
     - rewrite parts of student papers
     - balance positive and negative comments
     - limit comments to what student has done well

- limit comments to student errors
- indicate mechanical errors and correct them
- indicate mechanical errors without correcting them
- comment on lapses in logic or organization
- suggest ways to improve the style of writing
- assign a single grade
- assign a split grade, one for content, one for form
• the test you give (describe)
  (probe in this question: comparison of Advanced Study course pre- and post-certification; comparison to other non-Advanced Study courses faculty member has taught)

7. What degree of impact do you think the workshop has had on your:
   - confidence in teaching writing
   - level of skill in teaching writing
   - own efficiency as a writer

8. What degree of impact do you think your participation in the workshop has had on your *students*?
   - ease in selecting a topic
   - doing research and taking notes
   - thinking through their ideas before writing
   - actually sitting down to write
   - deciding who is the audience
   - using correct grammar and punctuation
   - spelling
   - editing and rewriting drafts
   - style and originality
   - logic and organization
   - getting papers in on time

9. Since last semester, have you had any continuing contact or involvement with the staff who taught the workshop? (describe)

10. Now that you have had a chance to reflect, how would you rate the usefulness of the program in assisting you to incorporate a writing component into your Advanced Study course?

Of little use				A great deal of use
1	2	3	4	5

11. Have you incorporated any of the techniques/ideas from the workshop into your other courses? (describe which and how)

12. Were there any problems with attrition in your Advanced Study course? (describe). We would like to survey the students from your Advanced Study course. Do you have the class lists?

13. Do you have a sense of the general faculty reaction to Advanced Study courses? Is there a need for such courses? What are the major obstacles to identifying and certifying Advanced Study courses?

14. What do you see as the biggest problems facing you the next time you teach your Advanced Study course? (probe: lack of reader help)

15. What future do you think the program or associated activities (readers) have on this campus? (probe: barriers to institutionalization; problems in attracting participants)

16. What do you think is needed to improve student writing on this campus?

Exhibit 5

Survey Questionnaire for Comparison Faculty

As part of the evaluation of the Writing Workshops, we are interested in your candid assessments of students' writing skills and your reactions to the Advanced Study requirement. Your answers will be kept confidential and only summary results will be reported.

Name _____
Course _____ (1-2)

1. If you have proposed a course for Advanced Studies, what were the chief reasons for doing so?

2. Have you heard about the Writing Workshops for faculty?
____ (1) no   ____ (2) not sure   ____ (3) yes   (3)

3. Did you consider participating in the workshops?
____ (1) no   ____ (2) yes   (4)

4. Below are some reasons faculty members might not participate in the workshop program. Please check all that apply to you.

____ didn't want to use readers   (5)
____ required too much time
____ workshops met too frequently over the semester
____ workshop topics did not sound interesting or appropriate
____ couldn't fit workshops into my schedule
____ already feel competent to introduce writing in my courses
____ didn't know about the program
____ other (please describe)   (12)

5. Would you consider participating in the workshops in the future?   (13)

____ (1) yes   ____ (2) not sure (please describe)
____ (3) no (please describe)

6. Would you participate if you were not given assigned time?

____ (1) yes   ____ (2) not sure   ____ (3) no   (14)

7. If you are teaching or have taught an Advanced Study course, which of

179

the following services do you feel you might need to strengthen the writing component of your course? Check all that apply.

    ____ individual consultations with a writing expert   (15)
    ____ small group sessions with other faculty teaching Advanced Study courses
    ____ reader assistance
    ____ articles, handbooks, or materials on teaching writing or responding to and grading student writing
    ____ writing experts providing instruction directly to students about their writing
    ____ tutoring for students having difficulties in the course
    ____ other (please describe)   (21)

8. In how many of the courses you have taught at this campus have you ever required students to do the following?

    a. write a research or term paper; in ____ courses   (22-24)
    b. write two or more short papers, essays, or reports; in ____ courses   (25-27)
    c. write lab reports; in ____ courses   (28-30)
    d. keep a journal; in ____ courses   (31-33)
    e. write stories, poems or plays; in ____ courses   (34-36)

9. If you plan to teach an Advanced Study course in the future, what specific problems, if any, do you anticipate?

10. How do you feel about the Advanced Study requirement? What advice, suggestions or recommendations would you like to pass on regarding this course?

11. Have you ever attended any other workshops to teach writing?

    ___ (1) no   ___ (2) yes   (37)

12. How would you rate your own:

	Very Low				Very High	
a. fluency/productivity as a writer	1	2	3	4	5	(38)
b. confidence in teaching writing	1	2	3	4	5	
c. enjoyment of writing	1	2	3	4	5	(40)

13. How descriptive of the way you mark students' papers is each of the following?

	Not At All Descriptive		Somewhat Descriptive		Very Descriptive	
a. write only general comments, either at the beginning or end of the paper	1	2	3	4	5	(41)
b. write comments throughout referring to specific aspects of the paper	1	2	3	4	5	
c. rewrite parts of student papers to show them how they might have written a phrase, sentence or paragraph more effectively	1	2	3	4	5	
d. try to balance positive and negative comments on each student's writing	1	2	3	4	5	
e. limit comments primarily to what the student has done well	1	2	3	4	5	
f. limit comments primarily to the errors or problems in student's writing	1	2	3	4	5	

g. indicate mechanical errors (spelling, grammar) and correct them	1	2	3	4	5
h. indicate mechanical errors without correcting them	1	2	3	4	5
i. comment on lapses in logic or organization	1	2	3	4	5
j. suggest ways to improve the style of writing	1	2	3	4	5
k. assign a single grade representing a combined evaluation of content and form (mechanics and usage)	1	2	3	4	5
l. assign a split grade: one for content, one for form	1	2	3	4	5 (52)

14. How much of a problem is each of the following for students in your courses?

	Not a Problem		Somewhat a Problem		A Major Problem	Don't Know	
a. selecting a topic	1	2	3	4	5	( )	(53)
b. doing research and taking notes	1	2	3	4	5	( )	
c. thinking through their ideas before writing	1	2	3	4	5	( )	
d. actually sitting down to write	1	2	3	4	5	( )	
e. deciding who is the audience	1	2	3	4	5	( )	
f. using correct grammar and punctuation	1	2	3	4	5	( )	
g. spelling	1	2	3	4	5	( )	
h. editing and rewriting drafts	1	2	3	4	5	( )	
i. style and originality	1	2	3	4	5	( )	
j. logic and organization	1	2	3	4	5	( )	
k. getting papers in on time	1	2	3	4	5	( )	(63)

15. Based on your experience with students on this campus, how would you rate the overall quality of student writing?

Extremely Poor				Excellent	
1	2	3	4	5	(64)

16. Below are some topics which could be covered in these workshops. For each one, please candidly assess your skill in that area.

	Not At All Skilled			Very Skilled		
a. giving constructive feedback to students	1	2	3	4	5	(65)
b. writing essay test questions	1	2	3	4	5	
c. diagnosing student writing problems	1	2	3	4	5	
d. designing writing assignments	1	2	3	4	5	
e. evaluating student writing holistically	1	2	3	4	5	
f. motivating students to write	1	2	3	4	5	
g. knowing when and where to refer students for tutoring	1	2	3	4	5	
h. avoiding plagiarism	1	2	3	4	5	
i. helping students structure and organize their papers	1	2	3	4	5	
j. convincing students to edit and rewrite their papers	1	2	3	4	5	
k. grading students' writing	1	2	3	4	5	(75)

17. Please attach on a separate sheet any other comments about the Workshop Program, the Advanced Study requirement or student writing on this campus.

Exhibit 6

Current Student Questionnaire—Pretest

The instructor of this course is participating in a workshop on writing in the disciplines. As one part of the evaluation of that workshop, your cooperation in responding to this brief questionnaire will be greatly appreciated.

Name of Instructor ———————————————————— (1-2)
Course No. ———————————————————— (3-4)

1. Listed below are reasons students might enroll in this course. Please indicate how important *each* reason was for you.

	Not At All Important		Somewhat Important		Very Important	
a. personal interest in subject matter	1	2	3	4	5	(5)
b. recommendation of advisor or other faculty member	1	2	3	4	5	
c. opportunity to improve my writing skills	1	2	3	4	5	
d. recommendation of a fellow student	1	2	3	4	5	
e. fulfillment of the general education advanced study requirement	1	2	3	4	5	
f. requirement for graduation in my major	1	2	3	4	5	
g. preparation for the writing proficiency examination	1	2	3	4	5	
h. other (please describe)	1	2	3	4	5	(12)

2. Approximately how many college-level courses have you taken to date?

____ courses   (13-14)

3. In how many of those courses were you required to do each of the following?

a. write a term paper; in ____ courses   (15)
b. write two or more short papers, essays, or reports; in ____ courses
c. write lab reports; in ____ courses
d. keep a journal; in ____ courses   (18)

4. In how many of those courses did you receive written or oral feedback from the instructor or readers which you found helpful in improving your writing skills?   In ____ courses   (19)

5. To what extent has your writing improved as the result of your job experience or extracurricular activities?

	Not At All		Somewhat		A Great Deal	
	1	2	3	4	5	(20)

6. To what extent has your writing improved as the result of taking college-level courses?

	Not At All		Somewhat		A Great Deal	
	1	2	3	4	5	(21)

7. Compared to other students at this university, overall how would you rate your writing skills?

	Poor				Excellent	
	1	2	3	4	5	(22)

8. Compared with your other classes this semester, how much time do you think you will spend on this course?

____ (1) much more time   ____ (2) somewhat more time   (23)
____ (3) same amount of time   ____ (4) somewhat less time
____ (5) much less time

9. How much time outside class do you expect to devote to each of the following in this course?

a. reading: ____ hours per week outside of class   (24-25)
b. other research: ____ hours per week outside of class   (26-27)
c. writing: ____ hours per week outside of class   (28-29)

10. In general, how much improvement do you feel you need to make in each of the following writing skills?

	Little or no improvement		Some improvement		A great deal of improvement	
a. choosing a topic which motivates me to write	1	2	3	4	5	(30)
b. doing research and taking notes	1	2	3	4	5	
c. thinking through my ideas before writing	1	2	3	4	5	
d. outlining or organizing my paper	1	2	3	4	5	
e. actually sitting down to write	1	2	3	4	5	
f. deciding who is my audience	1	2	3	4	5	
g. saying what I really want to say	1	2	3	4	5	
h. using correct grammar & punctuation	1	2	3	4	5	
i. spelling	1	2	3	4	5	
j. editing and re-writing drafts	1	2	3	4	5	
k. getting papers in on time	1	2	3	4	5	(40)

11. Please indicate whether you:

    a. are aware of the advanced   (1)＿＿ yes   (2)＿＿ no   (3)＿＿ not sure   (41)
       study requirement

    b. have already taken one   (1)＿＿ yes   (2)＿＿ no   (3)＿＿ not sure
       course which fulfills the advanced
       study requirement?

    c. will be required to fulfill the   (1)＿＿ yes   (2)＿＿ no   (3)＿＿ not sure   (43)
       advanced study requirement?

    d. will be required to take the   (1)＿＿ yes   (2)＿＿ no   (3)＿＿ not sure
       writing proficiency exam?

    e. have already taken the   (1)＿＿ yes   (2)＿＿ no   (3)＿＿ not sure   (45)
       writing proficiency exam?

12. What is your year in school?

    ＿＿ (1) Fresh.   ＿＿ (2) Soph.   ＿＿ (3) Junior
    ＿＿ (4) Senior   ＿＿ (5) Grad   (46)

13. What is your major (or most likely major)? ＿＿＿＿＿＿＿＿＿ (47-48)

14. Please check your age group.

    ＿＿ 18 or under   ＿＿ 19-20   ＿＿ 21-25   ＿＿ 26-29   ＿＿ 30 or above (49)

15. Please think of a high school or college assignment which you found to be especially educational. Describe the assignment briefly and analyze what it was that made it a valuable learning experience for you.

                                                     (50)

                                                     (51)

                                                     (52)

                                                     (53)

                                                     (54)

16. Your responses will be treated anonymously. However, in order that we can compare your responses from this questionnaire with those we will ask you to give toward the end of the semester, please print your mother's maiden name.

    My mother's maiden name is: ＿＿＿＿＿＿＿＿＿＿＿＿   (55-67)

THANK YOU FOR YOUR COOPERATION.

Exhibit 7

Current Student Questionnaire—Posttest

As you may remember, the instructor of this course is participating in a workshop on writing in the disciplines. As a final part of the evaluation of that workshop, your cooperation in responding to this brief questionnaire will be greatly appreciated.

Name of Instructor _____
               (1-2)
Course No. _____

1. Compared with your other classes this semester, how much time did you spend on this course?

      ___ (1) much more time   ___ (2) somewhat more time   (3)
      ___ (3) same amount of time   ___ (4) somewhat less time
      ___ (5) much less time

2. Approximately how much time outside class did you devote to each of the following in this course?

  a. reading: ___ hours per week outside of class   (4-5)
  b. other research: ___ hours per week outside of class   (6-7)
  c. writing: ___ hours per week outside of class   (8-9)

3. As a result of taking this course, to what extent, if any, did you improve in the following:

	Not At All		Somewhat		A Great Deal	
a. enjoyment of writing	1	2	3	4	5	(10)
b. confidence in writing	1	2	3	4	5	
c. fluency or productivity in writing	1	2	3	4	5	
d. overall writing skills	1	2	3	4	5	(13)

4. As a result of this course, how much improvement, if any, do you feel you made in each of the following writing or writing-related skills?

	Little or no improvement		Some improvement		A great deal of improvement	
a. choosing a topic which motivates me to write	1	2	3	4	5	(14)
b. doing research and taking notes	1	2	3	4	5	
c. thinking through my ideas before writing	1	2	3	4	5	
d. outlining or organizing my paper	1	2	3	4	5	
e. actually sitting down to write	1	2	3	4	5	
f. deciding who is my audience	1	2	3	4	5	
g. saying what I really want to say	1	2	3	4	5	
h. using correct grammar & punctuation	1	2	3	4	5	
i. spelling	1	2	3	4	5	
j. editing and re-writing drafts	1	2	3	4	5	
k. getting papers in on time	1	2	3	4	5	
l. other (please describe)	1	2	3	4	5	(25)

5. Looking back at Question 4, select up to 3 items (a through l) on which you made the *most* improvement as a result of this course. Please describe as concretely as possible what aspects of this course or the instructor's

teaching were most helpful to you in improving these aspects of your writing and explain why.

Item____because: (26-27)
Item____because: (28-29)
Item____because: (30-31)

6. Now, looking back at Question 4 once more, select up to 3 items on which you would like to have improved *more* than you did as a result of this course. Please describe whether and how the instructor might have helped you to improve those aspects of your writing.

Item____because: (32-33)
Item____because: (34-35)
Item____because: (36-37)

7. In any writing you may have done for other courses or on your job, have you been able to apply specifically any techniques or skills learned in this class?

____ (1) no ____ (2) not sure ____ (3) yes (which techniques or skills?)   (38)

8. In the course, how often were the following techniques used?

	Never	Infre-quently	Some-times	Fre-quently	Always	
a. students submitted first drafts for comments or grading	1	2	3	4	5	(39)
b. students were required to revise their writing	1	2	3	4	5	
c. students wrote assignments in class (other than midterms and exams)	1	2	3	4	5	
d. examples of student writing were discussed in class	1	2	3	4	5	(42)

9. How descriptive of the way the instructor and readers marked your papers is each of the following?

	Not At All Descriptive		Somewhat Descriptive		Very Descriptive	
The instructor and readers:						
a. wrote only general comments, either at the beginning or end of the paper	1	2	3	4	5	(43)
b. wrote comments through-out referring to specific aspects of the paper	1	2	3	4	5	
c. rewrote parts of my papers to show me how I might have written a phrase, sentence or paragraph more effectively	1	2	3	4	5	
d. wrote balanced (positive *and* negative) comments on my writing	1	2	3	4	5	
e. limited comments primarily to what I had done well	1	2	3	4	5	

f. limited comments primarily to the errors or problems in my writing	1	2	3	4	5	
g. indicated mechanical errors (spelling, grammar) and corrected them	1	2	3	4	5	
h. indicated mechanical errors without correcting them	1	2	3	4	5	
i. commented on lapses in logic or organization	1	2	3	4	5	
j. suggested ways to improve the style of writing	1	2	3	4	5	
k. assigned a single grade representing a combined evaluation of content and form (mechanics and usage)	1	2	3	4	5	
l. assigned a split grade: one for content, one for form	1	2	3	4	5	(54)

10. Compared to other students at this university, how would you rate your writing skills?

Poor				Excellent	
1	2	3	4	5	(55)

11. How successful was this course in integrating writing into the subject matter of the course?

Not At All Successful				Very Successful	
1	2	3	4	5	(56)

12. Your responses will be treated anonymously. However, in order that we can compare your responses from this questionnaire with those we asked you at the beginning of the semester, please print your mother's maiden name.

My mother's maiden name is: _____ (57-69)

AGAIN, MANY THANKS FOR YOUR COOPERATION.

Exhibit 8

Student Questionnaire

Dear student:

The instructor named below participated in a writing workshop. Because you were enrolled in his/her course last fall, your cooperation in responding to this brief questionnaire will be very helpful in evaluating the effectiveness of the workshop. A stamped, self-addressed envelope is enclosed for your convenience in responding.

In order that your responses can be summarized in a final report, please return the questionnaire by May 20. The questionnaire is coded so that we can send a follow-up reminder to non-respondents. Your responses will be treated as entirely confidential, however, and only summary results will be reported. Thank you so much for your help.

Name of Instructor ————————————————————————— (1-2)
Course No. —————————————————————————

1. Listed below are reasons students might have enrolled in this course. Please indicate how important *each* reason was for you.

	Not At All Important		Somewhat Important		Very Important	
a. personal interest in subject matter	1	2	3	4	5	(3)
b. recommendation of advisor or other faculty member	1	2	3	4	5	
c. opportunity to improve my writing skills	1	2	3	4	5	
d. recommendation of a fellow student	1	2	3	4	5	
e. fulfillment of the general education advanced study requirement	1	2	3	4	5	
f. requirement for graduation on my major	1	2	3	4	5	
g. preparation for the writing proficiency examination	1	2	3	4	5	
h. other (please describe)	1	2	3	4	5	(10)

2. Please indicate whether you:

   a. will be required to fulfill the advanced study requirement   (1)____ yes (2)____ no (3)____ not sure (11)

   b. have enrolled in at least two advanced study courses   (1)____ yes (2)____ no (3)____ not sure

   c. have passed at least one advanced study course   (1)____ yes (2)____ no (3)____ not sure

   d. have taken the writing proficiency exam?   (1)____ yes (2)____ no (3)____ not sure

   If "yes" did you: ____ (1) pass   ____ (2) not pass   ____ (3) don't know   (15)

3. Compared to other students at this university, overall how would you rate your writing skills?

Poor		Fair		Excellent	
1	2	3	4	5	(16)

4. As a result of this course, how much improvement, if any, do you feel you made in each of the following writing skills?

188

	Little or no improvement		Some improvement		A great deal of improvement	
a. choosing a topic which motivates me to write	1	2	3	4	5	(17)
b. doing research and taking notes	1	2	3	4	5	
c. thinking through my ideas before writing	1	2	3	4	5	
d. outlining or organizing my paper	1	2	3	4	5	
e. actually sitting down to write	1	2	3	4	5	
f. deciding who is my audience	1	2	3	4	5	
g. saying what I really want to say	1	2	3	4	5	
h. using correct grammar & punctuation	1	2	3	4	5	
i. spelling	1	2	3	4	5	
j. editing and re-writing drafts	1	2	3	4	5	
k. getting papers in on time	1	2	3	4	5	(27)

5. At the time you enrolled, how much time did you think you would spend on this course in comparison with your other courses?

_____ (1) much more time   _____ (2) somewhat more time   (28)
_____ (3) same amount of time   _____ (4) somewhat less time
_____ (5) much less time

6. Please check the *one* phrase which *best describes* your status in this course.

_____ (1) withdrew from the course (Fall) or intend to do so (Spring)
_____ (2) took an incomplete (Fall) or intend to do so (Spring)
_____ (3) passed the course (Fall) or expect to do so (Spring)
_____ (4) failed the course (Fall) or expect to do so (Spring)
_____ (5) audited the course (Fall) or auditing the course (Spring)
_____ (6) other, please explain.   (29)

If you checked #3, 4, 5, or 6 in Question 6 (above) please skip to Question 12.
If you checked #1 or 2 in Question 6 (above), please complete Questions 7 through 13.

7. At the time you withdrew or stopped attending this course, how much time were you spending on this course in comparison with your other classes?

_____ (1) much more time   _____ (2) somewhat more time   (30)
_____ (3) same amount of time   _____ (4) somewhat less time
_____ (5) much less time

8. To what extent was (or is) each of the following a factor in your withdrawing or not completing this course?

	Not At All A Factor			A Major Factor	
a. the amount of writing required	1	2	3	4	5	(31)
b. the amount of reading required	1	2	3	4	5	
c. the subject matter or instructor	1	2	3	4	5	
d. your grades on assignments or exams	1	2	3	4	5	
e. personal reasons (e.g., illness)	1	2	3	4	5	(35)
f. other, please explain:						

9. How many writing assignments, if any, had you completed before you left the course?

___ (1) none ___ (2) one ___ (3) two ___ (4) three
___ (5) four or more ___ (6) don't remember (36)

10. If you completed *one or more* writing assignments in this course, how helpful was the written and/or oral feedback you received from the instructor and readers?

Not at all helpful				Very helpful	
1	2	3	4	5	(37)

11. How successful was this course in integrating writing into the subject matter of the course?

Not at all successful				Very successful	
1	2	3	4	5	(38)

12. What is your year in school?

___ (1) Fresh. ___ (2) Soph. ___ (3) Junior
___ (4) Senior ___ (5) Grad (39)

13. What is your major (or most likely major)? _____ (40-41)

Many thanks again for helping us to evaluate these workshops. If you have any comments about the course or advanced study requirements, please write them here.

Exhibit 9

Former Student Questionnaire

The instructor named below participated in a writing workshop. Because you were enrolled in his/her course last fall, your cooperation in responding to this brief questionnaire will be very helpful in evaluating the effectiveness of the workshop. A stamped, self-addressed envelope is enclosed for your convenience in responding. Thank you so much for your help.

Name of Instructor _____ (1-2)
Course No. _____

1. Compared with your other classes this semester, how much time did you spend on this course?

___ (1) much more time ___ (2) somewhat more time (3)
___ (3) same amount of time ___ (4) somewhat less time
___ (5) much less time

2. Approximately how much time outside class did you devote to each of the following in this course?

a. reading: ___ hours per week outside of class (4-5)
b. other research: ___ hours per week outside of class (6-7)
c. writing: ___ hours per week outside of class (8-9)

3. As a result of taking this course, to what extent, if any, did you improve in the following:

	Not At All		Somewhat		A Great Deal	
a. enjoyment of writing	1	2	3	4	5	(10)
b. confidence in writing	1	2	3	4	5	
c. fluency or productivity in writing	1	2	3	4	5	
d. overall writing skills	1	2	3	4	5	(13)

4. As a result of this course, how much improvement, if any, do you feel you made in each of the following writing or writing-related skills?

	Little or no improve- ment		Some improve- ment		A great deal of improve- ment	
a. choosing a topic which motivates me to write	1	2	3	4	5	(14)
b. doing research and taking notes	1	2	3	4	5	
c. thinking through my ideas before writing	1	2	3	4	5	
d. outlining or organizing my paper	1	2	3	4	5	
e. actually sitting down to write	1	2	3	4	5	
f. deciding who is my audience	1	2	3	4	5	
g. saying what I really want to say	1	2	3	4	5	
h. using correct grammar & punctuation	1	2	3	4	5	
i. spelling	1	2	3	4	5	
j. editing and re-writing drafts	1	2	3	4	5	
k. getting papers in on time	1	2	3	4	5	
l. other (please describe)	1	2	3	4	5	(25)

5. Looking back at Question 4, select up to 3 items (a through l) on which you made the *most* improvement as a result of this course. Please describe as concretely as possible what aspects of this course or the instructor's teaching were most helpful to you in improving these aspects of your writing and explain why.

Item____because: (26-27)
Item____because: (28-29)
Item____because: (30-31)

6. Now, looking back at Question 4 once more, select up to 3 items on which you would like to have improved *more* than you did as a result of this course. Please describe whether and how the instructor might have helped you to improve those aspects of your writing.

Item____because: (32-33)
Item____because: (34-35)
Item____because: (36-37)

7. In any writing you may have done for other courses or on your job, have you been able to apply specifically any techniques or skills learned in this class?

_____ (1) no _____ (2) not sure _____ (3) yes (which techniques or skills?) (38)

8. In the course, how often were the following techniques used?

	Never	Infre-quently	Some-times	Fre-quently	Always	
a. students submitted first drafts for comments or grading	1	2	3	4	5	(39)
b. students were required to revise their writing	1	2	3	4	5	
c. students wrote assignments in class (other than midterms and exams)	1	2	3	4	5	
d. examples of student writing were discussed in class	1	2	3	4	5	(42)

9. How descriptive of the way the instructor and readers marked your papers is each of the following?

	Not At All Descriptive		Somewhat Descriptive		Very Descriptive	
The instructor and readers:						
a. wrote only general comments, either at the beginning or end of the paper	1	2	3	4	5	(43)
b. wrote comments through-out referring to specific aspects of the paper	1	2	3	4	5	
c. rewrote parts of my papers to show me how I might have written a phrase, sentence or paragraph more effectively	1	2	3	4	5	
d. wrote balanced (positive *and* negative) comments on my writing	1	2	3	4	5	
e. limited comments primarily to what I had done well	1	2	3	4	5	
f. limited comments primarily to the errors or problems in my writing	1	2	3	4	5	
g. indicated mechanical errors (spelling, grammar) and corrected them	1	2	3	4	5	
h. indicated mechanical errors without correcting them	1	2	3	4	5	
i. commented on lapses in logic or organization	1	2	3	4	5	
j. suggested ways to improve the style of writing	1	2	3	4	5	
k. assigned a single grade representing a combined evaluation of content and form (mechanics and usage)	1	2	3	4	5	
l. assigned a split grade: one for content, one for form	1	2	3	4	5	(54)

10. Compared to other students at this university, how would you rate your writing skills?

	Poor				Excellent	
a. your *present* level of skills	1	2	3	4	5	(55)
b. your level of skills *before* taking this course	1	2	3	4	5	(56)

11. Please indicate whether you:

    a. will be required to fulfill   (1)＿＿ yes (2)＿＿ no (3)＿＿ not sure (57)
       the advanced study
       requirement
    b. have enrolled in at least   (1)＿＿ yes (2)＿＿ no (3)＿＿ not sure
       two advanced study courses
    c. have passed at least *one*   (1)＿＿ yes (2)＿＿ no (3)＿＿ not sure
       advanced study course
    d. have taken the writing   (1)＿＿ yes (2)＿＿ no (3)＿＿ not sure (60)
       proficiency exam?
    If "yes" did you: ＿＿ (1) pass ＿＿ (2) not pass ＿＿ (3) don't know (61)

12. What grade did you receive in this course?

＿＿ (1) A   ＿＿ (2) B   ＿＿ (3) C   ＿＿ (4) D   ＿＿ (5) F   (62-63)
＿＿ (6) U   ＿＿ (7) CR ＿＿ (8) NC ＿＿ (9) I   ＿＿ (10) SP
＿＿ (11) W ＿＿ (12) RD ＿＿ (13) AU

13. If you checked "U," "NC," "I," "W," or "RD," what was the *primary* reason you did not complete the course?

14. Any other comments about this course or about improvements in your writing skills?

Exhibit 10

Interview Protocol for Campus Community

1. How do you feel about the Advanced Study requirement?
   Probes:
   Do you have a sense of other faculty's reaction to the requirement?
   Is there a real need for such courses?
   How severe is the problem of students' ability to write in upper-division courses?
   What are your expectations for the Advanced Study courses in relation to the problem?
   How would you measure progress toward those goals of expectation?
   What are the main obstacles to faculty participation?
   Do you have any concerns about the standards for Advanced Study courses?
   What relationship, if any, should the proficiency exam have to the Advanced Study requirement?

2. What problems, if any, *did* you anticipate with the new requirement?
   Probes:
   With the faculty? Within your own department? With students? With attrition?
   With the readers? With released time? With students' knowledge of new requirements?

3. Have any of these actually *become* problems to your knowledge?
   Probes:
   Which ones? Why?
   Have any unanticipated problems arisen to your knowledge?
   Any unanticipated benefits?

4. How much do you know about the workshops to help faculty members
   implement the Advanced Studies requirement?
   Probes:
   How needed are these workshops in your view?
   What should be the primary goals of the workshops?
   How well are the workshops accomplishing those goals?
   Should the workshops be limited to advanced study courses or be directed toward
      a broader goal of encouraging faculty to integrate writing into upper-division
      courses generally?
   Are readers necessary to the success of the workshops in your view?
   Is released-time necessary to faculty participation in your view?
   What future do you think the workshop or associated activities (e.g., readers)
      has on this campus? Are they barriers to institutionalization? To faculty
      participation?

References
Additional Reading
Glossary
Index
About the Authors

References

Alloway, E. *New Jersey Writing Project Observation Form*. Princeton, NJ: Educational Testing Service, 1978.

Applebee, A. *Tradition and Reform in the Teaching of English*. Urbana, IL: National Council of Teachers of English, 1974.

Applebee, A. Teaching conditions in secondary school English: Highlights of a survey. *English Journal*, 67(3), March 1978, 57–65.

Applebee, A. *Contexts for Learning to Write: Studies of Secondary School Instruction*. Norwood, NJ: Ablex, 1986.

Backer, T. *A Directory of Information on Tests*. TM Report 62. ERIC Clearinghouse on Tests, Measurement and Evaluation. Princeton, NJ: Educational Testing Service, 1977.

Balajthy, E. Artificial intelligence and the teaching of reading and writing by computers. *Journal of Reading*, 29, October 1985, 23–32.

Bamberg, B. Composition instruction does make a difference: A comparison of the regular and remedial classes. *Research in the Teaching of English*, 12(1), January 1978, 47–59.

Bamberg, B. Multiple-choice and holistic essay scores: What are they measuring? *College Composition and Communication*, 33(4), December 1982, 404–406.

Bay Area Writing Project Evaluation Staff. *The National Writing Project Evaluation Portfolio*. Berkeley: Bay Area Writing Project, U.C. Berkeley, 1983.

Beavan, M. H. Individualized goal setting, self-evaluation and peer evaluation. In *Evaluating Writing*, C. Cooper and L. Odell (eds.). Urbana, IL: National Council of Teachers of English, 1977.

Becker, G. *Evaluation of Innovative Approaches to English Composition Instruction*. 1972. ERIC ED 061944.

Berdie, D., and Anderson, J. *Questionnaires: Design and Use*. Metuchen, NJ: Scarecrow Press, 1974.

Bereiter, C., and Fillion, B. Surveys. *NWP Network Newsletter*, 2(1), November 1979.

Berman, P., and McLaughlin, M. *Federal Programs Supporting Educational Change*, Vols. I–VIII. Santa Monica, CA: Rand Corp., 1978.

Berthoff, A. E. *Forming, Thinking, Writing: The Composing Imagination*. Rochelle Park, NJ: Hayden Book Co., 1978.

Blake, R. W. Assessing English and language arts teachers' attitudes towards writers and writing. *English Record*, 27, Summer–Autumn 1976, 87–97.

Blake, R., and Tuttle, F. Composing as the curriculum: The Albion Writing Project. *English Record*, 30(2), Spring 1979, 9–14.

Borich, G., and Madden, S. *Evaluating Classroom Instruction: A Sourcebook of Instruments*. Reading, MA: Addison-Wesley, 1977.

Breininger, L. A visit to Professor CRAM. *College Composition and Communication*, 34, 1983, 358–361.

Breland, H. *A Study of College English Placement and the Test of Standard Written English*. RDR-76-77. Princeton, NJ: College Entrance Examination Board, 1977.

Breland, H. M. *The Direct Assessment of Writing Skills: A Measurement Review*. College Board Report No. 83-6. Princeton, NJ: Educational Testing Service, 1983.

Breland, H., and Gaynor, J. Comparison of direct and indirect assessments of writing skill. *Journal of Educational Measurement*, 16(2), Summer 1979, 119–127.

Britton, J. *The Development of Writing Abilities 11–18*. New York: Macmillan, 1975.

Bruner, J. *The Process of Education*. Cambridge, MA: Harvard University Press, 1960.

Buros, O. *Mental Measurements Yearbook*. 9th ed. Highland Park, NJ: Gryphon Press, 1985.

Caldwell, K. *Survey of Student Writing*. Berkeley: Bay Area Writing Project, School of Education, University of California, 1979.

California State Department of Education. *Practical Ideas for Teaching Writing as a Process*. 1986. Available from California State Department of Education, Publication Sales, P. O. Box 271, Sacramento, CA 95802–0271.

Camp, G. (ed.). *Teaching Writing: Essays from BAWP*. Upper Montclair, NJ: Boynton Cook, 1983.

Catano, J. Computer-based writing. *College Composition and Communication*, 36(33), October 1985, 309–315.

Centra, J. *Determining Faculty Effectiveness*. San Francisco: Jossey-Bass, 1979.

Chickering, A.; Halbuton, D.; Berquist, W.; and Lindquist, J. *Developing the College Curriculum*. Washington, DC: Council for Advancement of Small Colleges, 1977.

Cook, T., and Campbell, D. *Quasi-Experimentation: Design and Analysis Issues for Field Settings*. Chicago: Rand McNally, 1979.

Cooper, C., and Odell, L. (eds.). *Evaluating Writing*. Urbana, IL: National Council of Teachers of English, 1977.

Cooper, P. L. *The Assessment of Writing Ability: A Review of Research*. ETS Report 84-12. Princeton, NJ: Educational Testing Service, 1984.

Daiker, D.; Kerek, A.; and Morenberg, M. *Sentence Combining and the Teaching of Writing.* Conway, AR: University of Central Arkansas, 1979.

Daly, J., and Miller, M. The empirical development of an instrument to measure writing apprehension. *Research in the Teaching of English*, 9(3), Winter 1975, 250–256.

Davis, B. G., and Wood, L. *Evaluation of Teaching College Faculty Across Disciplines to Use Writing*, 1981. Available from the first author at the University of California, Berkeley.

Delbecq, A.; Van de Ven, A.; and Gustafson, D. *Group Techniques for Program Planning.* Glenview, IL: Scott, Foresman and Company, 1975.

Demaline, R., and Quinn, D. *Hints for Planning and Conducting a Survey and a Bibliography of Survey Methods.* Kalamazoo, MI: Evaluation Center, Western Michigan University, 1979.

Dent, R.; Jones, E.; MacKay, C.; and Taylor, P. *Righting Writing: UCLA Composition Guide.* Los Angeles: Department of English, UCLA, 1978.

Diederich, P. *Measuring Growth in English.* Urbana, IL: National Council of Teachers of English, 1974.

Diederich, P. Personal communication, 1978.

Donlan, D. Teaching writing in the content areas. *Research in the Teaching of English*, 8(2), Summer 1974, 250–264.

Donlan, D. A methodology inventory for composition instruction. *English Education*, 11(1), October 1979, 23–31.

Dusel, W. J. Determining an efficient teaching load in English. *Illinois English Bulletin*, 43(1), October 1955, 11–15.

Eliot, C. W. *Annual Report to the Harvard Board of Overseers 1873.* [Reported in Judy, S. Composition and rhetoric, 1840–1900. *English Journal*, 68(4), 1979, 35.]

Emig-King Student Attitude Questionnaire, 1978. Available from Barbara King, Douglas/Cook Writing Center, Douglas Library, New Brunswick, NJ 08901.

Emig-King Teacher Questionnaire, 1978. Available from Barbara King, Douglas/Cook Writing Center, Douglas Library, New Brunswick, NJ 08901.

Evans, W. H., and Jacobs, P. H. *Illinois Tests in the Teaching of English*, "Test of Attitude and Knowledge in Written Composition." Carbondale, IL: Southern Illinois University Press, 1972.

Fadiman, C., and Howard, J. *Empty Pages: A Search for Writing Competence in School and Society.* Belmont, CA: Fearon Pitman, 1979.

Fillion, B. *Surveys of Composition Instruction.* Paper presented at the Ontario Conference on Learning to Write. Summarized in *NWP Network Newsletter*, 2(1), November 1979.

Fishbein, M., and Ajzin, I. *Belief, Attitude, Intention, and Behavior: An Introduction to Theory and Research.* Reading, MA: Addison-Wesley Publishing Company, 1975.

Fishman, J. *The Politics of Bilingual Education.* Georgetown University Monograph Series on Language and Linguistics, 1, 1977, 47–58.

Fitz-Gibbon, C., and Morris, L. *How to Design a Program Evaluation.* Beverly Hills: Sage, 1978.

Flanigan, M. C. Observing teaching: Discovering and developing the individual's teaching style. *Writing Program Administration*, 3(2), Winter 1979, 17–24.

Ford, J., and Larkin, G. The portfolio system. *College English*, 39(8), April 1978, 950–955.

Forrest, A., and Steele, J. *College Outcome Measures Project: Assessment of General Education Knowledge and Skills*. Iowa City: American College Testing Program, 1977.

Frase, L. T. *Creating Intelligent Environments for Computer Use in Writing*. Paper presented at American Educational Research Association Meeting, San Francisco, April 1986.

Freedmen, S. W. The acquisition of written language: Response and revision. Washington, D.C.: Institute of Education, 1986. ERIC ED 265 553.

Frye, N. (ed.). *Literature: Uses of the Imagination*. New York: Harcourt Brace Jovanovich, 1973.

Gallagher, B. *Microcomputers and Word Processing Programs: An Evaluation and Critique*. New York: Instructional Resource Center, City University of New York, 1985.

Gere, A. R. Writing and writing. *English Journal*, 77(11), November 1977, 60–64.

Gere, A., and Smith, E. *Attitudes, Language and Change*. Urbana, IL: National Council of Teachers of English, 1979.

Glass, G.; Mcgaw, B.; and Smith, M. *Meta-Analysis in Social Research*. Beverly Hills: Sage, 1981.

Godshalk, F.; Swineford, E.; and Coffman, W. *Measurement of Writing Ability*. New York: College Entrance Examination Board, 1966.

Gorden, R. *Interviewing: Strategies, Techniques and Tactics*. Homewood, IL: Dorsey Press, 1975.

Graves, D. *Balance the Basics: Let Them Write*. New York: Ford Foundation, 1978.

Graves, D. *Growth and Development of First-grade Writers*. Paper presented at the Canadian Council of Teachers of English Annual Meeting, Ottawa, Canada, 1979.

Griffin, C. W. *Teaching Writing in All Disciplines*. San Francisco: Jossey-Bass, 1982.

Gronlund, N. *Measurement and Evaluation in Teaching*. 4th ed. New York: Macmillan, 1981.

Haggerty, S. *The Resource Approach to the Analysis of Educational Project Costs*. SN 017-080-01914-1. Washington, DC: U.S. Government Printing Office, 1978.

Hairston, M. What freshmen directors need to know about evaluating writing programs. *Writing Program Administration*, 3(1), Fall 1979, 11–16.

Halpern, J. W., and Liggett, S. *Computers and Composing*. Urbana, IL: National Council of Teachers of English, 1983.

Hancock, D., and Moss, A. (eds.). *Reading and Writing Programs within the Disciplines: A Preliminary Directory of Models*. Long Beach, CA: Chancellor's Office, Office of New Program Development, California State University and College System, 1979.

Harris, J. Student writers and word processing: A preliminary evaluation. *College Composition and Communication*, 36(3), October 1985, 323–330.

Hawkins, T. *Group Inquiry Techniques for Teaching Writing.* Urbana, IL: National Council of Teachers of English, 1976.

Healy, M. K. *Using Student Writing Response Groups in the Classroom.* Berkeley: Bay Area Writing Project, School of Education, University of California, 1980.

Henerson, M.; Morris, L.; and Fitz-Gibbon, C. *How to Measure Attitudes.* Beverly Hills: Sage, 1978.

Hershey, W. Idea processors. *Byte,* June 1985, 337–350.

Hillocks, G. *Research on Written Composition: New Directions for Teaching.* Urbana, IL: National Council of Teachers of English, 1986. ERIC ED 265 552.

Hoetker, J., and Brossell, G. Who (if anyone) is teaching them writing and how? *English Journal,* 68, October 1979, 19–22.

Hogan, T. P., and Mishler, C. Relationships between essay and objective tests of language skills for elementary school students. *Journal of Educational Measurement,* 17(3), Fall 1980, 219–227.

Hook, J. N. *A Long Way Together.* Urbana, IL: National Council of Teachers of English, 1979.

Hunt, K. W. Early blooming and late blooming syntactic structure. In *Evaluating Writing,* Cooper, C. and Odell, L. (eds.). Urbana, IL: National Council of Teachers of English, 1977.

Joyce, B., and Weil, M. *Models of Teaching.* 2nd ed. Englewood Cliffs, NJ: Prentice-Hall, 1980.

Joyce, B., and Associates. *The California Staff Development Study: Instruments and Guidelines for Implementation in the Schools.* Palo Alto, CA: Booksend Lab, 1982. ERIC ED 198 622.

Judy, S. Who resurrected bonehead English? *English Journal,* 64(4), 1975, 6–7.

Keech Student Questionnaire for Evaluating Writing Courses. Available from author, University of California, Berkeley: Bay Area Writing Project, School of Education, 1978.

Keech, C. *Comparative Methods Studies in Composition Research & Evaluation.* Berkeley: Bay Area Writing Project, School of Education, University of California, 1979a.

Keech, C. Holistic assessment and proficiency testing. *National Writing Project Network Newsletter,* 1(3), May 1979b, 4–6.

Keech, C. *Topics for Assessing Writing Through Writing Samples.* Bay Area Writing Project, School of Education, University of California, 1979c.

Keech, C., and Thomas, S. *Compendium of Promising Practices in Composition.* Berkeley: Bay Area Writing Project, School of Education, University of California, 1979.

Kirrie, M. Prompt writing is not impromptu. *National Writing Project Network Newsletter,* 1(3), May 1979, 6–7.

Kotler, L. A partnership of teachers and computers in teaching writing. *College Composition and Communication,* 34, 1983, 361–367.

Kowalski, J. *Evaluating Teacher Performance*. Arlington, VA: Educational Research Service, 1978.

Koziol, S. *Written Composing and Communication Skills: PCRP Assessment Survey II*. Harrisburg: Pennsylvania State Department of Education, 1982. ERIC ED 213 030.

Lambert, W. E. *Culture and Language as Factors in Learning and Education*. Paper presented at the annual Learning Symposium on Cultural Factors in Learning, Western Washington State College, 1973. ERIC ED 096820.

Larson, R., et al. Evaluating instruction in writing. *College Communication and Composition*, 33(2), 1983, 213–229.

Lawrence, G. *Patterns for Effective Inservice Education*. Chipley, FL: Panhandle Area Educational Cooperative, 1974.

Levin, H. M. *Cost-Effectiveness: A Primer*. Beverly Hills: Sage, 1983.

Lindemann, E. Evaluating writing programs: What an outside evaluator looks for. *Writing Program Administration*, 3(1), Fall 1979, 17–24.

Loban, W. *Language Development: Kindergarten Through Grade 12*. Research Report No. 18. Urbana, IL: National Council of Teachers of English, 1976.

Macdonald, N. H.; Frase, L. T.; Gingrich, P. S.; and Keenan, S. A. The Writer's Workbench: Computer aids for text analysis. *Educational Psychologist*, 17, 1982, 172–179.

McKeachie, W. Student ratings of faculty: A reprise. *Academe*, 65(6), 1979, 384–397.

Marcus, S. *Computers in Writing Classes*. South Coast Writing Project, School of Education, University of California at Santa Barbara, 1985.

Martin, C. The rhetoric program at the University of Iowa. In *Options for the Teaching of English*, Neel, J. (ed.). New York: Modern Language Association of America, 1978.

Mehrens, W., and Lehmann, I. *Measurement and Evaluation*. 3d ed. New York: Holt, Rinehart & Winston, 1979.

Mellon, J. A taxonomy of compositional competencies. In *Perspectives on Literacy: Proceedings of the 1977 Conference*, Beach, R. and Pearson, R. (eds.). Minneapolis: College of Education, University of Minnesota, 1978.

Modern Language Association, NCTE, and American Association of Junior Colleges. *The National Study of English in Junior College*. New York: ERIC Clearinghouse on the Teaching of English in Higher Education, 1969.

Moffett, J., and Wagner, B. J. *Student-Centered Language Arts and Reading, K–13*. (2d ed.). Boston: Houghton-Mifflin, 1976.

Morris, L., and Fitz-Gibbon, C. *Program Evaluation Kit*. Beverly Hills: Sage, 1978.

Murray, D. The feel of writing and teaching writing. In *Reinventing the Rhetorical Tradition*, Freedman, A., and Pringle, I. (eds.). Urbana, IL: National Council of Teachers of English, 1980.

Myers, M. *A Procedure for Writing Assessment and Holistic Scoring*. Urbana, IL: National Council of Teachers of English, 1980.

Myers, M., and Gray, J. *Theory and Practice in the Teaching of Composition:*

Processing, Distancing, Modeling. Urbana, IL: National Council of Teachers of English, 1983.

Myers, M., and Thomas, S. C. *The Interaction of Teacher Roles in the Teaching of Writing in Inner-city Secondary Schools: Executive Summary.* Berkeley, CA: University of California Department of Education, 1982. ERIC ED 228 648.

NCTE Composition Opinionaire: Students' Right to Write. Urbana, IL: National Council of Teachers of English, 1972. ERIC ED 091 729.

NIE Conference on Professional Development: Exploring Issues in Teacher Education: Questions for Future Research. Austin: Research and Development Center for Teacher Education, University of Texas at Austin, 1979.

Neel, J. P. *Options for the Teaching of English.* New York: Modern Language Association of America, 1978.

Nicholson, A., and Joyce, B. *The Literature on Inservice Teacher Education.* Syracuse, NY: National Dissemination Center, Syracuse University, 1977.

Nold, E. Interview questions available from author. Ellen Nold, School of Engineering, Stanford University, Stanford, CA. 1979.

Obenchain, A. Developing paragraph power through sentence-combining. In Daiker, N. et al. (eds.). *Sentence Combining and the Teaching of Writing.* Fayetteville: University of Arkansas Press, 1979, 123–134.

Oliver, L. J. Pitfalls in electronic writingland. *English Education,* 16(2), May 1984, 94–100.

Parker, R. G. *Aids to English Composition.* New York: D. Appleton, 1841. [Reported in Judy, S. Composition and rhetoric in American secondary schools. *English Journal,* 68(4), 1979, 35.]

Piche, G. L. Synopsis and prognosis. In *Perspectives on Literacy: Proceedings of the 1977 Conference,* Beach, R., and Pearson, R. (eds.). Minneapolis: College of Education, University of Minnesota Press, 1978.

Pike, K. L. Beyond the sentence. *College Composition and Communication,* 15, October 1964, 129–135.

Purves, A. et al. *Common Sense and Testing in English.* Urbana, IL: National Council of Teachers of English, 1975.

Questionnaire Brochure Series. Measurement Services Center, University of Minnesota, Minneapolis, 1978.

Reilly, R. *Use of Expert Judgment in the Assessment of Experiential Learning.* CAEL Working Paper no. 10. Princeton, NJ: Educational Testing Service, 1975.

Richards, I. A. *Practical Criticism.* New York: Harcourt Brace, 1956.

Roark, N. *Inservice Report, 1978.* Berkeley: Bay Area Writing Project, School of Education, University of California, 1978.

Rodrigues, D. Computers and basic writers. *College Composition and Communication,* 36(3), October 1985, 336–339.

Rossi, P., and Freeman, H. *Evaluation: A Systematic Approach.* (3d ed.). Beverly Hills: Sage, 1985.

Ruth, L., and Murphy, S. *Designing Writing Tasks for the Assessment of Writing*. Norwood, NJ: Ablex, 1986.

Schuessler, B.; Gere, A. R.; and Abbot, R. D. The development of scales measuring teacher attitude toward instruction in written composition. *Research in the Teaching of English*, 15(1), 1981, 55–63.

Schwartz, H. *Interactive Writing: Composition with Word Processors*. New York: Holt, Rinehart and Winston, 1985.

Scriven, M. The philosophical and pragmatic significance of informal logic. In *Informal Logic: The First International Symposium*, Blair, J. A. and Johnson, R. (eds.). Inverness, CA: Edgepress, 1980.

Scriven, M. et al. *Evaluation of the Bay Area Writing Project*. (19 reports). Berkeley: Bay Area Writing Project, School of Education, University of California.

Searling, A. E. P. Why college graduates are deficient in English. *Educational Review*, 16, 1898, 245. [Reported in *Perspectives on Literacy*, Beach, R., and Pearson, R. (eds.). Minneapolis: University of Minnesota Press, 1978.]

Serlin, R. *A Study of Las Lomas High School Writing Program*. Berkeley: Bay Area Writing Project, School of Education, University of California, 1977.

Seybold, J. W. Computer aids for authors and editors. *The Seybold Report*, 13, February 13, 1984, 1–18.

Simon, A., and Boyer, E. *Mirrors for Behavior III*. Wyncote, PA: Communications Materials Center, 1974.

Solomon, G. *Teaching Writing with Computers*. Englewood Cliffs, NJ: Prentice-Hall, 1986.

Spandel, V., and Stiggins, R. *Direct Measures of Writing Skill: Issues and Applications*. Portland, OR: Northwest Regional Educational Laboratory, 1980.

Squire, J., and Applebee, R. *High School English Instruction Today*. New York: Appleton Century Crofts, 1968.

Stahlecher, J. *Cost Analysis Report*. Berkeley: Bay Area Writing Project, School of Education, University of California, 1979.

Stibbs, A. *Assessing Children's Language: Guidelines for Teachers*. London: Ward Lock Educational, 1979.

Sudman, S., and Bradburn, N. *Asking Questions*. San Francisco: Jossey-Bass, 1982.

Tallmadge, G., and Horst, P. *A Practical Guide to Measuring Project Impact on Student Achievement*. Washington, DC: U.S. Government Printing Office, 1975.

Thomas, S. *Teacher Interview Report*. Berkeley: Bay Area Writing Project, School of Education, University of California, 1978.

Thomas, S. et al. *Interview and Questionnaire Forms*. Berkeley: Bay Area Writing Project, School of Education, University of California, 1979.

Thomas, S., and Keech, C. *Bay Area Field Studies Report*. Berkeley: Bay Area Writing Project, School of Education, University of California, 1979.

Thompson, B. *Evaluation of Teacher Change in the Arizona Writing Project*.

Unpublished doctoral dissertation, University of Arizona, Tempe, 1978.

Ward, C. S. *What Is English?* 1917 (Reported in Judy, S. Who resurrected bonehead English? *English Journal*, 64(4), 1975, 6).

White, E. M. *Teaching and Assessing Writing.* San Francisco: Jossey-Bass, 1985.

Wiswell, P. Wordprocessing. *PC Magazine*, August 20, 1985, 110–134.

Womble, G. Process and processor: Is there room for a machine in the English classroom? *English Journal*, January 1984, 34–37.

Wood, L., and Davis, B. G. *Designing and Evaluating Higher Education Curricula.* Washington, DC: American Association for Higher Education, 1978.

Wresh, W. (ed.). *The Computer in Composition Instruction: A Writer's Tool.* Urbana, IL: National Council of Teachers of English, 1984.

Young, R. E., and Larson, K. J. *College Teachers' Conceptions of Composition.* Paper presented at the American Educational Research Association Meeting, San Francisco, 1979.

Additional Reading

Select Bibliography Related to the Evaluation of Composition Instruction

Evaluating Writing Programs

Cazden, C., et al. Language assessment: Where, what, and how. *Anthropology and Education Quarterly*, 8(2), 1977, 83–91.

Houston, M. What freshman directors need to know about evaluating writing programs. *Writing Program Administration*, 3(1), 1979, 11–16.

Lindemann, E. Evaluating writing programs: What an outside evaluator looks for. *Writing Program Administration*, 3(1), 1979, 17–24.

Witte, S. P., and Faigley, L. *Evaluating College Writing Programs*. Carbondale: Southern Illinois University Press, 1983.

Composition Instruction and Research

Annotated Bibliography in the Teaching of English. *Research in the Teaching of English*, issued every May and December.

Braddock, R.; Lloyd-Jones, R.; and Schoer, L. *Research in Written Composition*. Urbana, IL: National Council of Teachers of English, 1974.

Caplan, R., and Keech, C. *Showing-Writing: A Training Program to Help Students Be Specific* (Classroom Research Study No. 2, Bay Area Writing Project). Berkeley: University of California, 1980.

Cooper, C., and Odell, L. *Research on Composing: Points of Departure*. Urbana, IL: National Council of Teachers of English, 1978.

Donovan, T., and McClelland, B. *Eight Approaches to Teaching Composition*. Urbana, IL: National Council of Teachers of English, 1980.

Emig, J. *The Composing Processes of Twelfth Graders*. Urbana, IL: National Council of Teachers of English, 1971.

Gray, S., and Keech, C. *Writing from Given Information* (Classroom Research Study No. 3, Bay Area Writing Project). Berkeley: University of California, 1980.

Keech, C., and Thomas, S. *Compendium of Promising Practices in Composition Instruction.* Berkeley: Bay Area Writing Project, School of Education, University of California, 1979.

Tate, G. *Teaching Composition: Ten Bibliographical Essays.* Fort Worth: Texas Christian University Press, 1976.

White, E. M., and Polin, L. G. *Research in Effective Teaching in Writing, Phase I: Final Report.* Los Angeles: California State University Foundation, 1983. ERIC ED 239 292 and ERIC ED 239 293.

Woodworth, P., and Keech, C. *The Write Occasion* (Classroom Research Study No. 1, Bay Area Writing Project). Berkeley: University of California, 1980.

Writing Assessment

American College Testing Program. *Alternative Strategies for the Assessment of Writing Proficiency.* Iowa City: Author, 1979.

Fagan, W.; Cooper, C. R.; and Jenson, J. *Measures for Research and Evaluation in the English Language Arts.* Urbana, IL: National Council of Teachers of English, 1975.

White, E. M. *Teaching and Assessing Writing.* San Francisco: Jossey-Bass, 1985.

Cost Analysis in Evaluation

Haller, E. Cost analysis for educational program evaluation. In *Evaluation in Education,* W. J. Popham (ed.). Berkeley: McCutchan, 1974.

Thompson, M. *Benefit-Cost Analysis for Program Evaluation.* Beverly Hills: Sage, 1980.

Computers and Composition

Halpern, J. W., and Liggett, S. *Computers and Composing.* Urbana, IL: National Council of Teachers of English, 1984.

Nancarrow, P. R.; Ross, D.; and Bridwell, L. *Word Processors and the Writing Process: An Annotated Bibliography.* Available from the first author, English Department, University of Minnesota, Minneapolis, MN 55455.

Schwartz, H. J., and Bridwell, L. S. A select bibliography on computers and composition. *College Composition and Communication,* 35(1), 1984, 71–77.

Wresh, W. (ed.). *The Computer in Composition Instruction: A Writer's Tool.* Urbana, IL: National Council of Teachers of English, 1984.

Journals and Newsletters

Creative Word Processing in the Classroom Newsletter. P. O. Box 590727, San Francisco, CA 94159.

National Writing Project Newsletter. Bay Area Writing Project, School of Education, University of California, Berkeley, CA 94720.

Notes from the National Testing Network in Writing. City University of New York, 535 East 80th Street, New York, NY 10021.

Journals published by the National Council of Teachers of English (NCTE), 1111 Kenyon Road, Urbana, IL 61801:

College Composition and Communication
English Journal
Language Arts
Research in the Teaching of English

Case Studies of Writing Project Evaluations and Local Writing Assessments

Reports on Writing Assessments

California State University and Colleges. *Comparison and Contrast: The 1980 California State University and Colleges Freshman English Equivalency Examination*. Edward M. White, 1980. (Available from Jane Winstead, New Program Development Evaluation, Office of the Chancellor, 400 Golden Shore, Suite 314, Long Beach, CA 90806 [$2.00])

Colorado writing assessment. Olson, M., and Swadener, M. *English Education*, 16(4), 1984, 208–219.

Modesto City Schools Writing Handbook for Teachers (Grades K–12), 1986. (From: Modesto City Schools, 426 Locust Street, Modesto, CA 95351)

New Mexico Writing Assessment. Howard J. Scheiber, 1981. (Available from New Mexico State Department of Education, Santa Fe, NM. ERIC ED 200 975)

Oakland Assessment of Student Writing Abilities (A procedure for writing assessment and holistic scoring). Miles Myers, 1982. ERIC ED 193 676.

The San Mateo Writing Project, K–8: The Story of Young Children Learning to Write. Johanne Graham, Laurie Williams, Miles Myers. Bay Area Writing Project, 1980. (Available from San Mateo Union High School District, 650 N. Delaware Street, San Mateo, CA 94401.)

Reports of Writing Program Evaluations

The Carleton Writing Project, Part I: The Writing Abilities of a Selected Sample of Grade 7 and 8 Students. Final Report.

Carleton Writing Project Report. 1978–1979.

Analysis of Writing—1978, Grades 7–8, Intermediate Writing Evaluation Project. Ontario Institute for Studies in Education.
(All of the above available from Aviva Freedman, Department of Linguistics, Carleton University, Ottawa, Ontario, Canada K1S 5B6.)

Davis, B. G., and Wood, L. *Evaluation of "Teaching College Faculty Across Disciplines to Use Writing,"* 1981. (Available from Barbara Gross Davis, Office of Educational Development, 273 Stephens Hall, University of California, Berkeley, CA 94720)

Webster Groves, Missouri, School District. *Better Teaching—Better Writing* (ESEA IV-C. Interim Report 35-78-20-1), August 1980. (Available from Max Wolfrum, Gateway Writing Project, 16 Selma Avenue, Webster Groves, MO 63119)

Technical Reports of the Bay Area Writing Project Evaluation

(Directed by Michael Scriven and funded by the Carnegie Corporation. All reports available from Bay Area Writing Project, School of Education, Tolman Hall, University of California, Berkeley, CA 94720.)

1. *Executive Summary of BAWP Evaluation.* M. Scriven, 1980. ($1.00)
2. *The Summer Invitational.* C. Keech, 1977. ($2.00)
3. *Inservice Report.* N. Roark, 1978. ($4.00)
4. *Teacher Interview Report.* S. Thomas, 1978. ($2.00) ERIC ED 191 061
5. *Writing Assessment Report.* C. Keech, 1978. ($3.00)
6. *Procedures for Running a Writing Assessment.* C. Keech, 1978. ($2.00)
7. *Topics for Assessing Writing Through Writing Samples.* C. Keech, 1979. ($3.00) ERIC ED 191 059
8. *Rubrics for Writing Assessment.* C. Keech, 1978. ($3.00)
9. *Long Term Follow-Up of Four BAWP Programs.* J. Stahlecker, 1979. ($3.00) ERIC ED 191 062
10. *Compendium of Promising Practices in Composition.* C. Keech and S. Thomas, 1979. ($2.00) ERIC ED 191 058
11. *Critical Competitors of BAWP's Inservice Model.* S. Thomas and P. Watson, 1979. ($2.00) ERIC ED 191 063
12. *Bay Area Field Studies Report.* S. Thomas and C. Keech, 1979. ($1.00) ERIC ED 191 060
13. *Cost Analysis Report.* J. Stahlecker, 1979. ($2.00) ERIC ED 191 064
14. *National Writing Project Evaluation Report.* C. Keech, J. Stahlecker, S. Thomas, and P. Watson, 1979 ($3.00) ERIC ED 191 065

Instruments for Evaluating Composition Instruction

Teacher Questionnaires
Davis, B. G., and Wood, L. College faculty questionnaire. (Available from Barbara Gross Davis, Office of Educational Development, 273 Stephens Hall, University of California, Berkeley, CA 94720)

Froegner language inquiry survey. In Gere, A., and Smith, E. *Attitudes, Language and Change.* Urbana, IL: National Council of Teachers of English, 1979.

Goodman communication questionnaire. In Skillings, L., *Motivation through Individual Projects in Freshman Composition.* 1976. ERIC ED 156 255.

Thomas, S. *Teacher Interview and Questionnaire Forms.* (Available from Bay Area Writing Project, School of Education, University of California, Berkeley, CA 94720).

Witte, S. P.; Daly, J. A.; Faigley, L.; and Koch, W. P. An instrument for reporting composition course teaching and effectiveness in college writing programs. *Research in the Teaching of English,* 17 (2), 1983, 243–261.

Writing Program Assessment Instrument. The Network, 290 S. Main, Andover, MA 01810.

Student Questionnaires

Davis, B. C., and Wood, L. *Student Writing Questionnaire.* (Available from Barbara Gross Davis, Office of Educational Development, 273 Stephens Hall, University of California, Berkeley, CA 94720)

Hoepfner, R., et al. *The CSE Test Evaluation Series.* Los Angeles: Center for the Study of Evaluation, UCLA Graduate School of Education, 1971–1976.

Holther, J., and Brossell, G. Who (if anyone) is teaching them writing and how. *English Journal,* 68 (7), October 1979.

Writing Assessment Instruments

Buros, O. K. (ed.). *English Tests and Reviews,* Highland Park, NJ: Gryphon Press, 1985.

Fagan, W. T., Cooper, C. and Jensen, J. *Measures for Research and Evaluation in the English Language Arts.* Urbana, IL: National Council of Teachers of English, 1975.

Grommon, A. (ed.). *Reviews of Selected Published Tests in English.* Urbana, IL: National Council of Teachers of English, 1976.

Glossary

Accountability: responsibility, typically for the justification of expenditures or for achieving certain objectives; requires a documented evaluation of some kind.

Adjunct courses: college-level composition courses offered through departments other than English and designed to teach writing skills in conjunction with a specific course. Part of the college version of **writing across the curriculum.**

Administrative design: the conceptualization and planning of the logistics of implementing a **scientific design,** so that it becomes a feasible and business-like process; typically involves timelines, cash flow, hiring procedures, and so forth.

Analytic evaluation: evaluation that provides diagnostic or explanatory information about the functioning of a program or its components.

Analytic scoring: scoring or rating of samples of writing according to key components or aspects such as organization, style, sentence structure, and so on.

Anchor papers: a set of representative or exemplar papers that illustrate the quality of responses typical of specific scores or ratings.

Articulation: regular and systematic communication among teachers at different grade levels regarding their curricula, teaching methods, and standards for evaluating student work.

Assessment: often used as a synonym for *evaluation* but sometimes refers to a process that is more focused on quantitative or testing approaches.

Attitude: predisposition to respond in a consistent manner with respect to a given object or experience based on one's values about that object or experience; attitudes often link mental states (beliefs) with behaviors.

Audience: the real or imagined group of readers to whom a piece of writing is directed.

Audience for the evaluation: a group, whether or not they are the **clients,** who will see or hear about the evaluation.

213

Baseline data: information about the performance of students (or teachers) prior to their participation in the program or sequence of instruction.

Basics: refers to skills considered essential for success in school or for entry-level jobs and adult life; specific skills identified as basic often vary from one context to another.

Bay Area Writing Project (BAWP): both a project and an innovative approach to composition inservice which has been available in the San Francisco Bay Area since 1974 and nationally through the National Writing Project sites since 1977. The Project is located at the UC Berkeley School of Education under the direction of James Gray.

Behavioral description: description in observable terms.

Behavioral intention: actions planned for the future.

Belief: information that one holds to be true about an object, and that links the object to some attribute.

Bias: a state or factor tending to produce erroneous results in an assessment; commonly confused with *commitment*, which may be due and proportional to the weight of evidence, and entirely justified.

Bias control: the attempt to exclude the influence of unjustified, premature, or irrelevant views in an evaluation design.

Blind scoring: the rating, scoring, or judging of students' work or performance by individuals who do not possess information that could bias or prejudice their response (e.g., student grade level, membership in treatment or control group).

Checklist approach to evaluation: process by which evaluators construct a list that identifies all significant relevant dimensions of value, preferably in measurable terms, and may also provide for weighting them according to importance, which is determined by a **needs assessment.**

Client: the individual who commissions the evaluation, and to whom one has technical, legal, and immediate responsibilities. *Moral* responsibility is primarily to those who can be affected by the evaluator's good and bad performance, typically the "ultimate consumers" of the program's services, which include both taxpayers and students.

Cognitive process(es): the variety of thought processes that include recalling, imagining, naming, describing, analyzing, evaluating, and so on.

Coherence: consistency or systematic connections and relationships in a piece of writing.

Comparison group: a group of people who do not receive the program or instruction under evaluation, but are administered the questionnaires and tests. The performance of the comparison group is useful in interpreting change among the experimental group.

Competence/competency: students' abilities to meet some predetermined standards or level of proficiency in writing.

Conferencing: a method of teaching writing popularized by Donald Murray of the University of New Hampshire in which student and instructor privately confer on writing in progress, with the instructor helping the student discover, shape, and polish written ideas and finally edit them into a finished piece.

Construct: a hypothesis, idea, or other synthesis intended to explain certain recurring human experiences.

Content validity: the extent to which the content of a test also represents a balanced and adequate sampling of the outcomes (knowledge, skills, and so forth) of the course or program it is intended to cover.

Context: The context of a writing *program* includes factors such as support services, administrative and peer encouragement (e.g., a rewards system), and parental support. The context of the *evaluation* of the writing program includes the spirit of cooperation or hostility exuded by the program staff, the sense of the importance of the evaluation results in decision making that is communicated by the administrators or other clients. The context of an evaluation often controls the selection of the focus for the investigation and for the report.

Correlations: the relationship between two variables—e.g., scores or measures; the tendency of one score to vary with the other, as in the tendency of students with high IQs to be above average in reading ability. The existence of a strong relationship (a high positive correlation) between two scores does not necessarily indicate that one has any causal influence on the other.

Cost analysis: an aspect of evaluation that involves calculating monetary and other costs and relating them to some outcome measure such as student achievement, overall benefits, or utility.

Cost benefit analysis: the comparison of the total or major costs and total or major benefits, each converted into monetary terms to determine whether costs exceed benefits.

Cost effectiveness analysis: a procedure in which costs are described in monetary figures, and benefits are calculated in terms of effectiveness (e.g., student achievement measures). This approach is used when benefits cannot be converted to monetary terms and allows comparisons among different alternatives.

Cost feasibility analysis: the comparison of a program's total monetary and nonmonetary costs to available resources, in order to determine whether the new program is affordable.

Cost utility analysis: a complex method of evaluating costs, used when effectiveness measures are in different metrics or when limited effectiveness data are available.

Credibility: the audience's *perception* of the **validity** of an assessment.

Criterion-referenced test: a type of test that provides information about an individual's (or group's) performance relative to certain independently defined standards rather than relative to the performance of others.

Criterion validity: the degree to which the test scores correlate with criterion.

Descriptive writing: writing that calls for impressions of an object, scene, place, or event.

Derived scores: scores that have been converted from one scale (raw score scale) to another scale (percentile ranks, grade equivalents, and so forth).

Direct assessment: the judging of student writing by the examination of actual examples of past assignments or essays written in response to teacher-developed or commercially published tests.

Discourse structure: a way of characterizing written expression according to various structures or organizational forms, such as levels of abstraction, cohesive ties, thematic units, genre forms, **tagmemic** units, and so on.

Empirical model of composing: information about the composing process derived from observation of composing activities or from a writer thinking aloud or reporting afterward on how he or she approached the writing task. (Called "protocol analysis" in other areas.)

Errors of central tendency: the tendency of people to give the average (middle) rating when judging student work or observing student performance.

Evaluand: the method, program, or object to be evaluated.

Evaluation: the process of determining the merit or worth or value of something; also, the product of that process.

Experience-based models of professional training: programs that link training activities directly to classroom practices and provide teachers with opportunities to try methods they are being trained to use.

Expository writing: writing that discusses, explains, analyzes, or argues ideas; typically considered academic writing.

External evaluator: an evaluator who is not part of the staff of the program or project being evaluated.

Forced-choice questions: multiple-choice items that require students to select one or more of the given choices.

Formative evaluation: evaluation done for the purpose of improving a program or product that is still in the process of development or implementation. The results of a formative evaluation are given to the people who can still effect improvement.

"Found" test data: tests that are routinely administered in school districts or postsecondary institutions that may provide useful evaluative information about students' language skills.

Frequency scale: a response format used in questionnaires that asks the respondent to indicate the strength of response on a scale marked by numbers or frequencies (e.g., 1 = "least satisfactory" to 5 = "most satisfactory").

Gain scores: the difference between pretest scores and posttest scores.

Generalizability: the extent to which the program under study, or the treatment it incorporates, can be used in a more general context—either in other places, or with other students, or with other instructors, or in slightly modified form.

Grade equivalents: scores representing typical or average performance of individuals classified according to grade in school. A grade equivalent of 5.8 is the average score obtained by students in the eighth month of the fifth-grade school year.

Growth-centered approaches: a method of teaching composition which emphasizes students' general progress, not necessarily their movement toward a single goal or set of objectives.

Halo effect: the influence that a rater's impression of a person or an aspect of a person's work exerts (positively or negatively) on ratings of other aspects of the person's performance.

Hawthorne effect: the changes in behavior that sometimes occur when participants in an evaluation are aware that they are being evaluated.

Heuristically guided composition instruction: a method of teaching composition through use of general guidelines about how to write appropriately for different *audiences* or different *purposes*, rather than the teaching of specific rules about usage and correctness.

Holistic evaluation: the determination of the overall value of a program or product, without reference to the value of its components or its merit on various dimensions of performance.

Holistic scoring: a scoring system in which a piece of writing receives a single score based on a general impression of the paper as a whole.

Implementation: the process by which the intentions, methods, and the like of a planned program are actually realized.

Impromptu writing: a writing assignment that students undertake within a fixed period of time (typically 20 to 30 minutes) during which they may or may not have time to revise their work; a measure of students' ability to create and organize material under time pressure.

Indirect assessment: the judging of student writing on the basis of student responses to multiple-choice tests or other measures that do not involve a writing sample.

Information-based models of inservice: efforts to improve teaching skills by presenting teachers with appropriate information, usually through print materials or lectures.

Inservice training: training teachers receive while they are carrying on their professional duties and responsibilities. (Also known as professional development or professional training.) Cf. **preservice training.**

Integrated curriculum: one that involves practicing all language arts skills—reading, writing, speaking, and listening—in combination with one another rather than separating them into distinct skills units or exercises.

Integrated skills learning: a method of composition instruction in which students write meaningful discourses rather than practice skills in separate exercises.

Interrater reliability: the extent to which different people, possibly using the same instrument or rating scale, produce similar results when judging the same piece of writing or the same situation. Cf. **test-retest reliability.**

Internal consistency: the extent to which the items on a test are correlated with one another, thus indicating that the test measures a common skill, behavior, or content area.

Internal evaluator: an evaluator on the staff or closely associated with the program or project being evaluated; the evaluation is then a component of the system being evaluated.

Isolated skills learning: a way of learning skills of correct writing by practicing them in workbook exercises rather than writing whole discourses.

Key evaluation checklist: a checklist that calls attention to the multidimensional characteristic of evaluation, involving considerations as diverse as cost analysis, side-effects searches, program description, and testing.

Knowledge-centered approach: a method of teaching writing skills that entails the study of linguistics, rhetoric, literature, or philosophy.

Lexical and syntactic fluency: a measure of students' ability to express ideas effectively based on their ability to choose words and use them in sentences whose syntax is correct and appropriate for the ideas being conveyed.

Likert scale: a type of rating scale in which respondents indicate the intensity with which they agree or disagree with a statement. Sample item: "Prewriting helps me organize my thoughts." Likert scale response choices would be "Strongly disagree," "Disagree," "Neither agree nor disagree," "Agree," "Strongly agree." Named after the man who invented the scale.

Literacy: the ability to read and write; the level of skills deemed literate depend on the group being measured (e.g., college students, nonnative speakers, high school graduates).

Literature-based approach: a method of teaching writing skills by having students imitate literary models, analyze different genres of literature, or in some cases write literary criticism.

Logic-based program: a method of teaching composition that emphasizes skills of logical analysis (using either informal or formal logic methods) as a necessary prerequisite for clear expression of ideas and their coherent organization in writing.

Market: the group of potential users of a program's services.

Matrix sampling: a method of testing in which each student receives a sample of a longer test, often quite different from the one received by the adjacent student. Used in evaluating programs, not for evaluating students.

Maturation: a possible rival explanation for observed results in an evaluation that did not use a comparison group. Maturation refers to the "natural" gain in intellectual performance that occurs in learners regardless of any instructional intervention.

Mean: the average of a set of scores obtained by summing the scores and dividing by the number of scores.

Meaning discovery approach: an instructional technique that uses writing as a tool for discovering and shaping meaningful experiences.

Meta analysis: a procedure for integrating data from a series of research or evaluation studies.

Method- or skills-centered approach: a way of teaching writing that emphasizes the use of specific instruction methods and having students practice specific skills.

Methodology inventory: an instrument used in training that measures teachers' perceptions of the usefulness of techniques presented in inservice training.

Mode: the score or value that occurs most frequently in a set of scores or measurements.

Models approach: a method of teaching writing in which students emulate or model examples of good writing drawn from published literature or other sources (e.g., other students' writing).

Narrative writing: a type of writing intended to tell a real or imagined story about an event, incident or happening.

NCTE: National Council of Teachers of English, the national professional organization for elementary and secondary English teachers.

Needs assessment: a systematic determination of the improvement in performance or of the services required to maintain an acceptable level of achievement.

Norms: aids or guides in the interpretation of test results that describe the typical or average performance of specified subgroups. Norms are not to be regarded as standards for each learner to meet nor as desirable levels of attainment.

Norm-referenced test: a type of test that provides information on how well an individual (or group) does in comparison to other individuals taking the same test. Examples: ranking of students in a class; percentile scores for a given grade level on a state test; describing work as "best in the class" or "below class average." Norm-referenced language says nothing about whether the work is good or bad according any external criteria.

NWP Network: the National Writing Project Network, an association of over 150 writing projects based on the inservice model developed by the Bay Area Writing Project. NWP Network publishes a newsletter, maintains regular communication among its directors, and sponsors teacher exchanges and other projects of interest to its members. For information contact: Bay Area Writing Project, School of Education, UC Berkeley, Berkeley, CA 94720.

Open-ended questions/format: test items that require respondents to write out some answers in their own words.

Opportunity costs: the benefits or advantages that one foregoes by engaging in any one particular activity.

Peer feedback: responses by students to another student's piece of written discourse.

Peer response group: small group of instructors or students (usually no more than six people) whose members listen to one another's written compositions read aloud and make suggestions for subsequent revisions.

Percentile ranks: whole-number percentage of students in the reference group equaled or surpassed by the individual. If a person obtains a percentile rank of 70, his or her standing is regarded as equaling or surpassing that of (about) 70 percent of the group on which the test was standardized.

Persuasive writing: writing that calls for an author to persuade a specific (hypothetical) audience to accept some viewpoint.

Pilot study: an activity undertaken prior to an evaluation to test out the procedures, instruments, and measures. The tests and questionnaires are administered to a small sample of individuals with characteristics similar to those in the evaluation. Pilot testing helps to identify potential problems in test administration, interpretation, and scoring.

Portfolio: collection of a student's writing taken from a series of tasks, such as essay assignments, in-class writing projects, term papers, and personal journals.

Posttest: measurements of participants' performance made after the program, project or period of instruction.

Practice effects: improvement in performance between successive administrations of tests with similar items even if no additional instruction or learning has taken place. A possible alternative explanation of improvement that challenges the possibility that the teaching was responsible.

Preformative evaluation: evaluation in the planning phase of a program of proposed versions of that program.

Preservice training: training that aspiring teachers receive before they assume professional duties.

Pretest: the measurement made before the program or project begins, to gain baseline data or diagnostic information about the program's participants.

Prewriting: activities that assist the writer in choosing a topic, becoming aware of ideas related to the topic, or shaping or refining ideas. Such activities include journal writing, brainstorming, and idea diagramming.

Primary trait scoring: a method of scoring writing samples in which the traits unique to a particular rhetorical task are identified and rated according to particular criteria. For example, the primary traits in writing directions for preparing a souffle differ from those in writing a business letter requesting a job interview.

Process-centered approach: a method of teaching composition that focuses on some type of process, either psychological or related to an instructional sequence. Some of these methods presume that writing skills are best used to facilitate naturally occurring cognitive and linguistic processes. Others promote writing through a sequence of developmental assignments.

Product-based approach: a method of teaching writing skills that focuses on the specific written product students are to produce.

Product-/performance-centered approaches: these approaches teach specific skill outcomes or focus on a particular kind of written product.

Professional development: continuing training for those actively teaching and working in the schools (see **inservice training**).

Proficiency tests: tests designed to test students' skills or competencies in specific areas. Some people use the term to mean minimal competency; others to mean a high degree of mastery.

Promising practice: a method, technique, or approach for teaching composition skills that has gained support among experienced practitioners and may have been validated in quasi-experimental research studies.

Prompt: the instructions or directions for a writing task. Example of a prompt: "Explain how to do something so that someone else could do it."

Random assignment: a method of selecting a sample that gives every individual in the population an equal chance of being chosen.

Rank order: placing individuals in an order on the basis of their relative performance on some test or measure.

Raw score: a score on a test, usually the number of right answers or good features, that has not been adjusted.

Reliability: the consistency of the results derived from an instrument; also the consistency of an individual's scoring. Cf. **validity.**

Replication: an effort to duplicate an experimental program or method under a new set of circumstances (at a different site, for a different population, and so forth).

Rhetoric-based programs: teaching students to write using methods that emphasize **rhetorical principles of communication.**

Rhetorical principles of communication: heuristics or guidelines that take into account the relations between speaker-writer, audience, purpose, subject matter, and context in formulating effective written or spoken communications.

Rival explanation or hypothesis: alternative interpretation of the results of an evaluation.

Rubric: in scoring writing samples, the set of guidelines for marking papers. The guidelines include an analysis of the task required and the generally expected response characteristics for each score.

Rule- or form-governed composition practice: writing exercises that specify rules to follow when writing, or the final form the writing is to take. (See also **product-based approach.**)

Scientific design: the design of an evaluation such that, if properly executed, it will answer the relevant crucial evaluation questions.

Self-report measures: any instrument or method of data collection that depends upon the reports of participants about their own activities—for example, questionnaires and interviews.

Sentence combining: a method of teaching students to write sentences of increasing syntactic complexity; the method involves combining shorter, simpler sentences into longer, more complex sentences.

Side effects: the unintended good and bad effects of the program or product being evaluated.

Staff development: activities to promote the professional skills of staff members working in a school; synonymous with inservice and professional development.

Standard deviation: a measure of the variability, dispersion, or "spread" of a set of scores.

Standardized test: tests that have prescribed instructions for administration, scoring, and interpretation.

Style sheet: a list of features of written discourse to be taught or emphasized; usually includes a set of correction symbols to note erroneous use of stylistic features.

Syntax: the arrangement of words and phrases within sentences and the rules governing their ordering.

Summative evaluation: evaluation done for the purpose of reporting on the quality and merit of a project. Summative evaluation is conducted for an external client or audience (not the project staff).

T-units: a method of scoring writing samples that measures syntactic fluency or sophistication in writing. A T-unit (terminal unit) is the smallest group of words that can be punctuated as a sentence.

Tagmemics approach: a method of teaching composition that requires students to consider their subject from three perspectives: static (a "particle") with unchanging, distinctive features; dynamic (a "wave"); and relative (a "field" or "network"). A series of questions based on these concepts encourages students to explore their subject matter more fully.

Teacher-proof curriculum materials: methods or curriculum materials that are supposed to be effective regardless of the skills of the teachers using them.

Teaching to the test: the practice of teaching just or mostly the particular items that will be tested, based on prior knowledge as to test content; a source of **bias.**

Test-retest reliability: consistency of results when the same judge or test is used to assess the same student on a series of occasions. Cf. **interrater reliability.** A necessary but not a sufficient condition for (high) **validity.**

Tutorial courses: special college courses conducted individually or for small numbers of students to work on specific skills.

Validity: the quality of a test that measures what it purports to measure. Valid tests are reliable, but reliable tests are not necessarily valid. Cf. **reliability.**

Writing across the curriculum: a school-wide program in which teachers in areas other than English emphasize writing and teach writing skills appropriate to their disciplines.

Writing as a process: applied to a variety of methods for teaching composition. (See **process-based approach.**) Most commonly used to describe approaches that view writing as a series of steps: prewriting, writing or composing, and revising.

Writing competency: an overall level of skill defined by establishing standards of performance in component skills, most often involving grammar and usage.

Writing for different audiences: a method by which students practice varied diction and syntactic and discourse structures by writing for a variety of audiences (preferably real-life).

Writing for different purposes: a method by which students are asked to write for different purposes (self-expression, communication of information, persuasion, and so forth).

Writing sample: a piece of writing done in response to a particular assignment or task.

Writing skills labs (laboratories): settings designed to allow students to practice various writing skills leading to fluency and correctness. Some labs allow individualized study of skills; others operate as more traditional classrooms in which students all work on the same assignments.

Writing with revision: a writing sample that students are allowed to revise at home or during a later timed session in class.

Index

Abbot, R. D., 125
Academic Competence Test, 83
Administrative designs, 26
Alloway, E., 119
American Association of Junior Colleges, 61
American College Testing Program, 83
Analytic evaluation, 4–6
Anderson, J., 100, 101, 102
Applebee, A., 40, 42, 45, 110
Applebee, R., 45, 52, 61, 138–139
Arizona Writing Project, 117
"Attitude and Knowledge in Written Composition" (Evans and Jacobs), 123
Attitudes and beliefs
  description of, 97–98
  from observations, 106–107
  problems in measurement of, 99
  from questionnaires and interviews, 99–105
  from review of program records, 107–108
  of students, 97–108
  about writing, 97–108, 123–125

Backer, T. A., 83
Balajthy, E., 47
Bamberg, B., 70, 98
Basic Skills Assessment, 81
Bay Area Writing Project (BAWP), 110, 129–130, 133, 135, 139, 145–146, 147, 148–150, 151

Bay Area Writing Project Evaluation Reports, 25
Bay Area Writing Project Evaluation Unit, 87, 117
Beavan, M. H., 97
Becker, G., 111
Berdie, D., 100, 101, 102
Bereiter, C., 42
Berman, P., 63, 127
Berquist, W., 72
Berthoff, A. E., 56
Bias control, 7
Black Studies programs, 7
Blake, R., 94, 97, 124
Borich, G., 107, 120
Boyer, E., 107, 118
Bradburn, N., 101, 102
Breininger, L. A., 48
Breland, H., 70, 73
Britton, J., 108–109, 113
Brossell, G., 120
Bruner, J., 58-59
Buros, O. K., 78, 82-83

Caldwell, K., 110
California State Department of Education, 56, 131
Camp, G., 56
Campbell, D., 77
Catano, J., 49-50
Center for the Study of Writing, 47

Centra, J., 120, 121, 134
Chickering, A., 72
Class loads, daily, 45
Classroom observations, 117–119
Coffman, W., 86
College Level Examination Program in
    English composition, 78
Common Sense and Testing in English
    (Purves et al.), 70
Comparison group design, 31–33
Comparisons, 21–22
Composition courses
    evaluation of writing assignment topics
        of, 121–122
    student enrollments in, 110–111
    student grades in, 80
Composition instruction/instructors, 30–33.
    See also Writing
    aspects of, 40–67
    attitudes and beliefs of, about writing,
        123–125
    classroom observations of, 117–119
    composition questionnaires for, 99–105,
        115–116
    contexts of, 60–61
    description of, 52–61
    English instruction vs., 41–42
    faculty members responsible for, 46
    issues in, 40–51
    methodology inventory for, 112–115
    other language arts and subject areas
        related to, 59–60
    overview of, 40–46
    perception of, by students, 119–121
    preliminary considerations for, 52–53,
        111-112
    process of, 111–123
    recent developments and, 46–47
    standardized measures of expertise in,
        122–123
    stated purposes of, 54
    structured interviews for, 116–117
    training activities of, 45–46, 61–67,
        126–136, 160–194
    working conditions of, 45–46
Composition programs/approaches, 53–61,
    107–108
    administration of, 26, 136–139
    description of, 53–55
    examples of, 55–59
    knowledge-centered, 58–59

method- or skills-centered, 56–58
    process-centered, 55–56
    product-performance-centered, 58
    side effects of, 146–150
Composition questionnaires, 115–116
Composition research. *See* Tests
Comprehensive Test of Basic Skills
    (CTBS), 78, 79
Computers
    instructional software for, 48
    reported benefits of, 50-51
    uses of, 48-50
    writing and, 47–51
    writing programs for, 48
Conference on College Communication and
    Composition (CCCC), 118, 121, 122
Conferencing (University of New Hamp-
    shire program), 56
Consumer Reports, 8, 21
Cook, T., 77
Cooper, C., 70, 83, 90, 92
Cooper, P. L., 70
Costs, cost analyses, 7–9, 14–15, 20–21,
    139–146
    description of, 139–140
    example of, 145–146
    guidelines for conducting, 142–145
    types of, 140
Creative writing, functional prose vs.,
    37–38
Credibility, 6–7
CSE Test Evaluation Series, The
    (Hoepfner et al.), 83

Daiker, D., 57
Daly, J., 97, 101, 104
Davis, B. G., 78, 164
Delbecq, A., 72
Delivery systems, 16–17
Demaline, R., 101, 102, 104, 124
Dent, R., 92
Diederich, P., 73, 84, 87, 90
Discourse structure, 42
Donlan, D., 110, 114–115, 127, 152
Drill and practice programs, 48
Dusel, W. J., 45

Educational Testing Service (ETS), 83, 119
Effort, 7–8
Eliot, Charles, 40

Emig-King Student Attitude Questionnaire, 104
Emig-King Teacher Questionnaire, 125
English instruction, composition instruction vs., 41–42
English Journal, 40, 44, 120–121
English Tests and Reviews (Buros), 82–83
ERIC, 83
Evaluand, effects of, 17–19
amounts of, 18
duration of, 18–19
unintended, 9–10
validity of, 19
Evaluation components, assembling,
153–194
case study on, 160–194
vignettes on, 153–160
Evaluation designs
administrative, 26, 136–139, 166
scientific, 26–34
Evaluation plans, 160–194
areas omitted from, 163
comments on design of, 166
focus of, 161–163
methodology of, 163–166
purposes of, 161
Evaluation questions, 27–33
Evaluations. *See also* Key evaluation
checklist
analytic, 4–6
aspects of, 68–152
assembling components of, 153–194
controlling bias in, 7
cost of, 7–9, 14–15, 20–21, 139–146
credibility of, 6–7
effort involved in, 7–8
formative, 3–4, 127–130
holistic, 4–6
of impact of professional development
activities, 135–136
implementation of, 25–26
intended effects of, 9–10
internal vs. external, 7
phases of, 10
preliminary considerations for, 1–3
summative, 3–4, 130–133
of training by nonparticipant evaluators,
134–135
utilization of, 25–26
of writing assignment topics, 121–122
of writing as skill, 34–39

Evaluators
issues for, 63–64
nonparticipant, 134–135
participant, 127–133
questions frequently faced by, xv–xvii,
153–160
Evans, W. H., 123, 125
Extra duties, 45

Fadiman, C., 46
Fagan, W. T., 83
Fillion, B., 110
Final reports, 24–25
Fishbein, M., 98
Fishman, J., 43
Fitz-Gibbon, C., 72, 73, 77, 82, 101, 102,
104, 106, 118, 124, 125, 138, 145
Five-paragraph essay, 58
Flanigan, M. C., 66
Ford, J., 94
Formative evaluation, 3–4
of training activities by participants,
127–130
Forrest, A., 83
Frase, L. T., 48, 49
Freedman, S. W., 45
Freeman, H., 140
Froegner Language Inquiry Test, 123
Frye, N., 58–59
Functional prose, creative writing vs.,
37–38

Gallagher, B., 48
Gaynor, J., 70
Gere, A., 43, 110, 125
Gingrich, P. S., 48
Glass, G., 151
Godshalk, F., 86
Gorden, R., 116
Graduate Record Examination, 78
Grammar, writing and, 34–35, 38–39, 42–43
Graves, D., 47, 117
Gray, J., 55
Griffin, C. W., 46, 56
Grommon, A., 83
Gronlund, N., 72, 73, 82, 85
Gustafson, D., 72

Hairston, M., 136
Hallibuton, D., 72
Halpern, J. W., 47

Harris, J., 50
Hawkins, T., 96
Hawthorne effect, 32–33
Healy, M. K., 96
Hemingway, Ernest, 1
Henerson, M., 101, 102, 104, 106, 118, 124,
    125
Hershey, W., 48
Hillocks, G., 47
Hoepfner, R., 83
Hoetker, J., 120
Holistic evaluation, 4–6
Hook, J. N., 40, 42, 54
Horst, P. A., 79
Howard, J., 46
Hunt, K. W., 92

Idea planners/processors, word-processing,
    48
Ideational fluency, 42–43
Illinois Tests in the Teaching of English,
    123, 125
Immediately impacted population, 17
Implementation, 25–26
Inland Area Writing Project, 114–115, 127
Inservice, information-based models of,
    66–67
Instructional goals, 44–45
Instructional software, 48
Integrative software, 48
Intended effects, 9–10
Interviews
    for collecting data about teachers,
        115–117
    on student attitudes about writing,
        99–105

Jacobs, P. H., 123, 125
James, Henry, 41
Jensen, J., 83
Jones, E., 92
Joyce, B., 63, 66, 131, 137
Judy, S., 40

Keech, C., 37–38, 46, 52, 77, 86, 92–93, 115
Keech Student Questionnaire, 104
Keenan, S. A., 48
Kerek, A., 57
Key evaluation checklist, 10–24
    background and context of evaluand,
        12–13

background and context of evaluation, 13
checkpoints all necessary, 10–11
comparisons, 21–22
cost analysis, 20–21
delivery system, 16–17
describing evaluand, 12, 27
describing evaluation, 12
effects of evaluand, 17–19
generalizability, 19–20
iterative nature of, 11
legal, ethical, and political constraints on
    evaluation, 14
legal, ethical, political, and other process
    considerations, 14
market, 17
need for evaluation, 15–16
needs assessment, 15
overall significance, 22–24
resources available for evaluand, 13
resources available for evaluation, 13–14
Kirrie, M., 89
Kotler, L. A., 49
Kowalski, J., 120, 121
Koziol, S., 115, 116, 125

Lambert, W. E., 43
Language experience approach, 56
Language learning, 54–55
Language standards, 42–43
Larkin, G., 94
Larson, K. J., 52
Larson, R., 118, 121
Lawrence, G., 63
Lehmann, I., 73, 85
Levin, H. M., 140, 144
Lexical and syntactic fluency, 42
Liggett, S., 47
Lindemann, E., 136, 137
Lindquist, J., 72
Linguistic demands, 42
Literacy, recurring crisis in, 40–41
Literature-based programs, 58–59
Loban, W., 97
Logic, rewarding of, 37–38
Logic-based programs, 59

Macdonald, N. H., 48
McGraw, B., 151
MacKay, C., 92
McKeachie, W., 120

McLaughlin, M., 63, 127
Madden, S., 107, 120
Marcus, S., 49, 50, 51
Marking systems, programs coordinated
    by, 58
Martin, C., 41
Matrix sampling design, 33
Meaning-discovery approach, 56
*Measures for Research and Evaluation in
    the English Language Arts* (Fagan,
    Cooper, and Jensen), 83
Mehrens, W., 73, 85
Mellon, J., 42
Mental Measurements Yearbook (Buros),
    82
Metaevaluations, 12, 23–24, 168
Methodology inventory, 112–115
Miller, M., 97, 101, 104
Mirrors for Behavior (Simon and Boyer),
    118
Models approach, 57
Modern Language Association, 61
Moffett, J., 56
Morenberg, M., 57
Morris, L., 72, 73, 77, 82, 101, 102, 104,
    106, 118, 124, 125, 138, 145
Motivation, 42
Murphy, S., 89
Murray, D., 56
Myers, M., 55, 60, 90

National Assessment of Educational
    Progress writing tests, 37
National Council of Teachers of English
    (NCTE), 42, 44, 45, 46, 53, 59, 61, 66,
    70, 116, 138
National Defense Education Act Institutes,
    62, 66
  Conference on Professional Development
    of, 63
National Science Foundation, 146
National Televised Models of Teaching
    Writing, 66
National Writing Project model, 64
National Writing Project Network, 46–47,
    62, 126–127, 145–146, 147
NCTE Composition Opinionaire, 123, 125
Neel, J. P., 52, 53, 59, 61, 65
New Jersey Writing Project, 119, 125
News on Tests, 83
Nicholson, A., 63

Nold, E., 117
Nonparticipant evaluators, 134–135
Northern Virginia Writing Project, 129

Obenchain, A., 57, 66
Observations
  of attitudes and beliefs of students,
    97–108
  of writing teachers, 117–119
Odell, L., 70, 90, 92
Oliver, L. J., 50
Ontario Institute for Studies in Education,
    110

Parker, Richard Green, 41
Participant evaluators, 127–133
PCRP, 125
Philosophical issues, 36–37
Piche, G. L., 40
Pike, K. L., 57
Practice competencies, 43
Professional development/development
      programs, 45–46, 61–67. *See also*
      Training activities
  case study on evaluation of, 160–194
  at college level, 65–66, 160–194
  description of, 160–161
  evaluation of impact of, 135–136
  examples of, 64–67
  experience-based models of, 64
  issues for evaluators of, 63–64
  models of training approach of, 65–66
  research staff development and, 62–63
Program administration, 136–139
  guidelines for, 137–139
  key dimensions of, 137
  preliminary considerations for, 136
Project English, 58–59
Psychological competencies, 42–43
Purves, A., 70, 72

Questionnaire Brochure Series, 102, 104
Questionnaires
  for collecting data about teachers,
    115–116
  on student attitudes about writing,
    99–105
Quinn, D., 101, 102, 104, 124

Reilly, R., 73, 93
Replications, 150–152

Replications *(continued)*

example of, 151–152
key issues in, 150–151
Report of the Committee on Composition
    and Rhetoric, 44
Research instruments. *See* Tests
Research staff development, 62–63
*Reviews of Selected Published Tests in
    English* (Grommon), 83
Rhetoric-based programs, 59
Richards, I. A., 57
Roark, N., 62–63, 126, 135, 139
Rodrigues, D., 50
Rossi, P., 140
Ruth, L., 89

Scholastic Aptitude Test-Verbal, 79
School budgets, 46
Schuessler, B., 125
Schwartz, H., 47
Scientific designs, 26–34
    comparison group design, 31–33
    definition of, 26
    evaluation questions answered by, 27–33
    external evaluators and, 34
    matrix sampling design, 33
    nontraditional parts of, 33–34
    for types of composition instruction,
        30–33
Scriven, M., 25, 59, 137
Searling, A. E. P., 41
Sentence combining, programs based on,
    57
Sequential Tests of Educational Progress,
    78
Serlin, R., 80
Seybold, J. W., 48
Shared style sheets, programs coordinated
    by, 58
Side effects, 9–10, 17–19
    of composition programs, 146–150
    example of, 148–150
    process for identification of, 147–148
Simon, A., 107, 118
Simulation software, 48
Skill, writing as, 34–39
Smith, E., 43, 125
Smith, M., 151
Solomon, G., 47

Spandel, V., 70, 90, 92
Spelling checkers, word-processing, 48
Squire, J., 45, 52, 61, 138–139
Stahlecher, J., 146, 149
Stanford Achievement Test, 78
Steele, J., 83
Stibbs, A., 70
Stiggins, R., 70, 90, 92
Structured interviews, 116–117
Students
    attitudes and beliefs of, about writing,
        97–108
    teachers described and evaluated by,
        119–121
Student writing performance, 68–97. *See
    also* Writing
    criteria for measures of, 72–75
    evaluation questions related to, 28–33
    measures for evaluation of, 70–71
    potential problems in evaluation of,
        75–78
    purposes of evaluation of, 69
    self- and peer-assessment of, 95–97
    standards of, 71–72
    surveys of, 108–110
Student writing problems, causes of, 53
Sudman, S., 101, 102
Summative evaluation, 3–4
    of training activities by participants,
        130–133
Surveys, 108–110
Swineford, E., 86
Synthesizing, warnings about, 22–23

Tagmemics approach, 57–58
Tallmadge, G., 79
Taylor, P., 92
Teaching writing. *See* Composition
    instruction/instructors
Test data, "found," 78–80
Test of Standard Written English, 81
Tests, 37, 47, 81–93
    locally developed, 85–93
    published, 81–85
Text editors, word-processing, 48
Thomas, S., 46, 52, 60, 63, 92–93, 115, 117,
    152
Thompson, B., 63, 115, 117, 128, 129
Thompson Methodology Inventory, 128,
    129

Topics
  evaluation of, 121–122
  selection of, 36–38, 88–89
Training activities, 126–136. *See also*
    Professional development/development
    programs
  evaluation of, by nonparticipant evalua-
    tors, 134–135
  formative evaluation of, by participants,
    127–130
  summative evaluation of, by partici-
    pants, 130–133
Tutorials, 48
Tuttle, F., 94, 97

Undergraduate Program Area Tests, 78, 80
Unintended effects, 9–10. *See also* Side
    effects
Utilization, 25–26

Van de Ven, A., 72
Vignettes
  on problems handled by assembling
    evaluation components, 153–160
  on questions evaluators frequently face,
    xv–xvii, 153–160

Wagner, B. J., 56
Ward, C. S., 44
Weil, M., 66

White, E. M., 70, 85–86, 90, 91, 92
Wiswell, P., 48
Womble, G., 50
Wood, L., 78, 164
Word-processing programs, 48
Working conditions, 45–46
Wresh, W., 47
Writing. *See also* Composition
    instruction/instructors; Student
    writing performance
  adjunct courses in, 58
  attitudes and beliefs about, 97–108,
    123–125
  computers and, 47–51
  evaluation of, as skill, 34–39
  grammar and, 34–35, 38–39, 42–43
  standards for, 38–39
  student attitudes and beliefs about,
    97–108
  topics for, 36–38, 88–89, 121–122
Writing Apprehension Questionnaire, 104
Writing Apprehension Scale, 101
Writing competencies, 42–43
Writing curricula, training accompanying
    development of, 65
Writing process approach, 56
Writing programs, 48
Writing samples, "found," 94–95
Writing skills labs, programs with, 57

Young, R. E., 52

About the Authors

Barbara Gross Davis is Director of the Office of Educational Development at the University of California, Berkeley.

Michael Scriven is Professor of Education at the University of Western Australia.

Susan Thomas is an evaluation consultant to education projects and a former composition teacher.